Benjamin the Waggoner

The Cornell Wordsworth

General Editor: Stephen Parrish
Associate Editor: Mark L. Reed

Advisory Editors: M. H. Abrams, Geoffrey Hartman, Jonathan Wordsworth

---

The Salisbury Plain Poems, edited by Stephen Gill
The Ruined Cottage and *The Pedlar*, edited by James Butler
The Prelude, 1798–1799, edited by Stephen Parrish
Home at Grasmere, edited by Beth Darlington
Benjamin the Waggoner, edited by Paul F. Betz

CENTER FOR
SCHOLARLY EDITIONS
AN APPROVED EDITION
MODERN LANGUAGE
ASSOCIATION OF AMERICA

Benjamin the Waggoner
by William Wordsworth

Edited by PAUL F. BETZ

Cornell University Press | Ithaca, New York
The Harvester Press, Ltd. | Brighton, Sussex

THIS BOOK HAS BEEN PUBLISHED WITH THE AID OF A GRANT FROM THE HULL MEMORIAL PUBLICATION FUND OF CORNELL UNIVERSITY.

THE PREPARATION OF THIS VOLUME WAS MADE POSSIBLE IN PART BY A GRANT TO THE EDITORS FROM THE PROGRAM FOR EDITIONS, THE NATIONAL ENDOWMENT FOR THE HUMANITIES, AN INDEPENDENT FEDERAL AGENCY.

The Harvester Press Limited, *Publisher: John Spiers*
16 Ship Street, Brighton, Sussex, England

First printing 1981

Printed in the United States of America by Vail-Ballou Press, Inc.

British Library Cataloguing in Publication Data

Wordsworth, William
Benjamin the Waggoner.–(The Cornell Wordsworth; 5).
I. Title II. Betz, Paul F
821′.7 PR5869.W3
ISBN 0-85527-513-8

The Cornell Wordsworth

The individual volumes of the Cornell Wordsworth series, some devoted to long poems, some to collections of shorter poems, have two common aims. The first is to bring the early Wordsworth into view. Wordsworth's practice of leaving his poems unpublished for years after their completion, and his lifelong habit of revision—Ernest de Selincourt called it "obsessive"—have obscured the original, often the best, versions of his work. These original versions are here presented in the form of clean, continuous "reading texts" from which all layers of later revision have been stripped away. The second aim of the series is to provide, for the first time, a complete and accurate record of variant readings, from Wordsworth's earliest drafts down to the final lifetime (or first posthumous) publication. The most important manuscripts are shown in full transcription; on pages facing the transcriptions of the most complex and interesting of these manuscripts, photographs of the manuscript pages are also provided. Besides the transcriptions and the photographs, on which draft revisions may be seen, and an *apparatus criticus* in which printed variants are collected, a third device for the study of revisions is adopted: when two versions of a poem match sufficiently well, they are arrayed on facing pages so that the steps by which one was converted into the other become visible.

Volumes in the series are unnumbered, but upon publication their titles are inserted into the list of volumes in print in the order in which the works were written. A more detailed introduction to the series may be found in the first volume published, *The Salisbury Plain Poems*, edited by Stephen Gill.

S. M. Parrish

Ithaca, New York

Contents

Preface

The development of *Benjamin the Waggoner* from its earliest manuscripts to its final printed form is a complicated matter: it involves the incorporation of pre-1806 fragments, one partial manuscript of the poem as first composed in 1806, three complete fair copies (all of which have been revised), a missing manuscript, and numerous changes in the printed versions that appeared between 1819 and 1850. The handwritings in the manuscripts include those of Wordsworth, Coleridge, Mary Wordsworth—who transcribed two of the fair copies that have been previously attributed to Sara Hutchinson—Dorothy Wordsworth, Sara Hutchinson, and even perhaps the bibliographer and forger T. J. Wise. Some sections of the manuscripts contain as many as three layers of erased, inked-out, and overwritten corrections and drafts; they can be very difficult to read.

This volume presents for the first time complete texts of the two primary prepublication stages of the poem (1806 and 1812) and reprints the long-unavailable text of the 1819 first edition. The standard text has been that of the final corrected lifetime edition, the six-volume *Poetical Works* of 1849–1850. Ernest de Selincourt printed this text in the second volume (1944) of his edition of *The Poetical Works of William Wordsworth*; although he gave many of the earlier manuscript and printed readings as variants, he missed some and misread others. Here, also for the first time, all readings from the manuscripts and from all authorized lifetime editions are presented together. I have generally avoided offering my own critical opinions, although the reader will easily detect my affection and admiration for *Benjamin*.

My account of the development of this poem draws upon my paper "The Development of *The Waggoner*: Wordsworth, Coleridge, and T. J. Wise," delivered at the South Atlantic Modern Language Association Annual Meeting in Atlanta on November 17, 1973. It also draws, in a limited way, on my review article "After the *Lyrical Ballads*: Wordsworth and Coleridge in 1801–1802," which appeared in *Studies in Romanticism*, 12, 2 (Summer 1973), 580–589. Appendix II, "T. J. Wise and *Benjamin the Waggoner* MS. 2," draws on my article "T. J. Wise and Gordon Wordsworth," which appeared in the *Bulletin of the New York Public Library*, 74, 9 (November 1970), 577–586.

Many fellow Wordsworthians have been generous with assistance and encouragement in the preparation of this edition. The late John Finch of

Cornell University was helpful when I first became interested in editing this poem; Jonathan Wordsworth of Exeter College, Oxford, was helpful and encouraging then, and has been since. Mark L. Reed of the University of North Carolina has been both friend and adviser, and has been continually generous with his own research. Stephen Parrish of Cornell University has helped the edition through its final stages with untiring encouragement and assistance.

I am grateful to a number of other people who have helped in various ways: Carolyn Ahern, Jennifer Martin Bienenstock, Elaine Booras, Dorothy Burrows, James Butler, Nesta Clutterbuck, Brenda Colijn, Jared R. Curtis, Beth Darlington, Kristine Dugas, Leona Fisher, Margaret Fletcher, Stephen Gill, John Hayden, G. R. Jackson, Hilton Kelliher, Carl Ketcham, Joseph Kishel, Carol Landon, Eleanor Nicholes, Joseph O'Connor, Jason Rosenblatt, H. V. Wilkinson, and Basil Willey.

Thanks are gladly offered to the trustees of Dove Cottage, to the British Library, to the Wellesley College Library (English Poetry Collection), and to Olin Library, Cornell University, for permission to publish manuscripts in their charge; to Her Majesty Queen Elizabeth II for her gracious permission to cite variants in the Royal Library at Windsor Castle; to Dr. Williams's Library, London; to Georgetown University for supporting my work with a summer research grant and a sabbatic leave; and to the Danforth Foundation for supporting my work with a postdoctoral fellowship.

I offer, finally, particular thanks to my wife, Dorothy, for typing and encouragement, and for tolerating my frequent absences while I worked at the Dove Cottage Wordsworth Library and at the British Library.

PAUL F. BETZ

Georgetown University
Washington, D.C.

Abbreviations

BL	British Library.
BL Ashley	From the Ashley Library, collected by T. J. Wise and now at the British Library.
Chronology: EY	Mark L. Reed, *Wordsworth: The Chronology of the Early Years, 1770–1799* (Cambridge, Mass., 1967).
Chronology: MY	Mark L. Reed, *Wordsworth: The Chronology of the Middle Years, 1800–1815* (Cambridge, Mass., 1975).
DC MS.	Dove Cottage manuscript (1785–1814, revised numbering).
DW	Dorothy Wordsworth.
EQ	Edward Quillinan.
EY	*Letters of William and Dorothy Wordsworth: The Early Years, 1787–1805*, ed. Ernest de Selincourt (2d ed.; rev. Chester L. Shaver; Oxford, 1967).
H at G	"*Home at Grasmere*": *Part First, Book First, of* "*The Recluse*," by William Wordsworth, ed. Beth Darlington (Ithaca, 1977).
Journals	*The Journals of Dorothy Wordsworth*, ed. Mary Moorman (Oxford, 1971).
LY	*Letters of William and Dorothy Wordsworth: The Later Years, 1821–1850*, ed. Ernest de Selincourt (3 vols.; Oxford, 1939).
Memoirs	Christopher Wordsworth, *Memoirs of William Wordsworth* (2 vols.; London, 1851).
MS. 1	Manuscript 1 of *Benjamin the Waggoner*, DC MS. 56.
MS. 2	Manuscript 2 of *Benjamin the Waggoner*, BL Ashley 4637.
MS. 3	Manuscript 3 of *Benjamin the Waggoner*, DC MS. 72.
MS. 1832/36	Wordsworth's *Poetical Works*, 4 vols., 1832, in the English Poetry Collection, Wellesley College Library, revised and used as printer's copy for the edition of 1836.
MS. 1836/45	Wordsworth's *Poetical Works*, 6 vols., 1836, in the Royal Library at Windsor Castle, in a proof state with revisions adopted 1836–1845.
MW	Mary Hutchinson Wordsworth.
MY	*Letters of William and Dorothy Wordsworth: The Middle Years, 1806–1820*, ed. Ernest de Selincourt (2 vols.; 2d ed.; Part I, 1806–1811, rev. Mary Moorman [Oxford, 1969]; Part II, 1812–1820, rev. Mary Moorman and Alan G. Hill [Oxford, 1970]).
Prelude	William Wordsworth, *The Prelude*, ed. Ernest de Selincourt (2d ed.; rev. Helen Darbishire; Oxford, 1959).

Prelude 1799	"*The Prelude,*" *1798–1799*, by William Wordsworth, ed. Stephen Parrish (Ithaca, 1977).
PW	*The Poetical Works of William Wordsworth*, ed. Ernest de Selincourt and Helen Darbishire (5 vols.; Oxford, 1940–1949; vols. I and II rev. 1952, vol. III rev. 1954, vol. IV rev. 1958, vol. V rev. 1959).
Quillinan MS	Drafts for the 1836 edition, in Edward Quillinan's hand, at Dove Cottage.
SPP	*The Salisbury Plain Poems of William Wordsworth*, ed. Stephen Gill (Ithaca, 1975).
RC & Pedlar	"*The Ruined Cottage*" *and* "*The Pedlar*" by William Wordsworth, ed. James Butler (Ithaca, 1979).
SH	Sara Hutchinson.
STC	Samuel Taylor Coleridge.
WW	William Wordsworth.

Benjamin the Waggoner

Introduction

I

Although *Benjamin the Waggoner* (entitled *The Waggoner* in its printed versions) has been known and held in affection by Wordsworthians since it was composed, it is known to a larger literary public mainly through Byron's mockery of its subject matter in *Don Juan*. We might better listen to the reaction of Charles Lamb, to whom Wordsworth read the poem in its earliest manuscript incarnation as *Benjamin the Waggoner and His Waggon* in 1806, and to whom the mock-heroic poem was dedicated when it was published, partly at his urging, in 1819:

> My dear Wordsworth,
> You cannot imagine how proud we are here of the dedication. We read it twice for once that we do the poem—I mean all through—yet Benjamin is no common favorite—there is a spirit of beautiful tolerance in it—it is as good as it was in 1806—and will be as good in 1829 if our dim eyes shall be awake to peruse it.[1]

Surviving records of various kinds seem to indicate that Charles and Mary Lamb's warm admiration was shared by an unusual number of the immediate and peripheral members of the Wordsworth circle, who by no means automatically approved of everything Wordsworth wrote. Among their number were Southey; Coleridge; Coleridge's wife Sara and his son Hartley; Wordsworth's wife Mary and his daughter Dora; Sara Hutchinson; Dorothy Wordsworth; and Henry Crabb Robinson. Wordsworth himself was very fond of the poem; he wrote to Hans Busk, in response to Busk's praise, that "the 'Waggoner' was written con amore, and as the Epilogue states almost in my own despite."[2] It seems to have been one of his poems that Wordsworth most enjoyed reading aloud. On October 10, 1836, Coleridge's young nephew, John Taylor Coleridge, who had come upon Wordsworth when the poet was revising proofs for the collected *Poetical Works* of 1836–1837, set down an account of one such occasion:

> Then [Wordsworth] read me some lines, which formed part of a suppressed portion of "The Waggoner;" but which he is now printing "on the Rock of Names," so called

[1] Letter 322: To William Wordsworth, June 7, 1819, in *The Letters of Charles Lamb to Which Are Added Those of His Sister Mary Lamb*, ed. E. V. Lucas (London, 1935), II, 249.

[2] Letter 548 (July 6, 1819) in *MY*, II, 547.

because on it they had carved out their initials: [W. W., M. H., D. W., S. T. C., J. W., S. H.]

This rock was about a mile beyond Wythburn Chapel, to which they used to accompany my uncle, in going from Keswick to Grasmere, and where they would meet him when he returned. This led him to read much of "The Waggoner" to me. It seems a very favourite poem of his, and he read me splendid descriptions from it. He said his object in it had not been understood. It was a play of the fancy on a domestic incident and lowly character: he wished by the opening descriptive lines to put his reader into the state of mind in which he wished it to be read. If he failed in doing that, he wished him to lay it down. He pointed out, with the same view, the glowing lines on the state of exhultation in which Ben and his companions are under the influence of liquor. Then he read the sickening languor of the morning walk, contrasted with the glorious uprising of Nature, and the songs of the birds.[3]

Many readers over the years have found in this poem the "spirit of beautiful tolerance" that Lamb saw there and a spirit of humanity as well, a sympathy for the poor and weak, gentle humor often based on the deft use of mock-heroic techniques, and several lyric passages of grace and power. *Benjamin the Waggoner* may not deserve the critical attention accorded, for example, *The Prelude*; but it possesses features that entitle it to more attention than it has received. While mock-heroic elements appear in various poems by Wordsworth, including *The Prelude* and, more extensively, *Peter Bell*, *Benjamin the Waggoner* is his most extended effort in this vein. The poem parodies certain patterns in *Paradise Lost* and its source in Genesis, and in classical tragedy and epic, while yet making a serious point: its story involves a trust given (by his master to Benjamin), a warning that the trust must be fulfilled, temptation, sin, a consequent fall, and suffering by others ("The lame, the sickly and the old") as well as by the sinner. And while not in form a ballad, the poem is suffused with the experimental approach and many of the dramatic and narrative techniques that have caused the lyrical ballads to become the objects of intense critical interest. The earliest recoverable text of the poem is in this edition intact for the first time,[4] as the reading text of MS. 1; in this version, with its style as yet unembellished, the connections between *Benjamin* and the lyrical ballads can be clearly seen.

The history of the composition and progressive revisions of the poem is complicated, spanning the years from 1802 to 1849.[5] The following sections of this Introduction reconstruct the consecutive stages of *Benjamin*'s growth: (1) pre-1806 fragments; (2) 1806–early 1807 *Benjamin the Waggoner* composition and revisions; (3) December 1811–March 1812 revisions; (4) December 1818–June 1819 revisions and publication of *The Waggoner*, first edition;

[3] *Memoirs*, II, 310.

[4] De Selincourt gives many readings from the text as variants to the version of the poem published in the 1849–50 *Poetical Works* (*PW*, II, 176–205).

[5] An outline of the history of the poem through 1815 appears in *Chronology: MY*, pp. 178–179 and pp. 311–313 (text and notes).

(5) 1820–1849 revisions and publication of the six subsequent lifetime editions of the poem. As prologue to this effort, a summary, keyed to the manuscripts, of the stages of the poem's development up to its first publication should here prove useful.

Pre-1806 Fragments Later Incorporated into Benjamin the Waggoner

May 4–early June 1802	Possible composition of some part of the "Rock of Names" passage (MS. 1, ll. 496–511).
June 13–ca. June 20, 1802 (especially June 15)	Probable composition of "The Owl as if he had learn'd his cheer" (MS. 1, ll. 582–587).
June 15–ca. June 20, possibly ca. July 7, 1802	"A few lines about the nighthawk and other images of the evening" perhaps become the basis for the opening of *Benjamin* (MS. 1, ll. 1–25, and possibly also 26–37).
March 1802–January 1, 1806 (especially spring and early summer 1802)	Possible composition of a few additional lyric and descriptive passages later drawn into the poem.

Benjamin the Waggoner: *January 1, 1806– Spring 1819*

January 1–ca. January 14, 1806	Earliest version of *Benjamin* is "thrown off under a lively impulse of feeling."
January 1–March 29, probably after January 14, 1806	1. Draft of MS. 1, ll. 424–437, in DC MS. 28 (although possibly part of the January 1–ca. January 14 earliest version). 2. Draft of MS. 1, ll. 413–416, in DC MS. 28. 3. Draft of MS. 1, ll. 651–657, in DC MS. 47.
January 14–March 29, 1806	1. *Benjamin* MS. 1 (DC MS. 56), the earliest surviving complete manuscript of the poem, is transcribed by Mary Wordsworth. 2. *Benjamin* MS. 2 (BL Ashley 4637) is transcribed by Mary Wordsworth, probably entirely after the completion of MS. 1.
Ca. March 1806–early 1807	A few early corrections and drafts in *Benjamin* MSS. 1 and 2.
October 25, 1806–April 17, 1807	Coleridge's proposed revisions to *Benjamin*, in MS. 1.
Ca. May–December 1809	Possible date of some corrections and drafts in *Benjamin* MSS. 1 and 2.
December 1811–March 29, 1812	1. Probable date of most corrections and drafts in *Benjamin* MSS. 1 and 2. 2. *Benjamin* MS. 3 (DC MS. 72) is transcribed by Sara Hutchinson, probably in March.

Early March–March 29, 1812	Drafts of 1819 lines [471]–473 and 480–483 in DC MS. 60, entered after the transcription of MS. 3.
December 1818–March 1819	1. Corrections in Mary Wordsworth's hand to *Benjamin* MS. 3. 2. Benjamin [MS. 4]—intended for the printer—is transcribed, probably by Mary Wordsworth.

Following publication in late May–early June 1819, Wordsworth revised the poem for the collected editions of 1820, 1827, and 1832; he made extensive and substantial revisions for the edition of 1836, and a few further revisions for the editions of 1845 and 1849.

II

When Wordsworth wrote the first version of *Benjamin the Waggoner*, "under a lively impulse of feeling during the first fortnight of the month of Jan[ua]ry 1806,"[6] he incorporated into the poem at least one earlier lyric fragment, probably a second, and possibly as many as four more.[7] They will be considered here in order of declining probability. For the first fragment, an independent text still exists; the text of the second is conjectural; and that the others even existed is uncertain. Of the first two fragments, one and probably both were absorbed into *Benjamin the Waggoner* in early 1806, but each seems to have enjoyed a separate existence when composed in 1802.

The first of these fragments appears in Dove Cottage MS. 44, leaf 82^{v},[8] directly preceding MS. 4 of *Peter Bell*; it was added, according to a manuscript note in the hand of Mary Wordsworth, "To fill up the blank" at the bottom of the leaf:

> The Owl as if he had learn'd his cheer
> On the banks of Windermere
> In his Tower is making merry
> Mocking the Man who keeps the ferry
> Hallooing from an open throat
> Like one shouting for a Boat

When Wordsworth composed the first version of *The Waggoner* in January 1806, these lines were incorporated in a somewhat altered form. For example, the owl's location has necessarily been changed, since at this point in *Benjamin*

---

[6] From Wordsworth's MS. note in *Waggoner* MS. 2 (BL Ashley 4637), leaf 1^{r}.

[7] See Paul F. Betz, "After the *Lyrical Ballads*: Wordsworth and Coleridge in 1801–1802," *Studies in Romanticism*, 12 (Summer 1973), 580–589, on which most of the following discussion of the first two fragments is based.

[8] Formerly MS. Verse 25, before the recent chronological renumbering of the 1785–1814 Dove Cottage papers. This bound collection of poems is often referred to as MS. M, since it includes that manuscript of *The Prelude*.

the two travelers are nowhere near the Windermere ferry, but are past the Rock of Names and moving north on the road to Keswick. The Sailor has just expressed his fear that "Yon screech Owl" portends the coming of ghosts, and Benjamin the Waggoner responds:

"I know his station
I know him and his occupation
The jolly Bird has learnt his cheer
On the Banks of Windermere
Where a tribe of them make merry
Mocking the Man that keeps the Ferry
Hallooing from an open throat
Like Traveller shouting for a Boat
The tricks he learn'd at Windermere
This lonely Owl is playing here
That [is the worst of] his employment
He's in the height of his enjoyment."[9]

Of the thirteen poems that just precede "The Owl as if" in DC MS. 44, ten and part of an eleventh seem to have been written during the first half of 1802; the tone and general character of this poem suggest a similar date. (Compare it, for example, to *The Tinker*, "The sun has long been set," and another poem of this period, *The Barberry Tree.*) Further evidence is provided by the following 1802 entries from Dorothy Wordsworth's journal:

Tuesday June 8th. Ellen and I rode to Windermere. . . . Then we went to the Island, walked round it, and crossed the lake with our horse in the Ferry.

Sunday June 13th. . . . In the evening we [William and Dorothy] walked first on our own path. . . . We walked to our new view of Rydale, but it put on a sullen face. There was an Owl hooting in Bainriggs. Its first halloo was so like a human shout that I was surprized when it made its second call, tremulous and lengthened out, to find that the shout had come from an owl.[10]

The lines about the owl were probably composed, then, between June 13 and about June 20, 1802, with June 15 the most likely date, as Dorothy's journal entry reveals:

Tuesday 15th. . . . We walked a long time in the Evening upon our favourite path. The owls hooted, the night hawk sang to itself incessantly, but there were no little Birds, no thrushes. I left William writing a few lines about the night-hawk and other images of the evening, and went to seek for letters.[11]

That a text of the second fragment has survived is possible but far from certain. Primary evidence of its composition is confined to the June 15 entry from Dorothy's journal. If the "few lines" she alludes to still exist, they

[9] *Benjamin the Waggoner* MS. I, 580–591 (DC MS. 56, leaf 24^r^). Here, as in subsequent quotations from manuscript, punctuation is sometimes modified, for clarity, as in the reading text.

[10] *Journals*, pp. 133 and 135.

[11] *Journals*, p. 136.

probably do so in modified form as the opening thirty-seven (or possibly only the first twenty-five) lines of *The Waggoner*; the hooting owls make it seem likely that "The Owl as if" lines were also involved. If Wordsworth used his earlier work to begin the poem, at least two changes would have been necessary: on June 15, 1802, there were no children in the Wordsworth household, while in January 1806 there were two (ll. 8–12); and while the waggon may have made one of the evening sounds, lines 26–37 are developing rapidly into narrative.

At last this loitering day of June
This long, long day is going out
The Night-hawk is singing his frog-like tune
Twirling his watchman's rattle about
That busy busy Bird
Is all that can be heard
In silence deeper far than that of deepest noon.

Now that the Children are in their Beds
The little Glow-worm nothing dreads
Pretty playthings as they would be
Forth they come in company
And lift their fearless heads
In the sky and on the hill
Every thing is hush'd and still
The clouds shew here and there a spot
Of a star that twinkles not
The air is like a Lion's den
Close and hot, and now and then
Comes a tired and sultry breeze
With a haunting and a panting
Like the stifling of disease
The mountains [?seem] of wondrous height
And in the heavens there is a weight
But the dews allay the heat
And the silence makes it sweet.

Hush! there is some one on the stir
'Tis Benjamin the Waggoner
From the side of Rydale mere
Hither he his course is bending
With a faint and fretful sound
Such as marks the listening ear
Now he leaves the lower ground
And up the craggy hill ascending
Many a stop and stay he makes
Many a breathing fit he takes
Steep the way and wearisome
Yet all the while his whip is dumb.[12]

[12] *Benjamin the Waggoner* MS. 1, ll. 1–37 (DC MS. 56, leaves 1^{r} and 2^{r}).

The first twenty-five lines of this passage seem almost to be a companion piece to "The sun has long been set," composed on June 8, 1802; and Dorothy clearly still had that poem and the evening on which it was written in mind on June 15, as her complete journal entries for June 13 and 15 demonstrate. In addition, the variation in rhyme scheme and—especially at the beginning—the variation in length of lines distinguish this section from most of the remainder of the poem.

Although June 15 seems the likely date of composition for most of these opening lines, at least a few of them may date from July 7 or possibly 8 (on July 9 William and Dorothy set out on a journey to the Hutchinson farm at Gallow Hill, and further composition became unlikely). Lines 8–12 of the poem are similar to an entry in Dorothy's journal:

> *Wednesday* [*July 7th*]. . . . Walked on the White Moss. Glow-worms. Well for them children are in bed when they shine.[13]

She refers to the glowworms again the following night. While the verse lines about the glowworms may already have existed and Dorothy may be recalling them, it was more usual for Wordsworth to borrow from her.

A third section of the poem with pre-1806 origins could be the "Rock of Names" passage. The following 1802 entries from Dorothy Wordsworth's journal may be relevant:

> *Tuesday May 4th*. . . . We parted from Coleridge at Sara's Crag[14] after having looked at the Letters which C. carved in the morning. I kissed them all. Wm deepened the T with C.'s penknife.
>
> *Saturday* [*May*] *15th* [Written on the blotting paper facing the date:]
>
> S. T. Coleridge
> Dorothy Wordsworth William Wordsworth
> Mary Hutchinson Sara Hutchinson
> William Coleridge Mary
> Dorothy Sara
> 16th May
> 1802
> John Wordsworth
>
> *Saturday May 22nd*. . . . We met Coleridge, he was sitting under Sara's Rock when we reached him.[15]

---

[13] *Journals*, p. 145. Dorothy actually wrote by mistake "Wednesday 6th."

[14] The Rock of Names was occasionally referred to as Sara's Crag or Sara's Rock.

[15] *Journals*, pp. 120, 126, and 127.

The friends' current interest in the familiar rock with its "slender Spring" and the relationship implied by the initials carved on the rock may have led to Wordsworth's composition of some version of these lines from *Benjamin*:

> Ah! dearest Spot! dear Rock of Names
> From which our Pair thus slaked their flames!
> Ah! deem not this light strain unjust
> To thee and to thy precious trust,
> That file which gentle, brave, and good,
> The [?de]ar in friendship and in blood,
> The hands of those I love the best
> Committed to thy faithful breast!
> No, long as I've a genial feeling
> Or one that stands in need of healing
> I will preserve thy rightful power
> Inviolate till life's final hour.
> A[?ll take with kind]ness then as said
> With a fond heart though playfull head,
> And thou thy record duly keep
> Long after they are laid asleep.[16]

If earlier lines from the period of May through early June 1802 have here been drawn upon, they have been altered to suit this poem; the "light strain" and "playfull head" clearly refer to *Benjamin* and the tone of geniality and whimsy that the poet has adopted in most of it. Evidence for an 1802 date of composition is weak and hypothetical, however, and it is important to note contrary evidence. On February 5, 1805, John Wordsworth had been drowned in the wreck of the *Earl of Abergavenny*, and in early 1806 Coleridge was still abroad. The elegiac tone of the "Rock of Names" passage seems distinctly more appropriate to these circumstances than to those that prevailed in the spring of 1802.

That additional fragments of verse were drawn into *Benjamin the Waggoner* is unlikely, but the possibility should at least be considered. Parts of three descriptive passages in particular seem to be characterized by a somewhat greater variety in meter, in length of line, and in rhyme scheme than characterizes the poem as a whole: (1) the thunderstorm, MS. 1, lines 134–189; (2) the Wythburn merry-night, 318–335; and (3) some of the description of the moving cloud, 608–666. Such variety also characterizes the opening of the poem and the lines on the owl. It is not possible to say more on the basis of the slight evidence available, and even these connections are tenuous and conjectural.

As is often the case in Wordsworth's poetry, some stray images of an earlier date were drawn into *Benjamin*. A notable example appears in the second of seven lines of barely legible drafting in the Christabel Notebook (DC MS. 15, leaf 19^{r}): "The air works like a Lion's den[.]" These lines appear to be part

[16] *Benjamin the Waggoner* MS. 1, ll. 496–511 (DC MS. 56, leaves 20^{r} and 21^{r}).

of a previously unidentified "ballad poem never written" for which "The Danish Boy" was designed to serve as a prelude. (See Isabella Fenwick note in *PW*, II, 493.) They were composed before October 15, 1800; between June 15 and July 7 or 8, 1802, the "Lion's den" image was probably drawn into the "few lines about the night-hawk," and finally in early January 1806 it appeared in *Benjamin* MS. 1, line 17: "The air is like a Lion's den[.]"

III

The epilogue of the poem contains some evidence that Wordsworth may have contemplated writing *Benjamin the Waggoner* for several years before he actually did so:

A [?sad] Catastrophe, say you—
Adventure never worth a song?
Be free to think so, for I too
Have thought so many times and long. . . .
Nor is it I who play the part,
But a shy spirit in my heart
That comes and goes, will sometimes leap
From hiding-places ten years deep.
Sometimes, as in the present case,
Will shew a more familiar face,
Returning like a Ghost unlaid
Until the debt I owe be paid.[17]

Since the Wordsworths moved to Dove Cottage in the vale of Grasmere on December 20, 1799, and since further lines in the epilogue imply long familiarity with Benjamin and his waggon, the "Catastrophe" and Wordsworth's earliest impulse to write about it could not have occurred much before 1802. As its first line informs us, the events of the poem take place in June; and Wordsworth wrote the "few lines about the night-hawk and other images of the evening" on June 15, 1802. Benjamin's waggon may have made one of the sounds that the poet heard that evening, or—if the Waggoner's catastrophe had been a recent event—the absence of the sound may have stirred Wordsworth even more than its presence would have done. It is thus possible that the plan for *Benjamin* was conceived in June 1802.

When Wordsworth finally wrote the poem, he did so in the depth of the Grasmere winter, the very season when he especially felt the loss of Benjamin and his waggon:

But most of all, thou lordly Wain,
I wish to have thee here again
When windows flap and chimney roars
And all is dismal out of doors. . . .[18]

---

[17] MS. 1, ll. 752–755 and 758–765 (leaves 30^r and 31^r). See also the lines addressed to Lamb which were added to the epilogue in 1812.

[18] MS. 1, ll. 793–796 (leaf 32^r).

It was in winter that

> The lame, the sickly and the old,
> Men, Women heartless with the cold
> And Babes in wet and starvling plight[19]

most suffered from the loss of good Benjamin, who had allowed them shelter in his waggon from the wind and weather. That the poet's "emotion recollected in tranquillity" was rapidly succeeded by a genuine "spontaneous overflow of powerful feelings" his note in *Benjamin* MS. 2 testifies:

> This Poem was at first ~~writ~~ thrown
> under
> off ~~from~~ a lively impulse of feeling
> during
> ~~in~~ the first fortnight of the month
> of Jan^{ry} 180[6] and has since
> at several times been carefully revised
> retouched &
> and with the Author's best efforts, inspirited
> W Wordsworth[20]

This note, added to the manuscript perhaps in 1836, constitutes Wordsworth's fullest statement about the composition of the poem. It contradicts the "1805" placed by Wordsworth at the end of the fifth (1836) and all subsequent editions. There is a problem with the manuscript note, however: the "6" in "1806" was added in pencil, and there is evidence that it was added much later, probably by the celebrated bibliographer and forger T. J. Wise. (For an account of the history of this manuscript and evidence bearing on the added date, see Appendix II: "T. J. Wise and *Benjamin the Waggoner* MS. 2," below.)

Nonetheless, Wordsworth's later memory of the chronology of composition was often faulty, and 1806 is certainly the correct year. During the "first fortnight" of January 1806 Wordsworth was in Grasmere, while from about January 2 until January 10 or 15, 1805, he, Dorothy, Mary, and the children were on a visit to Park House, and Wordsworth was suffering from an inflammation of the eyes. During January 1806 Wordsworth was actively composing; on January 19 Dorothy wrote to Lady Beaumont that "my Brother though not actually employed in his great work, is not idle, for he almost daily produces something. . . ."[21] References to *Benjamin* survive from 1806, but none

---

[19] MS. 1, ll. 807–809 (leaves 32^{r} and 33^{r}).

[20] MS. 2, note on title page (leaf 1^{r}). Here and elsewhere, reduced type is used to indicate revisions.

[21] *MY*, I, 2. It may be worth noting that both *Benjamin* and another poem of this period, *The Character of the Happy Warrior* ("Probably composed between c 6 Dec 1805 and early Jan 1806": *Chronology: MY*, 41), allude to Lord Nelson, who had recently died.

from before then. Finally, MSS. 1 and 2 are both on hunting-horn-in-crowned-shield / 1798 paper, which was used by the family throughout 1806 but was not used at all before late 1805.[22]

It seems likely that no manuscripts survive from this early stage of composition. Two fragments containing three brief passages in Wordsworth's hand do survive from the period, but they seem less likely to be connected to Wordsworth's January 1–ca. January 14 composition of *Benjamin* than to the period of ca. January 14–March 29, during which he corrected and recopied to prepare the poem for transcription by Mary. Of the three passages, the one most likely to have been written before about mid-January occurs on the first interleaf of a manuscript that is composed of three gatherings of an interleaved copy of Coleridge's *Poems*, 1796:

Heard and in opposition quaff'd
A deep, determin'd, desperate, draft.
Nor did the batter'd Tar forget
Or flinch from what he deem'd *his* debt
Then like a Hero crown'd with laurel
Back to her place the ship he led
Wheel'd her back in full apparel
And so, flag flying at mast-head
Reyok'd her to the Ass—anon
Cries Benjamin we must be gone.
Thus after two hours hearty stay
Again behold them on their way
          Right gladly had the horses stirr'd
When they the smack of greeting heard[23]

This fragment has every appearance of being a fair copy. It is carefully written, and it contains no corrections. It breaks off at line 437 and thus is not a fragment of a complete fair copy, but was probably written to set some difficult lines in order before Mary transcribed them in MS. 1. Here the passage takes virtually the form in which it appears in MS. 1, although one spelling change suggests the sequence of transcription: "draft" as written here becomes "draft" corrected to "draught" in MS. 1, and is finally spelled "draught" in MS. 2.

A considerable number of fair-copy and draft lines preceding line 424 may have been present on the lost interleaved gatherings F through I from this volume, but it is impossible to be sure. It is probable, however, that lines immediately preceding 424 were present on the verso of the lost interleaf that faced the first surviving leaf of the manuscript, since the recto of that leaf

[22] Further information about this paper is provided in the headnote to the MS. 2 transcription.

[23] DC MS. 28, leaf 2^r (the first surviving interleaf); MS. 1, ll. 424–437. For detailed information about this and other *Benjamin the Waggoner* manuscripts mentioned in the Introduction, see the headnotes to the individual manuscripts.

contains a hastily written draft probably written to correct or add to the lost fair-copy lines:

> {a
> A bowl {of bowl of [?double] measure
> Cries Benjamin a draft of length
> ll Britains
> We drink to Englands pride and treasure
> Her bulwark & her tower of strength[24]

Unlike lines 424–437, this passage is carelessly written, contains corrections, and is entirely without punctuation.

The second manuscript fragment from this period contains a single passage, neither so careful as lines 424–437 nor so hastily written as lines 413–416:

> Straining sinews every horse
> To the utmost of his force
> And the smoke respiration
> Rises like an exhalation
> Which the merry merry sun
> Takes delight to play upon
> Never surely old Apollo[25]

This passage appears on an otherwise blank page in *Prelude* MS. X, in what seems to be a late, casual use of that manuscript. Although the lines are quite legible, the absence of other *Benjamin* material from this manuscript, the omission of "and" from line 653, and the absence of punctuation indicate that this is drafting rather than a section of fair copy. In MS. 1, "Straining sinews" becomes "Last and foremost," perhaps because "strain" is used three lines earlier.

Up to this point there probably existed no complete and satisfactory fair copy of the poem; the next step was to prepare one. The task became urgent shortly before March 2, when Dorothy wrote to Lady Beaumont:

> My Brother has thoughts of going to London before the end of this month: he desires me to say that if you have a bed for him he hopes to have the pleasure of spending the greater part of his time with you in Grosvenor Square. . . . He talks of staying about a month or five weeks. We have great delight in thinking of the possibility of Coleridge's reaching London before his return and all meeting under your roof.[26]

Wordsworth had completed *Benjamin* quite recently, and later events show that he wished to have a copy of it with him in London to read to friends. After the recent theft of a *Prelude* manuscript from the carrier's cart,[27] he

---

[24] DC MS. 28, leaf 1r; MS. 1, ll. 413–416.
[25] DC MS. 47, leaf 11r; MS. 1, ll. 651–657.
[26] *MY*, I, 12–13.
[27] See *EY*, p. 653, and *MY*, I, 2–4, for the story of this minor disaster. Since it happened just before *Benjamin* was written, it may have been a factor in the dislike that Wordsworth expresses at the end of the epilogue for the small carts that replaced Benjamin's waggon.

would have been especially careful to retain a clean copy at Dove Cottage for security. Almost invariably when such fair copies were needed, one or more of the women of the Wordsworth household were enlisted, and on this occasion the transcriber of both manuscripts was Mary.[28]

Although the work of transcription may have begun at any time after mid-January, both manuscripts were probably begun about March 2 or shortly thereafter and finished by March 29. Before March 2 the women were busy transcribing other texts, as Dorothy indicates in a letter to Catherine Clarkson: "[We have] been engaged in making two copies of William's poem [*The Prelude*], and I also in recopying my journal in a fair hand. . . . These works are finished, and also Sara's copy for Coleridge. . . ."[29] Both manuscripts must have been complete by the morning of March 29, when Wordsworth left for London, his date of departure apparently partly determined by "the chance of Southey's being going at this time."[30]

That de Selincourt was incorrect in assigning BL Ashley 4637 (MS. 2) priority of transcription over DC MS. 56 (MS. 1)[31] can be readily demonstrated. Although the manuscripts may appear at first to be duplicate fair copies, in their earliest states DC MS. 56 (MS. 1: 818 lines) was twenty lines shorter than BL Ashley 4637 (MS. 2: 838 lines). Twenty-three additional lines are present in the BL Ashley 4637 fair copy.[32] Without exception, these lines were entered neatly by Mary Wordsworth in MS. 1 as corrections to the initial fair copy, while they were present from the beginning in MS. 2. Only two lines from the earliest state of MS. 1 are absent from the MS. 2 fair copy: lines 532 and 533 were carefully but heavily deleted in MS. 1, probably before MS. 2 was transcribed. The sequence of transcription is thus clear, and it seems likely that MS. 1 was entirely transcribed before MS. 2 was begun. Two other distinctions between the manuscripts should be noticed: MS. 1 is divided into parts while MS. 2 is divided into cantos, as all succeeding manuscript and printed versions were to be; and in MS. 2 the first line of each verse paragraph is indented.

While one cannot be certain which manuscript Wordsworth took with him to London, the slightly neater and slightly more recent MS. 2 would seem

---

[28] De Selincourt incorrectly attributes both manuscripts to Sara Hutchinson (*PW*, II, 498). In the past, several manuscripts in the hand of Mary Wordsworth have been wrongly attributed to Sara Hutchinson because of a long-standing confusion about their hands, which at times can be quite similar. In addition to *Benjamin the Waggoner* MSS. 1 and 2, these manuscripts include DC MS. 24 (*Nutting* fragment only), DC MS. 44 (all that is not in DW's hand; this MS includes *Prelude* MS. M), DC MS. 53 (*Prelude* MS. B), DC MS. 62, DC MS. Verse 70, and DC MS. Verse 71.

[29] *MY*, I, 10. The letter is dated March 2.

[30] DW to Catherine Clarkson, March 28, 1806 (*MY*, I, 18).

[31] *PW*, II, 498.

[32] One line between MS. 1, ll. 202 and 203; four lines at 302/303; two lines after 411, with 412 deleted; four lines at 477/478; two lines at 503/504; four lines at 519/520; four lines at 545/546; two lines at 556/557.

more suitable. That one of the manuscripts was retained at Dove Cottage is evident from a comment by Mary to Wordsworth written shortly after April 6: "I have been reading Benjamin to Mrs C[oleridge] & Hartley—we were all delighted—will tell you about it tomorrow—."[33] Wordsworth passed much of his stay in London with the Beaumonts, and Dorothy wrote to Lady Beaumont on April 20 that she longed "to know your opinion and Sir George's of Benjamin, the Waggoner; I *think* you will be pleased with it, but cannot be so sure of this—."[34] Wordsworth may have read the poem aloud to the Lambs and other company on April 25 or 26.[35] There is no record of the Beaumonts' opinions, but Lamb's, as we have seen, was so favorable and encouraging that Wordsworth eventually dedicated the poem to him.

Of the two 1806 *Benjamin* manuscripts, MS. 2 was used much more extensively for drafts and revisions, and this edition therefore provides a complete transcription with facing photographs. MS. 1 received only limited use for this purpose, and readings that vary from those of MS. 2 are thus given in an *apparatus criticus* to the MS. 2 transcription; but the relatively few corrections and drafts in MS. 1 are often quite early ones, as, for example, the twenty-three lines in the MS. 2 fair copy which are present in MS. 1 only as revisions. Line numbers in MS. 1, by Mary in ink through 380 and by Wordsworth in pencil thereafter, were almost surely entered part way through the process of tidying up MS. 1 in preparation for the transcription of MS. 2; the numbers take into account added lines 202/203, [412], and 477/478, but do not take into account 302/303, probably 503/504, 519–520, 545/546, and 556/557. They do take into account lines 532 and 533, which apparently were then deleted and consequently omitted from the MS. 2 fair copy. Five lines that replace 186–189, drafted by Mary and Wordsworth and then entered to replace the original lines by Mary in MS. 1 and by Wordsworth in MS. 2, also seem to be early because of the presence of Mary's hand, although later than the MS. 2 fair copy and not counted in the line numbers.[36]

Probably no more than a few other corrections and drafts in MSS. 1 and 2 were made as early as 1806–1807. The major instance of drafting from this

---

[33] *MY*, I, 21. Unfortunately, the "long letter" that was to have contained Mary's account of the reading of *Benjamin* has apparently been lost.

[34] *MY*, I, 24. Dorothy had been quite sure that Lady Beaumont "would be deeply impressed by the Ode."

[35] See *Chronology: MY*, pp. 316 and 320.

[36] In what seems to be the single such instance, l. 311 has been included in the MS. 1 line numbers, although it was neither present in the initial MS. 2 fair copy nor deleted from MS. 1. The line is essential to the rhyme; Mary apparently either could not read it or could not find it, and left a gap in MS. 1, but counted it as she knew that it ought to be entered. When she transcribed MS. 2, the line was apparently still not available, and she again left a gap. The line was finally entered (following a facing draft by Wordsworth) in MS. 1 by Mary and in MS. 2 by Wordsworth.

period is, however, of distinct interest. An unsigned note and two passages of verse in MS. 1 are in the hand of Samuel Taylor Coleridge.

It is remarkable that Coleridge's involvement in the revisions to *Waggoner* MS. 1 was so long unrecognized. The two moderately long entries in DC MS. 56, though not signed, are clearly in Coleridge's hand, and were probably written between December 21, 1806, and April 17, 1807, when the Wordsworths and Coleridge were together at Coleorton.[37] Although Ernest de Selincourt examined this manuscript and made use of it in his edition of the *Poetical Works*, he does not include these notes; nor does he mention them. Readers will find what they need to appraise Coleridge's contributions to *Benjamin the Waggoner* in Appendix I of the present edition. It provides a brief commentary on some implications of the proposed changes, followed by complete transcriptions and facing photographs of the original fair-copy passages and earliest drafts, Coleridge's proposed revisions to them, and Wordsworth's complex corrections and drafts in response.

IV

The delight that Wordsworth's friends and family took even in the earliest version of *Benjamin the Waggoner* did not deter the poet from repeatedly revising it, as he did most of his long poems. It is possible that some of the next corrections and drafts in MS. 1, and the much more extensive ones in MS. 2, were made ca. May–December 1809; on May 1 of that year Dorothy wrote to Thomas De Quincey:

> My Brother has begun to correct and add to the poem of the White Doe, and has been tolerably successful. He intends to finish it before he begins with any other work, and has made up his mind, if he can satisfy himself in the alterations he intends to make, to publish it next winter, and to follow the publication by that of Peter Bell and the Waggoner.[38]

As *The White Doe of Rylstone* was not published until 1815, however, and as there is no other evidence to indicate that Wordsworth worked on *Benjamin* during this period, it is likely that the project never advanced very far.

Most of the revisions in MSS. 1 and 2 seem rather to be associated with the transcription of *Benjamin the Waggoner* MS. 3 (DC MS. 72) by Sara Hutchinson in early 1812, by and probably shortly before March 29. It is possible that Wordsworth had begun to revise the poem by December 1811. On December 4 (or possibly 3) Sara Hutchinson wrote to Mary Monkhouse, in words that assume her cousin's familiarity with *Benjamin*:

> It was fair when we set off but the *seasons returned* before we had gone far, & after Harry being completely drenched he arrived about an hour after me at Luffs where I

[37] See *Chronology: MY*, pp. 336 and 343.

[38] *MY*, I, 325.

was sitting Mistress of the House over a blazing stick fire in their nice little parlour with the Tea things before me in complete comfort having thought of Ben & the Sailor at the Cherry Tree. & repeated the lines many times.[39]

The weather itself may have been quite enough to cause her to think of this familiar poem, but the poem would also have been in her thoughts if Wordsworth had been actively revising it at the time, and the extensive drafts in MS. 2 are clearly not the work of a few days.

Most by far of the drafts in MS. 2 are in Wordsworth's hand, as the transcription and photographs in this edition indicate. Although Mary has made some neat corrections to the MS. 2 fair copy, probably contemporaneous with its transcription, her hand appears only once in the drafts, in a line of six X's between lines 383 and 384 on leaf 18[r] and in two lines on the facing verso meant to be inserted at that point:

> Ships stouter, loftier, ride the Sea
> But none so far renown'd as She

Both hand and ink differ from those of the fair copy, and although the lines (which are not present in MS. 1) may date from before 1812, they are probably later than her fair-copy corrections both here and in MS. 1. In her only involvement in any of the surviving *Benjamin* manuscripts, Dorothy Wordsworth's hand appears three times in the MS. 2 drafts:

1. In three lines of draft toward a replacement of line 61 on leaf 5[r]:

> Why need our Traveller then, (though frail
> Then why need Benjamin, (though frail
> His best resolves) be on his guard

2. In two lines of draft on leaf 24[v] related to lines 557–558:

> Hard passage forcing on with head
> Against the storm, & canvas spread

3. In "For" preceding line 756 on leaf 33[r] to replace "But," and in ten lines of pencil draft, to which a cross directs us, on leaf 31[v]:

> Accept O Friend for praise or blame
> The gift of this adventurous Song
> A record which I dared to frame
> Tho' timid scruples check'd me long
> They check'd me & I left the theme
> Untouch'd in spite of many a gleam

---

[39] Kathleen Coburn, ed., *The Letters of Sara Hutchinson from 1800 to 1835* (London, 1954), p. 36. See *Chronology: MY*, p. 487n, for evidence that the letter was probably written on December 4. Sara Hutchinson was probably thinking especially of *Benjamin* MS. 1, ll. 336–341.

Of fancy which thereon was shed
Like pleasant sun beams shifting still
Upon the side of a distant hill
But Nature might not be gainsaid

The dedication to Lamb is later than Wordsworth's drafts in pencil on leaf 32^{r}, and Wordsworth then entered it in ink on leaves 33^{r} and 32^{v}.

Following most of this activity and probably in conjunction with the final stage of it, Sara Hutchinson transcribed MS. 3, the next complete manuscript of *Benjamin the Waggoner*. She probably did so during March 1812 or shortly before, and certainly by March 29. In DC MS. 72, a commercially produced bound notebook composed of paper watermarked "1808," *Benjamin* MS. 3 was entered first and followed immediately by *Peter Bell* MS. 6. On March 28 Sara wrote to her cousin John Monkhouse that "I am at present busily employed in transcribing for William"; the following morning she added: "I have been transcribing the *Peter Bell* which is now completely finished and improved—and I intend to make another copy for myself when William has done with my Pen—."[40] MS. 6 is the only known manuscript of *Peter Bell* that could have come from this period, and the details of format, ink, and handwriting indicate that *Benjamin* MS. 3 was probably transcribed just before *Peter Bell* MS. 6 was begun.

In an interesting departure from the format that she uses elsewhere in MS. 3, Sara wrote the "Rock of Names" passage (MS. 1, ll. 496–511) in very small handwriting below ruled lines on leaves 22^{v} and 23^{r} (see photographs facing the transcription). She did so in response to a note by Wordsworth opposite these lines in MS. 2, leaf 23^{r}: "Checks I think the interest and stops the progress, therefore better out, do as you think best, Let [?the] the lines however be inserted put in the Margin." It seems likely that the very personal nature of this passage, with its implied references to his dead brother John and his now alienated friend Coleridge, was also a factor in Wordsworth's wish to remove it from the main text; his treatment of the three John Wordsworth elegies of 1805 provides an analogy.[41]

Two brief passages from *Benjamin* serve to illustrate how closely the transcription of *Benjamin* MS. 3 probably preceded that of *Peter Bell* MS. 6. Both passages appear on the first page of *Peter Bell* MS. 5 (DC MS. 60, leaf 1^{r}). The first is in Wordsworth's hand:

Earth spangled sky & lake serene
Involved & restless all—a scene
Pregnant with rare imagination
Rich change & multiplied creation

---

[40] Coburn, ed., *Letters of Sara Hutchinson*, pp. 42 and 46.

[41] See Betz, "After the *Lyrical Ballads*," p. 585n.

It opens

> There's something in a flying horse
> There's something in a huge balloon
> But through the clouds I'll never float
> Until I have a little boat
> Whose shape is like the crescent Moon.

This little boat is poetic fancy, at least it *may* be considered as such. The poet at once finds himself seated in his canoe and rapidly takes flight — [Robinson then quotes selected passages from MS. 6 of *Peter Bell*, accompanying them with his own marginal gloss.]

Benjamin the Waggoner has far less meaning. It is, says Wordsworth purely fanciful. The good Waggoner is addicted to liquor, but on the Night of the adventure resists temptation—he gives shelter to a Sailor's Wife during a storm and the Sailor will treat him at the Alehouse. The Model of a Ship the Sailor has with him is shown to the frolicking peasants but the hours are lost and the Waggoners Master is so enraged at seeing his Waggoner return with the Sailor and his Wife, and his own dog wounded by a kick from the Sailors Ass that he turns off poor Benjamin—the horses will obey no one else so the poet loses both Waggon and Waggoner—But this tale is told with grace and has delightful [*del to* passages][50] of description and elegant playfulness. The poem opens with an exquisite of an Evening after a hot day.

Here Robinson quotes lines 8–27 from MS. 3, with a few changes in accidentals,[51] then goes on to copy out another section of the poem, lines 333–342. He concludes by remarking:

This is in the Spirit of kindness and indulgence Wordsworth praises in Burns Tam OShanter—In describing the dancing and joy in the Ale house the Poet concludes

> As if it heard the fiddles call
> The pewter clatters on the Wall
> The very bacon shows it's feeling
> Swinging from the smoky ceiling

I must put a limit to copying or I shall have taken more than Wordsworth might wish to have in writing out of his possession.[52]

Later, on June 4, Crabb Robinson himself read *Peter Bell* at Flaxman's, until interrupted by the poet Samuel Rogers,[53] and on June 6 he read both poems to another friend:

Breakfasted with Parken to whom I read Wordsworths two poems. He was worthy to hear them read and was no niggard of his praise. Indeed he has a lively sense of all

---

[50] See "Editorial Procedure," below.

[51] William Knight, in his edition of *The Poetical Works of William Wordsworth*, III (London, 1896), 77, quotes twelve variant lines of the poem "from a MS. copy of the poem in Henry Crabb Robinson's *Diary, etc.*—1812." The lines at first appear to have been drawn from an unknown manuscript, but in fact they are MS. 3, ll. 8–19, quoted from Crabb Robinson's June 4 entry, with further changes in accidentals and two misreadings: "Sooth they come" rather than "Forth they come" (l. 11) and "In the play" rather than "In the sky" (l. 15).

[52] Crabb Robinson's diary, leaves 94^r–97^v. All or part of this analysis was probably written two days later; see the entry for June 6, quoted below.

[53] Crabb Robinson's diary, leaf 98^r.

excellence and retains more companionable qualities than any person of his religious feelings—At Chambers and early in the morning writing the preceding Analysis of the poems which occupied me till 2.[54]

After dinner that day, Crabb Robinson was "With C Lamb Lent him Peter Bell—To my Surprise he finds nothing in it good";[55] even before *Benjamin* was dedicated to him, Lamb preferred it to the more serious and overtly ambitious *Peter Bell.*

Wordsworth's excursion to the south came to an end when he learned, probably on June 10, of the sudden death of his daughter Catharine. He departed from London on June 12 to be with Mary at Hindwell in Wales, and they returned to Grasmere on or about July 5,[56] doubtless carrying *Benjamin* with them.

V

The next tentative stirring of the still unpublished *Benjamin the Waggoner* apparently took place while the printing of *The Excursion* was under way. On April 24, 1814, Dorothy wrote to Catherine Clarkson:

We are all most thankful that William has brought his mind to consent to printing so much of his work; for the MSS. were in such a state that, if it had pleased Heaven to take him from this world, they would have been almost useless. I do not think the book [*The Excursion*] will be *published* before next winter; but, at the same time, will come out a new edition of his poems in two Volumes Octavo, and shortly after—Peter Bell, The White Doe, and Benjamin the Waggoner. This is resolved upon, and I think you may depend upon not being disappointed.[57]

The Excursion did in fact appear in July, while both the new edition of Wordsworth's shorter poems (*Poems, including Lyrical Ballads*) and *The White Doe of Rylstone* were published in 1815; but *Peter Bell* and *Benjamin* still failed to appear, and Mary Moorman has suggested that Wordsworth may have been discouraged from publishing them by his "disappointment over the reception of *The Excursion* and *The White Doe.*"[58]

On May 2, 1815, Wordsworth set out on another trip to London, and again he seems to have taken *Benjamin* along.[59] On May 22 the Lambs wrote to Mrs. Morgan and Charlotte Brant: "Has Wordsworth told you that coming to town he lost the manuscript of 'The Waggoner' and 'Peter Bell' and two hundred lines of a new poem, and that he is not certain he can by any means recover a correct copy of them."[60] The manuscript involved was

---

[54] Crabb Robinson's diary, leaf 98^{v}. This account, omitted by Morley, is here published for the first time.

[55] Crabb Robinson's diary, leaf 98^{v}.

[56] *Chronology: MY*, pp. 504–507.

[57] *MY*, II, 140.

[58] *MY*, II, 140n.

[59] See *Chronology: MY*, pp. 599–609, for a full account of this journey and the stay in London.

[60] Edwin W. Marrs, Jr., ed., *The Letters of Charles and Mary Anne Lamb*, III (Ithaca, 1978), 161.

almost surely DC MS. 72, which contains *Benjamin the Waggoner* MS. 3, *Peter Bell* MS. 6, and *Artegal and Elidure*. It was apparently recovered, since there is no further reference to the loss, and since MS. 72 is now safely at the Dove Cottage Wordsworth Library.

The next reference in family letters to the intended publication of *Benjamin* was not, as it was in April 1814, merely a false alarm. On May 7, 1819, shortly after the publication of *Peter Bell* in April, Sara Hutchinson wrote to John Monkhouse:

> You will have seen by the Newspapers that *Peter Bell* is published—as also a spurious Peter who made his appearance a week before the true one. . . . The false one is very stupid, but I have no doubt that it has helped the sale of the true one—which has nearly all been sold in about a week, now a new Ed: is called for—Some good-natured person—the Author no doubt—sent William a No. of the '*Literary Gazzette*' in which is a most abominably abusive critique—it can only be written from personal *malice*—for the most beautiful passages are selected for ridicule. . . . This critique made us advise him to publish the *Waggoner*, just to give them another bone to pick, which he has consented to—and it will come out as soon as possible I hope with the second Ed: of *Peter*.[61]

The sudden demand for a second edition of *Peter Bell* and the wish of the Wordsworth family to show their contempt for critical malice were no doubt factors in the final decision to proceed with publication. Very little time intervened, however, between the publication of *Peter Bell* in April and the publication of *The Waggoner* in late May or early June. It seems likely that Wordsworth was willing to proceed with such speed partly because he had a satisfactory text in readiness. When was that text prepared?

There seems to be no firm evidence with which to answer the question, but it is possible to argue toward a tentative conclusion through analogy with *Peter Bell*. Although *Benjamin* and *Peter Bell* are connected in certain other ways as well, their textual histories became intertwined in March 1812 when Sara Hutchinson transcribed revised versions of each into the same notebook. The layers of revision in both manuscripts, *Benjamin* MS. 3 and *Peter Bell* MS. 6, are so similar in character that it seems probable that they were entered at approximately the same time. Aside from a few very early corrections to the fair copy by Sara Hutchinson, all revisions are in the hands of Mary Wordsworth or of the poet. Both manuscripts contain some pencil drafts by Wordsworth. There are pencil revisions in both hands, often later erased after being entered in ink. In a great majority of cases, the final layer of revisions was entered in ink by Mary.

One might expect to find this work being done in the winter or early spring of 1818–1819, shortly preceding the publication of both poems; and indeed,

[61] Coburn, ed., *Letters of Sara Hutchinson*, p. 154.

during this period Wordsworth and Mary were at Rydal Mount while Sara was at Hindwell in Wales. The fair copies of the poems transcribed for the printer apparently do not survive. However, a fragment in Mary's hand, discarded from the *Peter Bell* transcription that was sent to the printer and unknown to previous editors, does survive.[62] It is watermarked with a distinctive "1816"; the same watermark appears in five Wordsworth and Mary Wordsworth letters at the Dove Cottage Wordsworth Library, all written between December 1, 1818, and January 12, 1819.[63] Thus Mary Wordsworth apparently transcribed the final manuscript of *Peter Bell* within this fairly brief period. Mary also entered most of the final corrections to *Peter Bell* MS. 6 and *Benjamin* MS. 3; it is likely that between November 1818 and March 1819 she transcribed the text of *Benjamin* which went to the printer.

When the poem was finally published in late May–early June 1819, its title had been altered to *The Waggoner*. Although its working title had always previously been *Benjamin the Waggoner*, it appears earlier to have possessed a longer title. In MSS. 1 and 2 the poem is called *Benjamin the Waggoner &c*; the "&c" is probably explained in MS. 3, leaf 7[r], where beneath "Benjamin the Waggoner" Sara Hutchinson seems to have written the now thoroughly erased "and his Waggon." If there is an element of self-parody here, the longer title also recognizes the central role of the waggon itself in the narrative.

The second change in title, from *Benjamin the Waggoner* to *The Waggoner*, seems to have been made just before publication. In the *London Literary Gazette* of May 22, 1819, the publisher had already announced the forthcoming publication of *Benjamin the Waggoner*, and on the verso of the flyleaf before the engraved frontispiece in the second edition of *Peter Bell*, which was published almost simultaneously with *The Waggoner*, appears the notice:

In a few Days will be published,

BENJAMIN THE WAGGONER,

A Poem,

BY WILLIAM WORDSWORTH.

"What's a NAME?
"Brutus will start a Spirit as soon as Cæsar!"

---

[62] This fragment, composed of two conjugate leaves, was turned upside down and used for drafting toward "To the Nab Well" ("Composed when a Probability existed of our being obliged to quit Rydal Mount as a Residence"), and is now the final two leaves of DC MS. Verse 73. It was probably discarded from the *Peter Bell* transcription because of three corrections that made it no longer acceptable as fair copy. The *Peter Bell* lines (721–750) are all in Mary Wordsworth's hand, and the corrected readings are the same as those of the first edition, 1819.

[63] Letter 524 (December 4) in *MY*, II; letters 21 (December 1), 22 (December 6), 23 (December 18), and 24 (January 12) in *The Letters of Mary Wordsworth*, 1800–1855, ed. Mary E. Burton (Oxford, 1958).

John Hamilton Reynolds had seized on the announced title of *Peter Bell* to write and publish his own parody of Wordsworth under the same title, even before the genuine *Peter* had appeared. Although the ensuing publicity increased the sale of Wordsworth's poem, perhaps concern that the announcement of *Benjamin* might call forth a similar parody determined the change of title. Indeed, between June 19 and 26, shortly after the publication of *The Waggoner*, an anonymous parodist, who was probably John Gibson Lockhart of *Blackwood's*, published *Benjamin the Waggoner: A Ryghte Merrie and Conceitede Tale in Verse, a Fragment*, a good general parody of Wordsworth which has nothing to do with *Benjamin* beyond the title.[64]

Charles Lamb responded with delight to Wordsworth's dedication to him of *The Waggoner*. In his letter to Wordsworth of June 7, 1819, after the paragraph quoted at the beginning of this Introduction he continues:

> Methinks there is a kind of shadowy affinity between the subject of the narrative and the subject of the dedication—but I will not enter into personal themes—else, substituting ******* **** for Ben, and the Honble United Company of Merch[ts] trading to the East Indies for the Master of the misused Team, it might seem by no far fetched analogy to point its dim warnings hitherward—but I reject the omen—. . . .[65]

It was evident by July 25 that *The Waggoner* would not achieve the minor publishing success of *Peter Bell*. As Sara wrote to Thomas Monkhouse:

> We are sorry that the false Benjamin, & the 'battered Tar' have not had the same agreeable effect upon the true Benjamin as the false *Peter* had upon the true—for there has been no call for a second Ed: We had a most droll letter from Lamb concerning Ben: & the Dedication—It was worth while to have written the poem for the sake of the Letter.[66]

Although Lamb's was surely the most notable one, it was not the only enthusiastic letter written to Wordsworth about *The Waggoner*. Hans Busk, who had written to the poet on April 29 to praise *Peter Bell* (a copy of which Wordsworth had sent him), wrote on June 24 to thank him for his "kind and esteemed present" of a copy of *The Waggoner* and to praise the "simplicity" of the poem and the "naivetés of rural scenery & primitive rustic habit sketched by the hand of science, taste & sensibility."[67] On July 6 Wordsworth responded: "The Waggoner was written con amore, and as the Epilogue

---

[64] See Jack Benoit Gohn, "Who Wrote *Benjamin the Waggoner?*: An Inquiry," *The Wordsworth Circle*, VIII, 1 (Winter 1977), 69–74. Gohn presents evidence that the parody's author was probably Lockhart, and not as has generally been assumed John Hamilton Reynolds.

[65] Lucas, ed., *Letters of Charles Lamb*, II, 249–251. Haydon was also sent a copy; see M.H. to Thomas Monkhouse, June 15, 1819, *in Letters of Mary Wordsworth*, ed. Burton, p. 51.

[66] Coburn, ed., *Letters of Sara Hutchinson*, pp. 157–158.

[67] These letters are among the correspondence at the Dove Cottage Wordsworth Library addressed to Wordsworth.

states almost in my own despite; I am not therefore surprized that you read it with pleasure; composing wide[ly] as you do from unborrowed feelings—. . . ."[68] William Pearson, describing himself as one of "your less learned admirers," wrote on July 30 that

the Waggoner is a good deal different from your other poems—it is more light, and merry, and humourous, and if I am not mistaken promises to be more generally acceptable. In taking a less elevated flight, and appealing to more universal sympathies, it comes more home to the business and bosoms of *every-day* Man. . . . not its least charm arrises from its allusions to and communion with the history and feelings of the Poet and his family. There is a kindly sympathy with human nature in the lower walks of life spread over the poem,—this is one of the excellent moral effects of your poetry. In the Waggoner we perceive how often the vices of Man may be combined with amiable qualities of heart, and, perhaps in part arrise from them—so that by seeing more clearly into the causes of some of his immoral wanderings we view him with more indulgence and pity, and certainly feel great regret that a man like "mild Benjamin" should be ruined by a single infirmity.[69]

Although Wordsworth had finally ventured to submit to public scrutiny this poem written "almost in my own despite," the text had not yet assumed its final form. Before 1850 *The Waggoner* was to pass through six further editions, three of them involving substantial revisions.

VI

Except for the extensive alterations that Wordsworth made to *The Waggoner* in 1836, the history of the poem's development during the remaining thirty-one years of the poet's life can be told briefly. As early as autumn 1819 Wordsworth was already planning the second edition of the poem. During November or December 1819 Sara wrote to John Monkhouse:

William intends to publish a batch of small poems immediately—& when a new Ed: of the other poems is called for, which will be in a few months, these with *The White Doe*, Benjamin, *Peter*, & the Odes, will make a third volume—this ed: will be a small octavo in a cheaper style. . . .[70]

This octavo edition was expanded to four volumes and became *The Miscellaneous Poems of William Wordsworth*, published in 1820; it included the second edition of *The Waggoner*, with substantial revisions to the 1819 text.

The alterations made in 1820 were primarily of three sorts: (1) the expansion of contractions, primarily "'d" to "ed"; (2) changes in punctuation from the inconsistently punctuated first edition; and (3) several additions and revisions to the text (see, for example, ll. 3–5, 98n, 183/184, 300–301,

---

[68] *MY*, II, 547.

[69] This letter is also among the correspondence at the Dove Cottage Wordsworth Library addressed to Wordsworth.

[70] Coburn, ed., *Letters of Sara Hutchinson*, p. 165.

and 604n). Most of the changes then made were retained in all further lifetime editions.

Very few changes were made in the third edition, published in the five-volume *Poetical Works* of 1827. Some of Crabb Robinson's comments in a letter to Dorothy Wordsworth (May 21, 1827) upon receiving a gift of this edition are worth recording, however, since they apply so aptly to *The Waggoner* as well as to many of Wordsworth's other poems:

> I have received the new edition and am indeed grateful for it. . . . In the work of collation I have yet been able to make but little progress But I have seen enough to rejoice both in the quantity of the new and the quality of the alterd The variations of the three editions I possess are a matter of very interesting remark—A time will come, may it be very remote! when variorum editions will be published And the variations given—But an author himself cannot do this for obvious reasons—I have sometimes thought that Mr. W: on looking over his various readings must feel as a mother does who while caressing her youngest child, doubts whether she is not wronging the elder that is away—. . . .[71]

Although still few, a greater number of changes was made in the fourth edition, published in the four-volume *Poetical Works* of 1832; these are primarily further changes in punctuation.

For the fifth edition of *The Waggoner* in the six-volume *Poetical Works* of 1836–1837, Wordsworth undertook extensive revision. The unpublished diary of Edward Quillinan, who acted as Wordsworth's amanuensis during the process of revision and who later became the poet's son-in-law, tells part of the story:[72]

Wednesday, August 3, 1836	Mr. W. & Poems—
Thursday, August 4	Walked with Mr. W Poems tinkered
Friday, September 2	Desc. Sk. The Waggoner
Saturday, September 3	The Waggoner
Saturday, September 10	The Waggoner to the end.
Monday, September 12	Waggoner in the morng Note to Rock of Names Afternoon drove to John Fletcher's: walked to Rock of Names—the several initials—

Two brief manuscripts survive from this period: (1) a manuscript at Cornell University containing drafts corresponding to 1819, lines 683–692, and a draft of 1836 Note 3; and (2) a manuscript among the Quillinan papers containing drafts corresponding to 1819, lines 650–651, 655–656, 667–668, 682–692, 698–699, and 703–707, and also two drafts of 1836 Note 1 and a draft of 1836 Note 3.[73]

---

[71] Edith J. Morley, ed., *The Correspondence of Henry Crabb Robinson with the Wordsworth Circle (1808–1866)*, I (Oxford, 1927), 183–184.

[72] The diary is among the Quillinan papers at the Dove Cottage Wordsworth Library.

[73] For a description of these manuscripts, see the headnote to the Manuscripts of 1836.

The rest of the story is revealed in the printer's copy of 1836, which was a set of the four volumes of 1832 heavily revised by Wordsworth and his amanuenses (John Carter, Edward Quillinan, Mary, and Dora). The revisions swarm between the lines, in the margins, and occasionally onto paste-overs and interleaved scraps.

Work on the proof sheets of Volume I, which was to contain *The Waggoner*, apparently went forward during September and October. This work must have been completed by October 20, for on that date Wordsworth sent to his publisher Edward Moxon "by this Post a list of Errata and emendations for Mr Evans,"[74] of the printing firm of Bradbury and Evans. In November 1836 the heavily revised fifth edition of *The Waggoner* was published with the addition of three notes, one printing for the first time the "Rock of Names" passage and the lines that introduce it. On October 20 Wordsworth wrote to T. J. Judkin promising to have Moxon send the volumes of the new edition as they came out, and adding:

> If you think it worth while to compare the pieces entitled "Evening Walk," "Descriptive Sketches," and "The Waggoner," you will find I have made very considerable alterations, which I trust will be found to be improvements—at all events they ought to be so, for they cost me much labour.[75]

With these "very considerable alterations," most parts of *The Waggoner* took on what was to remain substantially their final form.

In another entry probably made on or about September 4, while he was assisting Wordsworth in copying out changes to *The Waggoner*, Quillinan wrote:

> W. places the Waggoner among the poems of *Fancy*.—The introductory passage about the glowworms was intended to shew the principle on which it was composed & to put the reader in the state of mind favourable for the perusal of a poem of fancy—It is all fancy [to *del*] "the very bacon has a feeling."
>
> Peter Bell may be contrasted with it as a Poem of *Imagination*.[76]

In 1820 *The Waggoner* had been placed first among the "Poems of the Fancy," while in 1827, 1832, and 1836 it was placed between "Poems of the Affections" and "Poems of the Fancy," and in 1845 and 1849 it was made the last of the "Poems of the Fancy."

A graphic summary of a few major changes made in the course of the poem's development should here be useful. Except where noted, line numbers are from MS. 3, since that text is the fullest.

---

[74] *LY*, II, 808.

[75] *LY*, II, 809.

[76] This entry is on leaf 16r of a notebook that Quillinan used during this period; on the cover is written: "RYDAL / MOUNT. / 1836." It is among the Quillinan papers at the Dove Cottage Wordsworth Library.

MS. 1 (818 lines)	*MS. 2* (838 lines)	*MS. 3* (945 lines)	*Waggoner 1819* (847 lines)	*Waggoner 1836* (864 lines)
—	Canto 1.st	—	CANTO FIRST.	CANTO FIRST.
Second Part	Canto 2.^{d}	—	CANTO SECOND.	CANTO SECOND.
Third Part	Canto 3.^{d}	—	CANTO THIRD.	CANTO THIRD.
←———— Benjamin's boast (MS. 1, ll. 548–560)	————	——“Rock of Names” (ll 534–551) much expanded (ll. 595–621) (break between ll. 668 and 669)	passage dropped	restored in note
		—	CANTO FOURTH.	CANTO FOURTH.
←———— The rising mist (MS. 1, ll. 608–627)	————	——Muse's excursion (ll. 675–724) much expanded (ll. 725–746)		
←————	————	——Dedication to Lamb (ll. 872–881)		

In 1845, for the sixth edition, in the one-volume *Poems of William Wordsworth*, fairly substantial alterations were made, and Wordsworth revised for a final time such problem lines as 262–263, 319, 657/658, 658, and 683–689. The seventh edition of *The Waggoner*, the final one during Wordsworth's lifetime, appeared in the six-volume *Poetical Works* of 1849–1850. This text has generally been treated as standard and has been reprinted since then in anthologies and volumes of Wordsworth's poetry. The changes embodied in it are minor, and fewer than in any other lifetime edition.

Charles Lamb's enthusiastic response to *Benjamin the Waggoner* as he first encountered it in 1806, and as he knew it again in its 1812 and 1819 versions, opened this account, and the account may be closed with an entry that Henry Crabb Robinson made in his diary during this final period:

> July 19th [1849] . . . . I read early Wordsworth's *Waggoner* in bed with great pleasure. [William Bodham] Donne had praised it highly. It did not used to be a favourite with me, but I discovered in it to-day a benignity and gentle humour, with a view of human life and a felicity of diction which rendered the dedication of it to Charles Lamb peculiarly appropriate. . . .[77]

I hope that this edition of *Benjamin the Waggoner* will help these qualities to shine forth.

---

[77] Morley, ed., *Henry Crabb Robinson on Books*, II, 691. "William Bodham Donne, later librarian of the London Library and Examiner of Plays. He became an intimate friend of Crabb Robinson" (p. 660n).

Editorial Procedure

Like other volumes in this series, this edition provides two kinds of texts: (1) "reading texts," from which all complexities and variant readings, if present, are stripped away, and (2) transcriptions of manuscripts, with facing photographic reproductions of the manuscripts if those manuscripts are complex and difficult to read. Editorial procedures have been adapted to the different aims of these two styles of presentation.

In this volume, the two reading texts face one another and represent distinct stages in the textual history of the poem. The reading text of the earliest complete manuscript of *Benjamin the Waggoner*, DC MS. 56, is designed to present the poem in its earliest recoverable form. When possible, therefore, only the earliest readings are given; overwritings are not shown except in fourteen cases, all enclosed in brackets, where the deleted words or words could not be recovered. The second reading text is of the first edition of *The Waggoner*, and it is presented as published in 1819, with a few obvious errors corrected. The accidentals of the *Waggoner* 1819 reading text, therefore, have not been modified; but the reading text drawn from DC MS. 56 required a different strategy. As with all *Benjamin the Waggoner* manuscripts, this text is generally but inconsistently underpunctuated. The original punctuation has here always been retained, but editorial punctuation has been added in accordance with the principle outlined in the headnote to the reading texts.

The other main type of text is the transcription of a manuscript (MSS. 2 and 3 are presented in this form), and is more complicated. Here the aim is to show with reasonable typographic accuracy everything in the manuscript that could be helpful to a study of the poem's growth and development. Even false starts and corrected letters can sometimes reveal the writer's intention, and they are here recorded, though reinforced letters and random marks are normally not. Passages in Wordsworth's hand are printed in roman type; passages in the hands of amanuenses are printed in italic with footnotes identifying the copyist, although identification of hands must occasionally be conjectural, especially in the case of scattered words or parts of words. Revisions are shown in type of reduced size, and an effort has been made to show deletion marks, spacing, and other such physical features so that they resemble those of the manuscript itself, although some minor adjustments of those features have been made in the interest of clarity. In the transcriptions of MS. 2, which face photographs of the manuscript pages, run-over lines are shown approximately as they appear in the manuscript. In the numbering of leaves, stubs are counted. Line numbers of the transcriptions are keyed to the MS. 1 reading text. In MS. 2 transcriptions of fair copy these numbers are carried in the left margin, while in transcriptions of drafts the range of roughly corresponding line numbers is shown within brackets at the upper right of each page. MS. 3 diverges much farther from MS. 1: while it is keyed to the MS. 1 reading text by bracketed numbers in the right margin, it has also been given line numbers of its own in the left margin. Further details of presentation are given in the headnote to each transcription.

To avoid unnecessary elaboration in textual notes, all quotations from manuscripts are printed in roman type.

The following symbol is used in the MS. 1 reading text only:

[inspiration]	Revised version; underlying reading deleted and not recovered.

The following symbol is used in the MS. 1 reading text, in transcriptions, and in the *apparatus criticus*:

[?Once more]	Conjectural reading of word or words.

The following symbols are used in transcriptions; the first three also appear in the *apparatus criticus*:

Y{ou / e}	An overwriting: original reading, "Ye," converted to "You" by writing "ou" upon the "e."
{ ;	A short addition, sometimes only a mark of punctuation.
[? ?]	Illegible word or words; each question mark represents one word.
[ ]	Gap or blank in the manuscript.
[—?—?—]	Deleted and illegible word or words; each question mark represents one word.
Stormy and dark	Word or words written over an erasure; the original is now illegible. Notes record the reading of the most closely related manuscript, and any visible letters are shown in boldface type.

The following symbols are used in the *apparatus criticus*:

{ pride / [?peace]	Word or words written over an erasure; the original is now legible or partly legible.
alt	Alternate reading; the original reading is not deleted.
del	Reading deleted.
del to	Reading changed to another reading; the original is deleted.

Benjamin the Waggoner MS. 1 (1806)

The Waggoner, First Edition (1819)

with Manuscript and Printed Variants
through 1849 in an *Apparatus Criticus*

Facing Reading Texts

The Cherry Tree Inn, Wythburn, about 1830–1835. Drawing, perhaps by Dora Wordsworth, preserved among the Wordsworth family papers at The Stepping Stones, Ambleside, until 1970; now in the possession of the editor.

Benjamin the Waggoner MS. 1 (1806) and *The Waggoner*, First Edition (1819)

The text on the left-hand pages is drawn from Mary Wordsworth's fair-copy transcription of *Benjamin the Waggoner* (DC MS. 56), MS. 1. Where the fair copy has been altered, the earliest readings, except for obvious miswritings corrected by the copyist, are shown when they are recoverable; when they are not recoverable, the later readings are bracketed and footnoted. Conjectural recoveries, also within brackets, are preceded by a question mark. Spelling, capitalization, and paragraphing are taken from MS. 1 without modification. Since this text faces the printed text of 1819, in which the verbal endings "'d" and "ed" irregularly appear, the few instances here of "'d" have been retained.

As is pointed out in Editorial Procedure, above, *Benjamin the Waggoner* manuscripts are generally but inconsistently underpunctuated. Here the original punctuation has always been retained, but editorial punctuation has been added, with an effort to be as consistent as possible while retaining the rather informal flavor (such as results from frequent use of dashes) of the original. In the adding of punctuation, first MS. 2 has been consulted, then when necessary MS. 3 and the first edition, in that order of authority.

Lines are numbered consecutively, by fives, in the left margin. Although previous editors have numbered this poem by cantos, to have followed this precedent in a variorum edition would have led to unnecessary complication: the poem was first divided into three parts (later called cantos), then into four; and in the fourth part (or canto) the conclusion of the regular narrative is separated from the epilogue addressed to Charles Lamb.

The facing text, on the right-hand pages, is reproduced from the first edition of *The Waggoner*, 1819, with all accidentals such as spelling, capitalization, and paragraphing, and punctuation intact; a few obvious printer's errors have been mended. The lines, numbered consecutively by fives in the right margin, have been keyed to the facing MS. 1 reading text with bracketed line numbers in the left margin.

The *apparatus criticus* records all variant readings found in editions of *The Waggoner* published in England during Wordsworth's lifetime, as follows:

1820 *The Miscellaneous Poems of William Wordsworth* (4 vols.; London, 1820).
1827 *The Poetical Works of William Wordsworth* (5 vols.; London, 1827).
1832 *The Poetical Works of William Wordsworth* (4 vols.; London, 1832).
1836 *The Poetical Works of William Wordsworth* (6 vols.; London, 1836–1837).
1840 *The Poetical Works of William Wordsworth* (6 vols.; London, 1840; a stereotyped reissue of the volumes of 1836 with various alterations; again reissued, with a few alterations, in 1841 and 1843).

1845 *The Poems of William Wordsworth* (London, 1845; reissued in stereotype, 1847 and 1849).

1846 *The Poetical Works of William Wordsworth* (7 vols.; London, 1846; another stereotyped reissue of the six volumes of 1836, incorporating further alterations, with an additional volume incorporating *Poems, Chiefly of Early and Late Years,* 1842; reissued, again with a few alterations, 1849).

1849 *The Poetical Works of William Wordsworth* (6 vols.; London, 1849–1850).

In the *apparatus criticus*, a citation of each volume in the list above implies its stereotyped reissues as well, unless otherwise noted, as follows:

1840 implies 1841, 1843
1841 implies 1843
1845 implies 1847, 1849 (1 volume)
1846 implies 1849 (7 volumes)
1847 implies 1849 (1 volume).

The *apparatus criticus* also records all variants found in two brief manuscripts (at Cornell University and at the Dove Cottage Wordsworth Library) which contain drafts made in preparation for the edition of 1836, and variants found in MS. 1832/36, the printer's copy for the 1836 edition (in the Wellesley College Library, English Poetry Collection). Variants in MS. 1832/36 are recorded only when they differ from the 1836 printed readings; in the absence of a note to the contrary, it may be assumed that the readings of MS. 1832/36 and 1836 are identical. Where portions of these various manuscripts of 1836 are transcribed in full in a separate section of this edition, a note to that effect is entered in the *apparatus criticus* in place of the variants themselves.

Finally, all variants found in MS. 1836/45, an annotated copy of the six-volume *Poetical Works* of 1836–1837 in the Royal Library at Windsor Castle (see Helen Darbishire, *Some Variants in Wordsworth's Text*, Oxford, 1949), are also recorded here. This set, which includes a proof state of *The Waggoner*, contains revisions to the accidentals in pencil in the hand of John Carter, who also added a few directions. When adopted at all, these revisions appear in the regular issue of the 1836–1837 printing (where they are corrections of typographical errors in the proof state) and, more often, in the first stereotype reissue of the edition in 1840. MS. 1836/45 also contains five pencil revisions to the text of the poem, ranging from one word to six lines, in the hand of Wordsworth. They represent, somewhat roughly, a step toward the next extensive revision of the poem in the one-volume *Poems* of 1845.

A limited number of explanatory notes is provided beneath the MS. 1 text; they are supplemented by a few notes beneath the 1819 text when that text has diverged from MS. 1.

The three notes first printed in 1836, the third of which presents the "Rock of Names" passage, follow the two reading texts. The *apparatus criticus* to the three notes records all variants found in manuscript drafts from 1836 and later and all subsequent printed variants to 1850.

THE

WAGGONER,

A Poem.

TO WHICH ARE ADDED,

SONNETS.

BY

WILLIAM WORDSWORTH.

"What's in a NAME?"

— — — — — — — — —

"Brutus will start a Spirit as soon as Cæsar!"

LONDON:
Printed by Strahan and Spottiswoode, Printers-Street;
FOR LONGMAN, HURST, REES, ORME, AND BROWN,
PATERNOSTER-ROW.
1819.

TO

CHARLES LAMB, Esq.

MY DEAR FRIEND,

WHEN I sent you, a few weeks ago, the Tale of Peter Bell, you asked "why THE WAGGONER was not added?" —To say the truth,— from the higher tone of imagination, and the deeper touches of passion aimed at in the former, I apprehended, this little Piece could not accompany it without disadvantage. In the year 1806, if I am not mistaken, THE WAGGONER was read to you in manuscript; and, as you have remembered it for so long a time, I am the more encouraged to hope, that, since the localities on which it partly depends did not prevent its being interesting to you, it may prove acceptable to others. Being therefore in some measure the cause of its present appearance, you must allow me the gratification of inscribing it to you; in acknowledgment of the pleasure I have derived from your Writings, and of the high esteem with which I am

Very truly yours,

WILLIAM WORDSWORTH.

RYDAL MOUNT,
May 20th, 1819.

---

dedication 2, ESQ.] ESQ. *1832–*
3 MY DEAR FRIEND,] MY DEAR FRIEND, *1820– but* DEAR] DEAR *1836– but not MS. 1832/36*
5 "why] 'why *1836– but not MS. 1832/36* added?"] added?' *1836– but not MS. 1832/36*
7 apprehended,] apprehended *1849*
9 manuscript;] manuscript, *1836– but not MS. 1832/36*
10 it] the Poem *1836– but not MS. 1832/36*
11 depends] depends, *1820*
16–17 with which / I am / Very truly yours, *1836–1840, 1846 but not MS. 1832/36* with which / I am very truly yours, *1845, 1849*
18 WILLIAM WORDSWORTH. *1820–*
19–20 RYDAL MOUNT, / May 20. 1819. *1820– but all on one line 1832– and Rydal Mount, 1836–1846 but not MS. 1832/36*
20 *May 20th,*] *May* 20. *1820–1832 May* 20, *1836– but not MS. 1832/36*

Benjamin the Waggoner &c

At last this loitering day of June
This long, long day is going out
The Night-hawk is singing his frog-like tune
Twirling his watchman's rattle about
That busy busy Bird
Is all that can be heard
In silence deeper far than that of deepest noon

Now that the Children are abed
The little Glow-worm nothing dreads

In the sky and on the hill
Every thing is hush'd and still
The clouds show here and there a spot
Of a star that twinkles not
The air is like a Lion's den
Close and hot, and now and then

DOVE COTTAGE TRUST

MS. 1, 1^r

THE WAGGONER.

CANTO FIRST.

'Tis spent — this burning day of June!
Soft darkness o'er its latest gleams is stealing;
The buzzing dor-hawk, round and round, is
wheeling, —
That solitary bird
Is all that can be heard
In silence deeper far than that of deepest noon!

Benjamin the Waggoner &c

At last this loitering day of June,
This long, long day is going out;
The Night-hawk is singing his frog-like tune,
Twirling his watchman's rattle about.
That busy, busy Bird
Is all that can be heard
In silence deeper far than that of deepest noon.

---

title The first title of the poem was probably "Benjamin the Waggoner and his Waggon"; "and his Waggon" was written, then erased, in MS. 3, and was reduced to "&c" here and in MS. 2. It may be relevant to Wordsworth's choice of a name for his hero that a "benjamin" was a weatherproof overcoat, favored by waggoners.

1 See Introduction, p. 7, for the possible connection of the opening of this poem with June 15, 1802.

3–4 This is an accurate description of the characteristic call of the night hawk (*Caprimulgus europaeus*), also called dor-hawk or nightjar.

THE WAGGONER.

CANTO FIRST.

'Tis spent—this burning day of June!
Soft darkness o'er its latest gleams is stealing;
The buzzing dor-hawk, round and round, is
  wheeling,—
[5] That solitary bird
Is all that can be heard
[7] In silence deeper far than that of deepest noon!

---

title THE WAGGONER. *1820–* *on half title of MS. 1832/36 are three penciled lines of instruction to the printer (EQ's hand):*

½ & blank
Ded & blank
  com.
each Canto‸a page

motto *omitted 1820–1836*

In Cairo's crowded streets
The impatient Merchant wondering waits in vain,
And Mecca saddens at the long delay. *1845– but* In] "In *1849* streets] streets, *1846* Merchant] Merchant, *1849* wondering] wondering, *1849* vain,] vain *MS. 1836/45* Mecca] M[?a]cca *MS. 1836/45* delay.] delay *MS. 1836/45* delay." / THOMSON. *1849*

title *no title between dedication and text 1845, 1849*

1–23 *see transcription of MS. 1832/36, below*

CANTO FIRST. 3–5

The dor-hawk, solitary bird,
Round the dim crags on heavy pinions wheeling,
Buzzes incessantly, a tiresome tune; [3]
That constant voice is all that can be heard *1820–1836 but* [3–4] With untired voice sings an unvaried tune; / Those buzzing notes are all that can be heard *1836*

Now that the Children are in their Beds
The little Glow-worm nothing dreads—
Pretty playthings as they would be,
Forth they come in company
And lift their fearless heads.
In the sky and on the hill
Every thing is hush'd and still;
The clouds shew here and there a spot
Of a star that twinkles not.
The air is like a Lion's den
Close and hot, and now and then
Comes a tired and sultry breeze
With a haunting and a panting
Like the stifling of disease.
The mountains [?seem] of wondrous height
And in the heavens there is a weight—
But the dews allay the heat
And the silence makes it sweet.

17 "The air works like a Lion's den" appears in the Christabel Notebook (DC MS. 15), 19[r], in what is probably a fragment of a poem related to "The Danish Boy." See Introduction, pp. 10–11.

Confiding Glow-worms, 'tis a night
Propitious to your earth-born light!
But, where the scattered stars are seen
In hazy straits the clouds between,
Each, in his station twinkling not,
Seems changed into a pallid spot.
[17] The air, as in a lion's den,
Is close and hot;—and now and then
Comes a tired and sultry breeze
[20] With a haunting and a panting,
Like the stifling of disease;
The mountains rise to wond'rous height,
And in the heavens there is a weight;
But the dews allay the heat,
[25] And the silence makes it sweet.

7–12
Now that the children's busiest schemes
Do all lie buried in blank sleep,
Or only live in stirring dreams,
The glow-worms fearless watch may keep;
Rich prize as their bright lamps would be,
They shine, a quiet company,
On mossy bank by cottage-door,
As safe as on the loneliest moor.
In hazy straits the clouds between,
And in their stations twinkling not,
Some thinly-sprinkled stars are seen,
Each changed into a pallid spot. *1836–1840*

7 Glow-worms,] Glow-worms! *1827–1832*

8 light!] light; *1827–1832*

9 But,] But *1832, 1846*

12/13
The mountains against heaven's grave weight
Rise up, and grow to wondrous height. *1836–*

15 tired] faint *1836–1840*

18–19 *omitted (see 12/13 1836) 1836–*

18 wond'rous] wonderous *1820–1827* wondrous *1832–*

19 is] hangs *1827–1832*

20 But the] But welcome *1836–1840*

Hush! there is some one on the stir—
'Tis Benjamin the Waggoner!
From the side of Rydale mere
Hither he his course is bending
With a faint and fretful sound
Such as marks the listening ear.
Now he leaves the lower ground
And up the craggy hill ascending
Many a stop and stay he makes,
Many a breathing fit he takes.
Steep the way and wearisome,
Yet all the while his whip is dumb.

The Horses have worked with right good will
And now are up at the top of the hill;
He was patient, they were strong,
And now they smoothly glide along
Gathering breath and pleased to win
The praises of good Benjamin.
Heaven shield him and from ill defend,
For he is their father and their friend,
From all mishap and every snare!

---

28 Rydal Water.
33 White Moss Common.

Hush, there is some one on the stir!
[27] 'Tis Benjamin the Waggoner;—
Who long hath trod this toilsome way,
Companion of the night and day.
That far-off tinkling's drowsy cheer,
[30] Mix'd with a faint yet grating sound
In a moment lost and found,
The Wain announces—by whose side
[28] Along the banks of Rydal Mere
He paces on, a trusty Guide,—
Listen! you can scarcely hear!
[29] Hither he his course is bending;—
[32] Now he leaves the lower ground,
And up the craggy hill ascending
Many a stop and stay he makes,
[35] Many a breathing fit he takes;—
Steep the way and wearisome,
Yet all the while his whip is dumb!

The Horses have work'd with right good-will,
And now have gain'd the top of the hill;
[40] He was patient—they were strong—
And now they smoothly glide along,
Gathering breath, and pleas'd to win
[43] The praises of mild Benjamin.
Heaven shield him from mishap and snare!

---

23 Waggoner:—] Waggoner; *1832*
25 *entire line del in pencil to* Through the [?night] [? ? ?] *then erased MS. 1832/36* and] or *1836–1840*
27 Mix'd] Mixed *1820–1840*
29 side] side, *1820–1840*
30 Mere] Mere, *1820–1840*
32 scarcely] hardly *1840*
33–37
Now he has left the lower ground,
And up the hill his course is bending,
With many a stop and stay ascending;— *1836–1840*
37 breathing fit] breathing-fit *1820–1832, 1845–*
40 work'd] worked *1820–*
41 now] so *1836–* gain'd] gained *1820–* hill;] hill, *1832*
42 patient— . . . strong—] patient, . . . strong, *1836–*
44 Gathering] Recovering *1836–* pleas'd] pleased *1820–*

---

26 See Thomas Gray's *Elegy Written in a Country Churchyard*, l. 8: "And drowsy tinklings lull the distant folds."

But why so early with this prayer?
Is it for threatenings in the sky,
Or for some other danger nigh?
No, none is near him yet, though he
Be one of much infirmity;
For at the bottom of the Brow
Where once the Dove and Olive-bough
Offered a greeting of good Ale
To all who entered Grasmere Vale
And tempted him who must depart
To leave it with a joyful heart,
There where the Dove and Olive-bough
Once hung, a Poet harbours now—
A simple water drinking Bard.
Then why need Ben be on his guard?
He [?amb]les by, secure and bold—
Yet thinking on the times of old
It seems that all looks wond'rous cold.
He shrugs his shoulders, shakes his head,
And for the honest Folks within
It is a doubt with Benjamin
Whether they be alive or dead.

No danger's here, no, none at all;
Beyond his wish is Ben secure.
But pass a mile and then for trial,
Then for the pride of self-denial,

---

52 The Brow is White Moss Common.

53 Dove Cottage, the Wordsworths' cottage at Town-End, Grasmere, had formerly been an inn called the Dove and Olive Branch.

60 Wordsworth here draws on the classical controversy between poetry as inspiration (exemplified by the wine-drinking bard) and poetry as craft (exemplified by the water-drinking bard).

[47] But why so early with this prayer?—
Is it for threatenings in the sky,
Or for some other danger nigh ?
[50] No, none is near him yet, though he
Be one of much infirmity;
For, at the bottom of the Brow,
Where once the Dove and Olive-bough
Offered a greeting of good ale
[55] To all who entered Grasmere Vale;
And called on him who must depart
To leave it with a jovial heart;—
There, where the Dove and Olive-bough
Once hung, a Poet harbours now,—
[60] A simple water-drinking Bard;
Why need our Hero then (though frail
His best resolves) be on his guard?—
[62] He marches by secure and bold,—
Yet, while he thinks on times of old,
It seems that all looks wond'rous cold;
[65] He shrugs his shoulders—shakes his head—
And, for the honest folk within,
It is a doubt with Benjamin
Whether they be alive or dead!

Here is no danger,—none at all!
[70] Beyond his wish is he secure;
But pass a mile—and *then* for trial,—
Then for the pride of self-denial;

---

47 prayer?—] prayer? *1849*
48 sky,] sky? *1820–*
50 No,] No; *1845–*
50–51
No;—him infirmities beset,
But danger is not near him yet; *1836–1840*
52 For,] For *1836–* Brow,] brow, *1836–*
57 heart;—] heart; *1836–*
59 now,—] now, *1836–*
62 guard?—] guard? *1836–*
63 by] by, *1820–* bold,—] bold; *1836–*
64 Yet,] Yet *1832–*
65 wond'rous] wonderous *1820–1827* wondrous *1832–*
66 shoulders— . . . head—] shoulders, . . . head, *1836–*
71 is he] he walks *1836–*
73 self-denial] self denial *1832*

If thou resist that tempting door
Which with such friendly voice will call,
Look at thee with so bright a lure,
For surely if no other where
Candle or lamp is burning there.

The place to Benjamin full well
Is known, and for as strong a spell
As used to be that sign of love
And hope, the Olive-bough and Dove.
He knows it to his cost, good Man!
Who does not know the famous Swan?
Uncouth although the object be,
An image of perplexity,
But what of that?—it is our boast,
For it was painted by the Host;
His own conceit the figure plann'd,
'Twas [?painte]d all by his own hand,
And Ben with self-dissatisfaction
Could tell long tales of its attraction.

---

73 The door of the Swan Inn, with light coming through its window.
84 The object is the inn's sign.

If he resist that tempting door
[74] Which with such friendly voice will call,
If he resist those casement panes
And that bright gleam which thence will fall
Upon his Leaders' bells and manes,
Inviting him with cheerful lure;
For still, though all be dark elsewhere,
Some shining notice will be *there*,
Of open house and ready fare.

[78] The place to Benjamin full well
Is known, and by as strong a spell
[80] As used to be that sign of love
And hope—the OLIVE-BOUGH and DOVE;
He knows it to his cost, good Man!
Who does not know the famous SWAN?
Uncouth although the object be,
[85] An image of perplexity;
Yet not the less it is our boast,
For it was painted by the Host;
His own conceit the figure plann'd,
[89] 'Twas colour'd all by his own hand;
And that frail Child of thirsty clay,
Of whom I frame this rustic lay,
[90] Could tell with self-dissatisfaction
Quaint stories of the Bird's attraction!*

* Such is the progress of refinement, this rude piece of self-taught art has been supplanted by a professional production.

---

74 door] door, *1820–*
75 call,] call; *1836– but not MS. 1832/36*
76 panes] panes, *1820–*
79 lure;] lure: *1832–*
83 full] right *1836– but not MS. 1832/36*
89–91 Object uncouth! and yet our boast, *1836–*
93 plann'd,] planned, *1820–*
94 'Twas] 'T was *1832* colour'd] coloured *1820–* hand;] hand *1832*
95 Child] child *MS. 1832/36*
96 frame] sing *1827–*
98 Bird's] bird's *1836–*
98 *note through* refinement,] *This rude piece of self-taught art (such is the progress of refinement) *1820–*

Well! that is past, and in despite
Of open door and shining light.
And now good Benjamin essays
The long ascent of Dunmal-raise
And with his Team is gentle here
As when he clomb from Rydale mere.
His whip they do not dread: his voice,
They only hear it to rejoice.
Their efforts and their time they measure,
To stand or go is at their pleasure—
He knows that each will do his best;
And while they strain and while they rest
He thus pursues his thoughts at leisure.

Now am I fairly safe to night
And never was my heart more light.
I've been a sinner, I avow,
But better times are coming now—
A sinner lately worse than ever—
But God will bless a good endeavour,
And to my soul's delight I find
The evil One is cast behind.
Yes, let my Master fume and fret,
I'm here, and with my Horses yet.
He makes a mighty noise about me
And yet he cannot do without me.
My jolly Team, he finds that ye
Will work for nobody but me—
Finds that with hills so steep and high
This Monster at our heels must lie
Dead as a cheese upon a shelf,
Or fairly learn to draw itself.

---

95 Dunmal-raise (now spelled Dunmail Raise) is the pass between Grasmere and Wythburn (see note to l. 270).

120 We are to understand that Benjamin's waggon is the largest in the Lake District.

Well! that is past—and in despite
Of open door and shining light.
And now the Conqueror essays
[95] The long ascent of Dunmail-raise;
And with his Team is gentle here
As when he clomb from Rydal Mere;
His whip they do not dread—his voice
[99] They only hear it to rejoice.
[101] To stand or go is at *their* pleasure;
[100] Their efforts and their time they measure
By generous pride within the breast;
[103] And, while they strain, and while they rest,
He thus pursues his thoughts at leisure.

[105] Now am I fairly safe to-night—
[106] And never was my heart more light.
[109] I trespass'd lately worse than ever—
[110] But Heaven will bless a good endeavour;
And, to my soul's delight, I find
The evil One is left behind.
Yes, let my Master fume and fret,
[114] Here am I—with my Horses yet!
[117] My jolly Team, he finds that ye
[118] Will work for nobody but me!
Good proof of this the Country gain'd,
One day, when ye were vex'd and strain'd—
Entrusted to another's care,
And forc'd unworthy stripes to bear.

---

101 Conqueror] conqueror *1836– but* Conqueror *MS. 1836/45*
103 Team] team *1836–*
113 light.] light, *1832* And with proud cause my heart is light, *1836– but* light: *alt* light; *MS. 1836–45* light: *1840–*
114 trespass'd] trespassed *1820–*
115 will bless] has blest *1836–*
116 delight,] delight *1820* content, *1836–*
118 Master] master *1820–*
119 Horses] horses *1836–*
120 Team,] team, *1836–*
122 Good] Full *1836–* gain'd,] gained, *1820–1832* gained; *1836–*
123 vex'd] vexed *1820–1832* strain'd] strained *1820–1832*
125 forc'd] forced *1820–1832*
123–125
It knows how ye were vexed and strained,
And forced unworthy stripes to bear,
When trusted to another's care. *1836– but* strained,— *MS. 1832/36*

When I was gone he [?knew] his lack
And was right glad to have me back.
Then grieve not, jolly Team! though tough
Our road be sometimes, steep and rough;
But take your time, no more I ask—
I know you're equal to your task;
And for us all I'll sing the praise
Of our good friend here Dunmal-raise
And of his brother Banks and Braes,
For plain it is that they're the tether
By which we have been kept together.

While Benjamin in earnest mood
His meditations thus pursued,
A storm which had been smothered long

Here was it—on this rugged spot
Which now contented with our lot
We climb—that piteously abused
Ye plung'd in anger and confused:
As chance would have it, passing by
I saw you in your jeopardy;
A word from me was like a charm—
The ranks were taken with one mind;
And your huge burthen safe from harm
Mov'd like a vessel in the wind!
—Yes, without me, up hills so high
'Tis vain to strive for mastery.
[125] Then grieve not, jolly Team! though tough
The road we travel, steep and rough.
Though Rydal heights and Dunmail-raise,
[131] And all their fellow Banks and Braes,
Full often make you stretch and strain,
And halt for breath, and halt again,
Yet to their sturdiness 'tis owing
That side by side we still are going!

[134] While Benjamin in earnest mood
[135] His meditations thus pursued,
A storm, which had been smother'd long,

---

126 spot] slope, *1836–*
127 now] now, *1820–1832* lot] lot, *1820–1832*
128 that] that, *1820–1832* abused] abused, *1820–1832*
129 plung'd] plunged *1820–1832*
127–129
Which now ye climb with heart and hope,
I saw you, between rage and fear,
Plunge, and fling back a spiteful ear,
And ever more and more confused,
As ye were more and more abused: *1836–*
131 your jeopardy;] your jeopardy: *1820–1832* that jeopardy *1836–*
132 charm—] charm; *1836–*
133 The ranks were taken] Ye pulled together *1836–*
134 burthen] burthen, *1820–* harm] harm, *1820–*
135 Mov'd] Moved *1820–*
138 Team!] team! *1836–*
139 The road we travel,] Our road be, narrow, *1836–1840* steep] steep, *1836–* rough.] rough, *1832* rough; *1836– but not MS. 1832/36*
140 Rydal heights] Rydal-heights *1827–*
141 Banks . . . Braes,] banks . . . braes, *1836–*
143 breath,] breath *1820–*
148 smother'd] smothered *1820–*

Was growing inwardly more strong,
And in its struggles to get free
Was busily employ'd as he.
The thunder had begun to growl—
He heard not, too intent of soul.
The air was now without a breath—
He mark'd not that 'twas still as death.
But now some drops upon his head
Fell, with the weight of drops of lead.
He starts, and at the admonition
Takes a survey of his condition.
The road is black before his eyes,
Glimmering faintly where it lies;
Black is the sky, and every hill
Up to the sky is blacker still—
A huge and melancholy room
Hung round and overhung with gloom—
Save that above a single height
Is to be seen a lurid light,
Above Helm-crag, a streak half-dead,
A burning of a sullen red;
And near that lurid light, full well
Th' Astrologer, dread Sydrofel,
Where at his desk and book he sits
Puzzling his wicked, wicked wits—
He who from quarter in the North
For mischief looks or sends it forth,
Sharing his wild domain in common

---

156 Helm Crag is directly north of Grasmere and west of the southern slope of Dunmail Raise.

159 Sydrofel (actually Sydrophel) is the astrologer in Samuel Butler's mock-heroic *Hudibras* (II, iii).

Was growing inwardly more strong;
And, in its struggles to get free,
Was busily employ'd as he.
[140] The thunder had begun to growl—
He heard not, too intent of soul;
The air was now without a breath—
He mark'd not that 'twas still as death
But soon large drops upon his head
[145] Fell with the weight of drops of lead;—
He starts—and, at the admonition,
Takes a survey of his condition.
The road is black before his eyes,
Glimmering faintly where it lies;
[150] Black is the sky—and every hill,
Up to the sky, is blacker still;
A huge and melancholy room,
Hung round and overhung with gloom!
Save that above a single height
[155] Is to be seen a lurid light,—
Above Helm-crag*—a streak half dead,
A burning of portentous red;
And, near that lurid light, full well
The ASTROLOGER, sage Sydrophel,
[160] Where at his desk and book he sits,
[161] Puzzling on high his curious wits;
[164] He whose domain is held in common

* A mountain of Grasmere, the broken summit of which presents two figures, full as distinctly shaped as that of the famous cobler, near Arracher, in Scotland.

---

151 employ'd] employed *1820–*
155 mark'd] marked *1820–* death] death. *1820–*
156 drops upon] rain-drops on *1836–*
158 and,] and takes, *1836–* the admonition] the'admonition *MS. 1832/36*
159 Takes a] A sage *1836–*
163 still;] still— *1832–*
164 Sky, hill, and dale, one dismal room, *1836– but* dale one *MS. 1832/36*
165 gloom!] gloom? *1832* gloom; *1836–*
167 light,—] light, *1820–*
168 *note* cobler,] Cobler, *1820* Cobbler, *1827–1832* Cobbler *1836– but not MS. 1832/36* Arracher,] Arroquhar *1832–*
170 And,] And *1832–*
171 Sydrophel] Sydropel *1827* Sidrophel *1832–*
173 on high] aloft *1836–*

With southern Neighbor, the old Woman,
A pair that [spite of] wind and weather
Still sit upon Helm-crag together.

The Astrologer was not unseen
By solitary Benjamin,
But total darkness came anon
And he and every thing was gone.
The rain rush'd down, the road was batter'd,
As with the weight of billows shatter'd.
The Horses scarcely seem'd to know
Whether they should stand or go,
[?For] Benjamin, though groping near them,
Sees nothing and can scarcely hear them.
He is astounded, wonder not,
With such a charge in such a spot—
Astounded in the mountain gap
[?With] peals of thunder, clap on clap,
With now and then a dismal flash
And some[?place], as it seems, a crash
Among the rocks with weight of rain,
And echoes long and violent

---

165 Part of the rock formation at the top of Helm Crag, when seen from a certain perspective, is said to resemble an old woman playing an organ.

[165] With no one but the ANCIENT WOMAN:
Cowering beside her rifted cell,
As if intent on magic spell;—
[166] Dread pair, that, spite of wind and weather,
Still sit upon Helm-crag together!

The ASTROLOGER was not unseen
By solitary Benjamin;
[170] But total darkness came anon,
And he and every thing was gone.
The rain rush'd down—the road was batter'd,
As with the force of billows shatter'd;
The horses are dismayed, nor know
[175] Whether they should stand or go;
And Benjamin is groping near them,
Sees nothing, and can scarcely hear them.
He is astounded, wonder not,
With such a charge in such a spot;
[180] Astounded in the mountain gap
By peals of thunder, clap on clap!
And many a terror-striking flash;—
And somewhere, as it seems, a crash,
[184] Among the rocks; with weight of rain,
And rattling motions long and slow,

---

175 WOMAN:] WOMAN, *1827–*
176 cell,] cell; *1820–1836* cell, *MS. 1832/36*
180–181 *order of lines reversed MS. 1832/36*
181 Benjamin;] Benjamin: *1820–1832*
183 gone.] gone: *1836– but not MS. 1832/36*
183/184
And suddenly a ruffling breeze,
(That would have sounded through the trees
Had aught of sylvan growth been there) [3]
Was felt throughout the region bare: *1820– but* [2] sounded through the] rocked the sounding *1836–* [4] Was felt throughout the region] Swept through the Hollow long and *1836–*
184 rush'd . . . batter'd,] rushed . . . battered, *1820–*
185 shatter'd;] shattered; *1820–*
190 astounded, . . . not,] astounded,— . . . not,—*1820–*
193–195
With thunder-peals, clap after clap,
Close-treading on the silent flashes—
And somewhere, as he thinks, by crashes *1836– but* clap,] clap! *MS. 1832/36*
197 rattling] sullen *1820–*

That when the thunder's force is spent
Yell and yell from Fell to Fell,
As if they would with might and main
Provoke it to begin again.

Meanwhile uncertain what to do
And oftentimes compell'd to halt,
The Horses cautiously pursue
Their way without mishap or fault,
And now have reach'd that pile of stones
Heap'd over good King Dunmal's bones—
He who had once supreme command
Our King in rocky Cumberland—
His bones and those of all his Power
Slain here in a disastrous hour.

When passing through this stony strait
('Tis little wider than a gate)
Benjamin can faintly hear
A female Voice, a voice of fear.
"Stop," says the Voice, "whoe'er ye be;
Stop, stop, good Friend, and pity me."
And less in pity than in wonder,
Amid the darkness and the thunder,
Good Benjamin with prompt command
Summons his Horses to a stand.

"Now tell," says he, "in honest deed
Who you are and what your need."
Careless of this adjuration
The Voice to move commiseration
Still prolonged its supplication:
"This storm that beats so furiously
This dreadful place! oh pity me!"

---

195 King Dunmal (usually spelled Dunmail), the last king of Cumberland, is, according to tradition, buried under the cairn at the top of Dunmail Raise.

That to a dreary distance go—
Till, breaking in upon the dying strain,
A rending o'er his head begins the 'fray again.

[190] Meanwhile, uncertain what to do,
And oftentimes compelled to halt;
The horses cautiously pursue
Their way without mishap or fault;
And now have reach'd that pile of stones,
[195] Heap'd over brave King Dunmail's bones;
He who had once supreme command,
Last king of rocky Cumberland;
His bones, and those of all his Power,
Slain here in a disastrous hour!

[200] When, passing through this narrow strait,
(Stony and dark and desolate,)
Benjamin can faintly hear
A voice that comes from some one near:
A female voice:—"Whoe'er you be,
[205] Stop," it exclaimed, "and pity me."
And, less in pity than in wonder,
Amid the darkness and the thunder,
The Waggoner, with prompt command,
[209] Summons his horses to a stand.

[213] The voice, to move commiseration,
Prolong'd its earnest supplication—
[215] "This storm that beats so furiously—
This dreadful place! oh pity me!"

197–198
Reverberations loud, or low;
And sullen mutterings long & slow *WW's pencil, del in pencil MS. 1836/45*
200 'fray] fray *1832–*
202 halt;] halt, *1827–*
204 way] way, *1820–*
205 reach'd] reached *1827–*
206 Heap'd] Heaped *1820–* bones;] bones *1849*
211 When,] When *1820*
212 *parentheses omitted 1827–* Stony . . . dark] Stony, . . . dark, *1827–*
214 near:] near *1827 but* near, *some copies of 1827, 1832–*
216 Stop,"] "Stop," *1819* me."] me!" *1836– but not MS. 1832/36*
222 Prolong'd] Prolonged *1820–1832*
224 This] "This *1819*

While this was said with sobs between
And many tears by one unseen
There came a flash and held the candle
To the whole bosom of Seat Sandal.
'Twas not a time for nice suggestion,
And Benjamin without further question,
Taking her for some way-worn Rover,
Said, "mount and get Ye under cover."

Another Voice that was as hoarse
As Brook with steep and stony course
Cried out, "good Brother why so fast?
I've had a glimpse of you, avast!
Let go, or since you must be civil,
Take her at once for good or evil."

"It is my Husband," softly said
The Woman, as if half afraid.
By this time she was snug within
Through help of honest Benjamin,
She and her Babe, for Babe she had—
No wonder then if she was glad.
And now the same strong Voice more near
Said cordially, "my Friend what cheer?
Rough doings these! as God's my judge
The sky owes somebody a grudge.

---

220 Seat Sandal is east of the southern slope of Dunmail Raise, north of Fairfield and south of Dollywaggon Pike.

[218] While this was said, with sobs between,
And many tears, by one unseen;
There came a flash—a startling glare,
And all Seat-Sandal was laid bare!
[221] 'Tis not a time for nice suggestion,
And Benjamin, without further question,
Taking her for some way-worn rover,
Said, "Mount, and get you under cover!"

[225] Another voice, in tone as hoarse
As a swoln brook with rugged course,
Cried out, "Good brother, why so fast?
I've had a glimpse of you—*avast!*
Or, since it suits you to be civil,
[230] Take her at once—for good and evil!"

"It is my Husband," softly said
The Woman, as if half afraid:
By this time she was snug within,
Through help of honest Benjamin;
[235] She and her Babe, which to her breast
With thankfulness the mother press'd;
And now the same strong voice more near
Said, cordially, "My Friend, what cheer?
Rough doings these! as God's my judge,
[240] The sky owes somebody a grudge!

---

225 *indented 1827–1832*
226 tears,] tears *1832*
221–226
While, with increasing agitation,
The Woman urged her supplication,
In rueful words, with sobs between—
The voice of tears that fell unseen; *1836– but* increasing] a growing *del to* encreasing *MS. 1832/36* between—] between, *MS. 1832/36*
230–231
And, kind to every way-worn rover,
Benjamin, without a question, *1836–1840*
230 further] a *1845–*
233 voice,] voice *1820*
236 I've] "I've *1819*
237 Or,] "Or, *1819*
238 Take] "Take *1819*
244 mother] Mother *1827–* press'd;] pressed; *1820–*
246 Said,] Said *1827–*
247 Rough] "Rough *1819*
248 The . . . grudge!] "The . . . grudge!" *1819*

We've had in half an hour, or less,
A twelvemonth's terror and distress;
But Kate, give thanks for this and ride
In quiet and be pacified."

Then Benjamin entreats the Man
Would mount too, quickly as he can.
The Sailor, Sailor now no more
But such he had been heretofore,
To courteous Benjamin replied,
"Go you your way, and mind not me,
For I must have, whate'er betide,
My Ass, and fifty things beside.
[?Haste—] I'll follow speedily."

The Waggon moves, and with its load
Descends along the sloping road;
And to a little tent hard by
Turns the Sailor instantly,
For when, at closing-in of day,
The Family had come this way,
Green pasture and the soft warm air
Had tempted them to settle there—
Green is the grass for Beast to graze
Around the stones of Dunmal-raise.

The Sailor gathers up his bed,
Takes down the canvas overhead,

We've had in half an hour or less
A twelve-month's trouble and distress!"

Then Benjamin entreats the Man
Would mount, too, quickly as he can:
The Sailor, Sailor now no more,
But such he had been heretofore,
To courteous Benjamin replied,
"Go you your way, and mind not me;
For I must have, whate'er betide,
My Ass and fifty things beside,—
Go, and I'll follow speedily!"

The Waggon moves—and with its load
Descends along the sloping road;
And to a little tent hard by
Turns the Sailor instantly;
For when, at closing-in of day,
The Family had come that way,
Green pasture and the soft warm air
Had tempted them to settle there.—
Green is the grass for beast to graze,
Around the stones of Dunmail-raise!

The Sailor gathers up his bed,
Takes down the canvas overhead;

---

250 twelve-month's] twelvemonth's *1827–* trouble] terror *1820–* distress!"] distress! *1819*
253 Sailor,] Sailor—*1836– but MS. 1832/36 as 1832*
254 heretofore,] heretofore—*1836– but MS. 1832/36 as 1832*
262–263 *see transcription of MS. 1832/36, below*
And to his tent-like domicile,
Built in a nook with cautious skill,
The Sailor turns, well pleased to spy
His shaggy friend who stood hard by
Drenched—and, more fast than with a tether, [5]
Bound to the nook by that fierce weather,
Which caught the vagrants unaware: *1836–1840 but* [4] friend] friend, *1840–1843, MS. 1836/45*
And the rough Sailor instantly
Turns to a little tent hard by: *1845–*
264 For when, at] For, when, ere *1836–1840 but* For when *MS. 1832/36*
265 Family] family *1836–*
267 Had tempted] Tempted *1836–*
271 canvas] canvass *1827–1846*

And after farewell to the place—
A parting word, though not of grace—
Pursues, with Ass and all his store,
The way the Waggon went before.

Second Part

If Wytheburn's lonely House of Prayer,
As lowly as the lowliest dwelling,
Had, with its Belfrey's humble stock—
A little Pair, that hang in air—
Been Mistress also of a Clock
(And one, too, not in crazy plight),
Twelve strokes that Clock would have been telling
Under the nose of old Helvellyn—
Its bead-roll of midnight—
Then, when the Hero of my Tale
Was passing by, and down the Vale
(The Vale now silent, hush'd, I ween,
As if a storm had never been)
Proceeding with an easy mind
And little thought of Him behind

---

270 Wythburn is a village at the southern end of Thirlmere, on the east side of the lake. The church still stands, but the village has been depopulated by the Manchester Water Corporation's conversion of Thirlmere into a reservoir.

275 Wordsworth may intend a humorous allusion to "those witty rhymes / About the crazy old church-clock" in his earlier poem *The Fountain*.

277 Helvellyn, the third highest peak in the Lake District, is east of Wythburn.

280 The Vale of Wythburn.

And, after farewell to the place,
A parting word—though not of grace,
Pursues, with Ass and all his store,
The way the Waggon went before.

CANTO SECOND.

If Wytheburn's modest House of Prayer,
As lowly as the lowliest Dwelling,
Had, with its belfrey's humble stock,
A little pair that hang in air,
Been mistress also of a Clock,
(And one, too, not in crazy plight)
Twelve strokes that Clock would have been telling
Under the brow of old Helvellyn—
Its bead-roll of midnight,
Then, when the Hero of my Tale
Was passing by, and down the vale
(The vale now silent, hush'd I ween
As if a storm had never been)
Proceeding with an easy mind;
While he, who had been left behind,

276 Prayer,] prayer, *1836–*
277 Dwelling,] dwelling, *1836–*
278 belfrey's] belfry's *1827–*
280 Clock,] clock, *1836–*
282 Clock] clock *1836–*
285 Tale] tale *1827–*
286 and] and, *1836– but MS. 1832/36 as 1832*
287 hush'd] hushed *1820–*
289 Proceeding] *alt* Following *in pencil* (*EQ*) *then del MS. 1836/45* an easy mind;] a mind at ease; *1836– but entered in pencil, with* ease, *MS. 1832/36* ease"; *1836 del to* ease, *MS. 1836/45*
290 he, who had been left behind,] the old Familiar of the seas *1836– but entered by EQ in pencil and by WW in ink MS. 1832/36*

Who, having used his utmost haste,
Gain'd ground upon the Waggon fast
And now is almost at its heels
And gives another [?hear]ty cheer,
For spite of rumbling of the wheels
A welcome greeting he can hear—
It is a fiddle in its glee
Dinning from the Cherry Tree.

Thence the sound, the light is there,
As Benjamin is now aware
Who neither saw nor heard—no more
Then if he had been deaf and blind—
Till rouz'd up by the Sailor's roar
He hears the sound and sees the light
And in a moment calls to mind
That 'tis the Village merry-night.

Although before in no dejection,
He gladden'd at the recollection,
For Benjamin is wet and cold
And there are reasons manifold
That make the good for which he's yearning
Look fairly like an honest earning.

Nor has thought time to come and go,
To vibrate between yes and no.

---

292 The Cherry Tree Inn, Wythburn, is no longer standing. See page 34 for a drawing of it in its prime, perhaps by Dora Wordsworth.

[285] Intent to use his utmost haste,
[286] Gain'd ground upon the Waggon fast—
[288] And gives another lusty cheer;
For, spite of rumbling of the wheels,
[290] A welcome greeting he can hear;—
It is a fiddle in its glee
Dinning from the CHERRY TREE!

Thence the sound—the light is there—
As Benjamin is now aware,
[295] Who neither heard nor saw—no more
Than if he had been deaf and blind,
Till, startled by the Sailor's roar,
He hears a sound and sees the light,
And in a moment calls to mind
[300] That 'tis the village MERRY-NIGHT!*

Although before in no dejection,
At this insidious recollection
His heart with sudden joy is fill'd,—
His ears are by the music thrill'd,
His eyes take pleasure in the road
Glittering before him bright and broad;
[303] And Benjamin is wet and cold,
And there are reasons manifold
[305] That make the good, tow'rds which he's yearning,
Look fairly like a lawful earning.

Nor has thought time to come and go,
To vibrate between yes and no;

* A term well known in the North of England, as applied to rural Festivals, where young persons meet in the evening for the purpose of dancing.

---

292 Gain'd] Gained *1820–* fast—] fast *1820* fast, *1827–*
294 For,] For *1827–*
300–301
Who, to his inward thoughts confined,
Had almost reached the festive door, *1820–*
302 Till,] When, *1820–*
305 MERRY-NIGHT!*] MERRY-NIGHT*! *1836–1840, 1846 but not MS. 1832/36*
305 *note* as] a *1820* and *1827–* Festivals,] Festivals *1827–*
308 fill'd,—] filled,—*1820–*
309 thrill'd,] thrilled, *1820–*

For cries the Sailor, "glorious chance
That blew us hither,—lucky dance!
Brave luck for us, my honest Soul;
I'll treat thee with a friendly Bowl."
He draws him to the door, "come in,
Come, come," cries he to Benjamin,
And Benjamin—ah! woe is me!—
Gave the word, the Horses heard
And halted, though reluctantly.

Blithe Souls and lightsome hearts have we,
Feasting at the Cherry Tree!
This was the outside proclamation,
This was the inside salutation;
What bustling, jostling, high and low—
A universal overflow!
What tankards foaming from the Tap!
What store of Cakes in every lap!
What thumping, stumping overhead!
The Thunder had not been more busy.
With such a stir, you would have said,
This little Place may well be dizzy.
'Twas who can dance with greatest vigour—
'Tis what can be most prompt and eager.
As if it heard the fiddle's call
The Pewter clatter'd on the wall;
The very Bacon shew'd its feeling,
Swinging from the smoky ceiling.

---

320 The sounds of music and merriment issuing from the Cherry Tree probably constitute the "outside proclamation."

"For," cries the Sailor, "Glorious chance
That blew us hither! Let him dance
Who can or will;—my honest Soul
Our treat shall be a friendly Bowl!"
He draws him to the door—"Come in,
Come, come," cries he to Benjamin;
And Benjamin—ah, woe is me!
Gave the word,—the horses heard
And halted, though reluctantly.

Blithe souls and lightsome hearts have we
Feasting at the CHERRY TREE!
This was the outside proclamation,
This was the inside salutation;
What bustling—jostling—high and low!
A universal overflow!
What tankards foaming from the tap!
What store of cakes in every lap!
What thumping—stumping—overhead!
The thunder had not been more busy:
With such a stir, you would have said,
This little place may well be dizzy!
'Tis who can dance with greatest vigour—
'Tis what can be most prompt and eager;—
As if it heard the fiddle's call,
The pewter clatters on the wall;
The very bacon shows its feeling,
Swinging from the smoky ceiling!

---

318 "For,"] For, *1836– but not MS. 1832/36*
319 hither! Let him dance] hither! dance, boys, dance! *1836–1840* hither!—let him dance, *1845–*
320 will;—] will!—*1845–* Soul] Soul, *1820–1832* soul, *1845–*
320–321
Rare luck for us! my honest soul,
I'll treat thee to a friendly bowl!" *1836–1840 but MS. 1832/36 has two versions, the first with* Soul, *and* Bowl!", *the second with* us, . . . Soul *and* bowl!", *then with* Soul *made lowercase*
321 Bowl!"] bowl!" *1845–*
323 Benjamin;] Benjamin! *1836– but not MS. 1832/36*
325 word,—] word—*1836– but not MS. 1832/36*
327 Blithe] "Blithe *1820–1832* 'Blithe *1836– but MS. 1832/36 as 1832* we] we, *1820–*
328 TREE!] TREE!" *1820–1832* TREE!' *1836– but MS. 1832/36 as 1832*
335 overhead!] over-head! *1820–1827*
337 stir,] stir *1836– but not MS. 1832/36*
340 eager;—] eager; *1836–*
343 its] it *1845, 1849*

A steaming Bowl, a blazing fire—
What greater good can heart desire?
'Twere worth a wise Man's while to try
The utmost anger of the sky,
To seek even thoughts of painful cast,
If such be the amends at last.
Now should you think I judge amiss,
The Cherry Tree shews proof of this;
For soon of all the happy there
Our Travellers are the happiest pair.
All care with Benjamin is gone—
A Caesar past the Rubicon.
He thinks not of his long, long strife—
The Sailor Man, by nature gay,
Has no resolves to throw away;
And he has now forgot his Wife,
Hath quite forgotten her, or may be
Knows what is the truth, I wis—
That she is better where she is,
Under cover,
Terror over,
Sleeping by her sleeping Baby.

With Bowl in hand
(It may not stand),

336 The "steaming Bowl" probably contains mulled ale. A hot poker is plunged into the ale to heat it.

A steaming Bowl—a blazing fire—
What greater good can heart desire?
'Twere worth a wise man's while to try
The utmost anger of the sky;
[340] To *seek* for thoughts of painful cast,
If such be the amends at last.
Now, should you think I judge amiss,
The CHERRY TREE shows proof of this;
For soon, of all the happy there,
[345] Our Travellers are the happiest pair.
All care with Benjamin is gone—
A Cæsar past the Rubicon!
He thinks not of his long, long strife;—
The Sailor, Man by nature gay,
[350] Hath no resolves to throw away;
And he hath now forgot his Wife,
[352] Hath quite forgotten her—or may be
Deems that she is happier, laid
Within that warm and peaceful bed;
[355] Under cover,
Terror over,
Sleeping by her sleeping Baby.

With bowl in hand,
(It may not stand)

---

345 Bowl— . . . fire—] bowl, . . . fire, *1836–*
348 sky;] sky: *1836– but not MS. 1832/36*
349 painful] a gloomy *1836–*
350 be the] the bright *1836– but revisions to lines 349–350 drafted in pencil, copied in ink MS. 1832/36*
351 Now,] Now *1832–* think] say *1836–*
352 this;] this: *1836 but not MS. 1832/36* this *1840*
353 soon,] soon *1836–* of all] among *1836–1840*
354 pair.] pair; *1836–1840*
355–356
And happiest far is he, the One
No longer with himself at strife, *1836–1840*
357 *omitted 1836–1840*
359 Found not a scruple in *his* way; *1836–1840*
362 Thinks her the luckiest soul on earth, *1836–*
363 bed;] berth, *1836–*
366/367 *no extra space 1820*
367 *further indented 1827–1832* With bowl that sped from hand to hand, *1836– but* hand,] hand *MS. 1836/45, then comma restored*
368 Refreshed, brimful of hearty fun, *1836–1840 but* Refreshed—*MS. 1832/36*

Gladdest of the gladsome band,
Amid their own delight and fun
They hear, when every dance is done—
They hear, when every fit is o'er—
The fiddle's squeak—that call to bliss
Ever follow'd by a kiss;
They envy not the happy lot
But enjoy their own the more.

While thus they sit and thus they fare
Up springs the Sailor from his chair,
Limps, (for I [?should] have told before
That he was lame) across the floor,
Is gone, returns, and with a prize—
With what? a Ship of lusty size,
A Vessel following at his heels
Upon a frame that goes by wheels,
A gallant stately Man of War
Sliding on a sliding car—
Surprize to all, but most surprize
To Benjamin, who rubs his eyes,
Not knowing that he had befriended
A Man so gloriously attended.

"This," cries the Sailor, "a first rate is;
Stand back and you shall see her gratis:
This was the Flag Ship at the Nile,
The Vanguard; you may smirk and smile,
But, pretty Maid! if you look near
You'll find you've much in little here!
A nobler Ship did never swim,

---

382 "First rate," "the highest of the 'rates' . . . by which vessels of war are distinguished according to size and equipment" and generally applied to "the old three-deckers carrying 74 to 120 guns" (*OED*), was corrected to "third rate" in MS. 2.

384–385 In 1798 the British fleet under Nelson won the battle of the Nile, thus winning control of the Mediterranean and cutting off the retreat of Napoleon's troops from Egypt. The *Vanguard* was Nelson's flagship.

[360] Gladdest of the gladsome band,
Amid their own delight and fun,
They hear—when every dance is done—
They hear—when every fit is o'er—
The fiddle's *squeak**—that call to bliss,
[365] Ever followed by a kiss;
They envy not the happy lot,
But enjoy their own the more!

While thus our jocund Travellers fare,
Up springs the Sailor from his chair—
[370] Limps (for I might have told before
That he was lame) across the floor—
Is gone—returns—and with a prize;
[373] With what?—a Ship of lusty size;
[376] A gallant stately Man of War,
Fix'd on a smoothly-sliding car.
Surprise to all, but most surprise
To Benjamin, who rubs his eyes,
[380] Not knowing that he had befriended
A Man so gloriously attended!

"This," cries the Sailor, "a third-rate is—
Stand back and you shall see her gratis!
This was the Flag Ship at the Nile,
[385] The Vanguard—you may smirk and smile,
But, pretty maid, if you look near,
You'll find you've much in little here!
A nobler Ship did never swim.

* At the close of each strathspey, or jig, a particular note from the fiddle summons the Rustic to the agreeable duty of saluting his Partner.

---

369 Gladdest] The gladdest *1836–*
371 done—] done, *1836*
372 They hear—when every fit] When every whirling bout *1836–*
373 *note* Partner.] partner. *1836– but MS. 1832/36 as 1832*
383 Man of War,] Man-of-war, *1836– but* Man-of-War *MS. 1832/36*
384 Fix'd] Fixed *1820–*
389 third-rate] Third-rate *1820–*
390 back] back, *1827–*
391 Flag Ship] Flag-Ship *1820–1832* Flag-ship *1836–*
393 maid,] Maid, *1832–*
395 Ship] ship *1836–* swim.] swim, *1820–*

And you shall have her in full trim;
I'll set, my Friends, to do you honour,
Set every inch of sail upon her."
So said, so done, and masts, sails, yards
He names them all and interlards
His speech, with uncouth terms of art,
Accomplish'd in the Showman's part,
And then as from a sudden check
Cries out, "'tis there the Quarter deck
On which brave Admiral Nelson stood—
A sight that would have done you good.
One eye he had which bright as ten
Burnt like a fire among his men.
Here lay the French and thus came we."
Let that be Land and that be Sea—
—[Hush'd was] by this the fiddler's sound;
[?Then all the Dancers] gather'd round,
And such the stillness of the house
[?You] might have heard a nibbling mouse;
While borrowing helps where'er he may
The Sailor through the story runs
Of Ships to Ships and Guns to Guns,
And does his utmost to display
[?The history of that wondrous day].

"A bowl, a bowl of double measure,"
Cries Benjamin, "a draft of length
To Nelson, England's pride and treasure,
Her bulwark and her tower of strength!"

397–403 "K[night] notes the similarity of this passage to Corporal Trim's exposition of the siege of Namur in *Tristram Shandy* (Bk. IX, ch. xxviii): 'And this,' said he, 'is the town of *Namur*—and this the citadel—and there lay the *French*—and here lay his honour and myself.' Doubtless W. had this passage at the back of his mind" (*PW*, II, 498–499).

And you shall see her in full trim;
[390] I'll set, my Friends, to do you honour,
Set every inch of sail upon her."
So said, so done; and masts, sails, yards,
He names them all; and interlards
His speech with uncouth terms of art,
[395] Accomplish'd in the Showman's part;
And then, as from a sudden check,
Cries out—" 'Tis there, the Quarter-deck
On which brave Admiral Nelson stood—
A sight that would have rous'd your blood!
[400] One eye he had, which, bright as ten,
Burnt like a fire among his men;
[403] Let this be Land, and that be Sea,
[402] Here lay the French—and *thus* came we!"

Hush'd was by this the fiddle's sound,
[405] The Dancers all were gathered round,
And such the stillness of the house
You might have heard a nibbling mouse;
While, borrowing helps where'er he may,
The Sailor through the story runs
[410] Of Ships to Ships and guns to guns;
[411] And does his utmost to display
The dismal conflict, and the might
And terror of that wondrous night!
[413] "A Bowl, a Bowl of double measure,"
Cries Benjamin, "A draught of length,
[415] To Nelson, England's pride and treasure,
Her bulwark and her tower of strength!"

---

396 trim;] trim: *1827–*
397 Friends,] friends, *1836–*
402 Accomplish'd] Accomplished *1820–* Showman's] showman's *1836–*
404 Quarter-deck] quarter-deck *1836–*
406 rous'd] roused *1820–*
408 Burnt] Burned *1836–*
409 Land, . . . Sea,] land, . . . sea, *1836–*
411 Hush'd] Hushed *1820–*
412 Dancers] dancers *1836–*
413 And . . . house] And, . . . house, *1820–*
417 Ships to Ships] ships to ships *1836–*
420 wondrous] wonderous *1820* marvellous *1836–*
421 Bowl, a Bowl] bowl, a bowl *1836–*
422 "A] "a *1827–*
424 strength!"] strength! *1832, MS. 1832/36*

When Benjamin had seiz'd the bowl
The Mastiff gave a warning growl;
The Mastiff from beneath the Waggon
Where he lay watchful as a Dragon
Rattled his chain—'twas all in vain;
For Benjamin, triumphant Soul!
He heard the monitory growl—
Heard, and in opposition quaff'd
A deep, determin'd, desperate draft.
Nor did the batter'd Tar forget
Or flinch from what he deem'd his debt.
Then like a hero crown'd with laurel
Back to her place the Ship he led—
Wheel'd her back in full apparel;
And so, [?Fl]ag flying at mast head,
[?He] yoked her to the Ass,—anon
Cries Benjamin, "we must be gone!"
Thus after two hours hearty stay
[?Once more] behold them on their way.

Third Part

Right gladly had the Horses stirr'd
When they the smack of greeting heard,

[417] When Benjamin had seized the bowl,
[419] The Mastiff, from beneath the waggon,
[420] Where he lay, watchful as a dragon,
Rattled his chain—'twas all in vain,
For Benjamin, triumphant soul!
He heard the monitory growl;
Heard—and in opposition quaff'd
[425] A deep, determined, desperate draught!
Nor did the battered tar forget,
Or flinch from what he deem'd his debt:
Then like a hero, crown'd with laurel,
Back to her place the ship he led;
[430] Wheel'd her back in full apparel;
And so, flag flying at mast-head,
Re-yoked her to the Ass:—anon,
Cries Benjamin, "We must be gone."
Thus, after two hours' hearty stay,
[435] Again behold them on their way!

CANTO THIRD.

Right gladly had the horses stirr'd,
When they the wish'd-for greeting heard;

---

426 Mastiff,] mastiff, *1836–*
428 chain—] chain;—*1836–*
431 quaff'd] quaffed *1820–*
433 tar] Tar *1827–*
434 deem'd] deemed *1820–*
435 Then . . . hero,] Then, . . . hero *1827* crown'd] crowned *1820–*
437 Wheel'd] Wheeled *1820–*
438 mast-head,] mast head, *1832–*
443 stirr'd,] stirred, *1820–*
444 wish'd-for] wished-for *1827–* heard;] heard, *1820–*

The smack of greeting from the door,
The sign that they might move once more.
You think these doings must have bred
In them disheartening doubts and dread?
No, not a Horse of all the eight,
Although it be a moonless night,
Fears either for himself or freight;
For this they know and know full well,
And this [?with] pleasure I may tell,
That Benjamin with half his brains
Is worth the best with all their pains;
And if they had a prayer to make
The prayer would be that they might take
With him whatever comes in course,
The better fortune with the worse—
That no one may have business near them
And drunk or sober he should steer them.
So forth in dauntless mood they fare,
And with them goes the guardian pair.

Now, Heroes, for the true commotion,
The blessing of your late devotion
—Can aught on earth impede delight
Still mounting to a higher height
And higher still, a greedy flight?
Can any low-born care pursue her,
Can any mortal clog come to her?
It can—if chance a strong desire
Such as did soon lay hold of these
Should rise and set the throat on fire
And nothing by to give us ease.
What wish you with that spacious mere
And all its weight of water near;
What nobler cup would ye be at?
No, no, they are too wise for that.
Once in, I put the question plain,
Who is to help them out again?

But Benjamin in *his* vexation
Possesses inward consolation.

468 The lake is Thirlmere.

The whip's loud notice from the door,
That they were free to move once more.
[440] You think, these doings must have bred
In them disheartening doubts and dread;
No, not a horse of all the eight,
Although it be a moonless night,
Fears either for himself or freight;
[445] For this they know (and let it hide,
In part, the offences of their guide)
[447] That Benjamin, with clouded brains,
Is worth the best with all their pains;
And, if they had a prayer to make,
[450] The prayer would be that they may take
With him whatever comes in course,
The better fortune or the worse;
That no one else may have business near them,
And, drunk or sober, he may steer them.
[455] So forth in dauntless mood they fare,
And with them goes the guardian pair.

Now, heroes, for the true commotion,
The triumph of your late devotion!
Can aught on earth impede delight,
[460] Still mounting to a higher height;
And higher still—a greedy flight!
Can any low-born care pursue her,
[463] Can any mortal clog come to her?

---

453 guide)] Guide) *1820–1832*
461/462 *extra space 1820–*
462 *indented 1820–* So] So, *1820–*

He knows his ground and hopes to find
A Spot with all things to his mind—
A slender Spring yet kind to Man,
A cordial true Samaritan,
Close to the highway pouring out
Its offering from a chink or spout
Whence all, however tired and drooping,
May drink at leisure without stooping.

Cries Benjamin, "where is it, where?
I know my treasure must be near."
—A Star declining to the west
Its image faintly had impress'd
Upon the smooth and dewy block,
The surface of the upright rock,
And he espies it by this sign
And both there take a draft divine.
Could happier, more convenient place
Be given in fortune's utmost grace?
They have a comfort in their madness
And feel that this is sober gladness.

Ah! dearest Spot! dear Rock of Names
From which our Pair thus slaked their flames!
Ah! deem not this light strain unjust
To thee and to thy precious trust,
That file which gentle, brave, and good,
The [?de]ar in friendship and in blood,
The hands of those I love the best
Committed to thy faithful breast!
No, long as I've a genial feeling
Or one that stands in need of healing

---

496 According to the Honourable Justice Coleridge, on October 10, 1836, WW

read me some lines, which formed part of a suppressed portion of 'The Waggoner;' but which he is now printing 'on the Rock of Names,' so called because on it they had carved out their initials:

W.W. Wm. Wordsworth. S.T.C. Samuel Taylor Coleridge.
M.H. Mary W. J.W. John Wordsworth.
D.W. Dorothy Wordsworth. S.H. Sara Hutchinson.

This rock was about a mile beyond Wythburn Chapel, to which they used to accompany my uncle, in going to Keswick from Grasmere, and where they would meet him when he returned. [*Memoirs*, II, 310]

I will preserve thy rightful power
Inviolate till life's final hour.
A[?ll take with kind]ness then as said
With a fond heart though playfull head,
And thou thy record duly keep
Long after they are laid asleep.

As winds by pausing do grow stronger
How fierce when they can pause no longer!
So now the tempest of delight
Broke forth with [?aggravated m]ight.
No notions have they, not a thought,
Not one that is not highly wrought.
Beside the Spring and silent Lake
Their [inspiration] I partake.
Oh! what a jubilee of fancy!
A braver world no Poet can see;
This sight to me the Muse imparts.
And then what kindness in their hearts,
What tears of rapture, what vow-making,
Profound entreaties, and hand-shaking,
What solemn vacant interlacing,
As if they'd fall asleep embracing!
Then in the turbulence of glee,
And in the excess of amity,
Cries Benjamin, "that Ass of thine,
He spoils thy sport and hinders mine.
Poor Beast! I know no harm is meant
But he's a sad impediment.
If he were tethered to the Waggon
He'd drag as well what he is dragging
And we, as Brother should with Brother,
Might travel along-side each other."
—So to the Waggon's skirts they tied
The creature by the Mastiff's side

[516] No notion have they—not a thought,
That is from joyless regions brought!
And, while they coast the silent lake,
[519] Their inspiration I partake;
Share their empyreal spirits—yea,
With their enraptured vision, see—
[520] O fancy what a jubilee!
What shifting pictures—clad in gleams
Of colour bright as feverish dreams!
Earth, spangled sky, and lake serene,
Involved and restless all—a scene
Pregnant with mutual exaltation,
Rich change, and multiplied creation!
[522] This sight to me the Muse imparts;
And then, what kindness in their hearts!
What tears of rapture, what vow-making,
[525] Profound entreaties, and hand-shaking!
What solemn, vacant, interlacing,
As if they'd fall asleep embracing!
Then, in the turbulence of glee,
And in the excess of amity,
[530] Says Benjamin, "That Ass of thine,
[531] He spoils thy sport, and hinders mine:
[534] If he were tether'd to the Waggon,
[535] He'd drag as well what he is dragging;
And we, as brother should with brother,
[537] Might trudge it alongside each other!"

Forthwith, obedient to command,
The horses made a quiet stand;
[538] And to the Waggon's skirts was tied
The Creature, by the Mastiff's side,

---

477 fancy] fancy, *1820* fancy—*1827–*
484 imparts;] imparts;—*1820–*
486 *defective punctuation after* vow-making *replaced by comma 1820–*
487 *defective punctuation after* hand-shaking *replaced by exclamation point 1820–*
492 Ass] ass *1827–1840*
494 tether'd] tethered *1820–* Waggon,] waggon, *1836–*
496 brother,] brother *1840–1846*
497 other!"] other! *1827–*
498 command,] command *1827*
500 Waggon's] waggon's *1836–*

(The Mastiff not well pleased to be
So very near such Company)
And staggering to the rock once more
They drank as deeply as before,
Their burning faces they bedew'd,
And thus their journey all renew'd,
The Vanguard following close behind
Sails spread as if to catch the wind.
"Thy Wife and Child are snug and warm.
Thy Ship [will travel without] harm;
I like," [said Ben, "her] make and stature
And this of mine, this bulky Creature
Of which I have the steering, this,
Seen fairly, is not much amiss.
We want your streamers, Friend! you know,
But altogether as we go
We make a kind of handsome show.

554 The scale model of the *Vanguard* still has "every inch of sail upon her" (l. 391) and "flag flying at mast head" (l. 431).

[540] (The Mastiff not well pleased to be
[541] So very near such company.)
This new arrangement made, the Wain
Through the still night proceeds again:
No moon hath risen her light to lend;
But indistinctly may be kenn'd
[546] The VANGUARD, following close behind,
Sails spread, as if to catch the wind!

"Thy Wife and Child are snug and warm,
Thy Ship will travel without harm;
[550] I like," said Benjamin, "her shape and stature
And this of mine—this bulky Creature
Of which I have the steering—this,
Seen fairly, is not much amiss!
We want your streamers, Friend, you know;
[555] But, all together, as we go,
We make a kind of handsome show!
Among these hills, from first to last,
We've weather'd many a furious blast;
Hard passage forcing on, with head
Against the storm and canvas spread.
I hate a boaster—but to thee
Will say't, who know'st both land and sea,
The unluckiest Hulk that sails the brine

502–503
The Mastiff wondering, and perplext,
With dread of what will happen next;
And thinking it but sorry cheer, [3]
To have such company so near! *1836–* *but* [1] perplext,] perplext *MS. 1832/36*, *MS. 1836/45*, *1840–* [2] will] may *del to* will *MS. 1832/36* next;] next *MS. 1832/36*

503/504 extra space *1836–*

504 indented *1836–*

505 again:] again; *1832–*

506 moon] Moon *1827–*

507 kenn'd] kenned *1827–*

510 Wife . . . Child] wife . . . child *1836–*

511 Ship] ship *1836–*

512 stature] stature; *1820–1827* stature: *1832–*

513 Creature] creature *1836–*

516 Friend,] friend, *1836–*

517 all together,] altogether, *1832* altogether *1836–*

520 weather'd] weathered *1820–*

522 storm] storm, *1827–* canvass] canvas *1827* canvass *with final* s *del MS. 1832/36*

523 boaster—] boaster; *1836–*

524 know'st] knowest *1832*

525 Hulk] hulk *1836–* sails] stems *1836–* brine] brin *1827 but corr errata*

Aye, long and long by night and day
Together have we ground our way
Through foul and fair, our task fulfilling,
And long shall do so yet, God willing!"

"Plague on the hooping and the howl,"
Replies the Tar, "of yon screech Owl."
But instantly began a fray
That called their thoughts another way.
The Mastiff, ill-condition'd carl,
What must he do but growl and snarl,
Still more and more dissatisfied
With the meek Comrade at his side,
Till, not incensed, though put to proof,
The Ass, [uplifting a fore hoof],
Salutes the Mastiff on the head;
And so were better manners bred
And all was calmed and quieted.

Is hardly worse beset than mine,
When cross winds on her quarter beat;
And, fairly lifted from my feet,
I stagger onward—Heaven knows how—
But not so pleasantly as now—
Poor Pilot I, by snows confounded,
And many a foundrous pit surrounded!
Yet here we are, by night and day
Grinding through rough and smooth our way,
[559] Through foul and fair our task fulfilling;
[560] And long shall be so yet—God willing!"
"Aye," said the Tar, "through fair and foul—
But save us from yon screeching Owl!"
[563] That instant was begun a 'fray
Which call'd their thoughts another way;
[565] The Mastiff, ill-conditioned carl!
What must he do but growl and snarl,
Still more and more dissatisfied
With the meek comrade at his side?
Till, not incensed though put to proof,
The Ass, uplifting a hind hoof,
[571] Salutes the Mastiff on the head;
And so were better manners bred,
And all was calmed and quieted.

---

527 cross winds] cross-winds *1836–*
529 Heaven . . . how—] heaven . . . how; *1836–*
530 now—] now: *1836– but* now; *MS. 1832/36*
531 Pilot] pilot *1836*
534 way,] way; *1836– but not MS. 1832/36*
537 indented *1820–* "Aye,"] "Ay," *1827–*
538 But] "But *1819* Owl!"] Owl! *1819* owl!" *1836–*
539 'fray] fray *1827–*
540 call'd] called *1820–* way;] way: *1832–*
541 Mastiff,] mastiff, *1836–*
544 side?] side! *1832–*
546 hind hoof,] hind-hoof, *MS. 1832/36*
547 Mastiff] *made lowercase, then marked* Stet *MS. 1832/36*

---

532 foundrous: capable of causing to founder or become mired.

"Yon screech Owl," cries the Sailor, turning
Back to his former cause of mourning,
"Yon Owl! pray God that all be well!
'Tis worse than any funeral bell.
As sure as I've the gift of sight
We shall be meeting Ghosts to-night."
"Pshaw, pshaw!" [?says] Ben, "I know his station!"
I know him and his occupation.
The jolly Bird has learnt his cheer
On the Banks of Windermere,
Where a tribe of them make merry
Mocking the Man that keeps the Ferry,
Hallooing from an open throat
Like Traveller shouting for a Boat.
The trick he learn'd at Windermere
This lonely Owl is playing here;
That [is the worst of] his employment,
He's in the height of his enjoyment."

This explanation still'd the alarm,
Cured the fore-boder like a charm—
This, and the manner and the voice,
Summon'd the Sailor to rejoice.
His heart is up, he fears no evil
From life or death, from Man or Devil.
He wheel'd, and making many stops
Brandished his crutch against the mountain-tops;

574–587 References to the ferryman and to the Sailor's fear of ghosts echo *The Aeneid*, Dante's *Inferno*, and other epics.

582–587 See Introduction p. 6, for the origin of this passage in 1802. The ferry crossed Windermere at Bowness.

598–599 See DW's *Journals*, p. 64, where two drunken soldiers "fought with the mountains with their sticks."

"Yon Screech-owl," says the Sailor, turning
[575] Back to his former cause of mourning,
"Yon Owl!—pray God that all be well!
'Tis worse than any funeral bell;
As sure as I've the gift of sight
[579] We shall be meeting Ghosts to-night!"
—Said Benjamin, "this whip shall lay
A thousand if they cross our way.
I know that Wanton's noisy station,
[581] I know him and his occupation;
The jolly Bird hath learn'd his cheer
On the banks of Windermere;
Where a tribe of them make merry,
[585] Mocking the Man that keeps the Ferry;
Hallooing from an open throat,
Like Travellers shouting for a Boat.
—The tricks he learn'd at Windermere
This vagrant Owl is playing here—
[590] That is the worst of his employment;
He's in the height of his enjoyment!"

This explanation still'd the alarm,
Cured the foreboder like a charm;
This, and the manner, and the voice,
[595] Summon'd the Sailor to rejoice;
His heart is up—he fears no evil
From life or death, from man or devil;
He wheel'd—and, making many stops,
Brandish'd his crutch against the mountain tops;

---

550 Screech-owl,"] screech-owl," *1836–*
552 "Yon] Yon *1819* Owl!—] owl!— *1836–*
554 sight] sight, *1827–*
555 Ghosts] ghosts *1836–*
556 "this] "This *1820–*
557 thousand] thousand, *1827–*
560 Bird] bird *1836–* learn'd] learned *1820–*
561 On] Upon *1836–*
563 Man . . . Ferry;] man . . . ferry; *1836–*
565 Travellers . . . Boat.] travellers . . . boat. *1836–*
566 learn'd] learned *1820–*
567 Owl] owl *1836–*
568 employment;] employment: *1832–*
569 in the height] at the top *1836–*
570 still'd] stilled *1820–*
573 Summon'd] Summoned *1820–*
576 wheel'd] wheeled—*1820–1832* wheels—*1836–*
577 Brandish'd] Brandished *1820–*

And while he talk'd of blows and scars
Ben beheld among the stars
Such a dancing and a glancing,
Such retreating and advancing
As, I ween, was never seen
In bloodiest battle since the days of Mars.

[Triumphant pair pursue your] sport
And let us cut our story short.

What is yon that glitters bright
Like a cloud of Rainbow-light?
Like!—it *is* a purple cloud,
Or a rainbow-coloured shroud
Such as doth round Angels blaze
Travelling along heavenly ways.
Slowly, slowly up the steep

And, while he talk'd of blows and scars,
Benjamin, among the stars,
Beheld a dancing—and a glancing;
Such retreating and advancing
As, I ween, was never seen
In bloodiest battle since the days of Mars!

CANTO FOURTH.

THUS they, with freaks of proud delight,
Beguile the remnant of the night;
And many a snatch of jovial song
Regales them as they wind along;
While to the music, from on high,
The echoes make a glad reply.—
But the sage Muse the revel heeds
No farther than her story needs;
Nor will she servilely attend
The loitering journey to its end.
—Blithe Spirits of her own impel
The Muse, who scents the morning air,
To take of this transported Pair
A brief and unreproved farewell;
To quit the slow-paced Waggon's side,
And wander down yon hawthorn dell,
With murmuring Greta for her guide.
—There doth she ken the awful form
Of Raven-crag—black as a storm—

---

578 talk'd] talked *1820–*
594 Spirits] spirits *1836–*
595 Muse,] Muse *1836, then* Muse, *MS. 1836/45, 1840–*
596 Pair] pair *1836–*
598 Waggon's] waggon's *1836–*

---

595 Compare the Ghost in *Hamlet*, I.v.58: "methinks I scent the morning air."
600 The River Greta runs from east to west through Keswick into Derwent Water.
602 Raven Crag is at the north end of Thirlmere, on the western side of the lake.

Glimmering through the twilight pale;
And Gimmer-crag, his tall twin-brother,
Each peering forth to meet the other:—
And, rambling on through St. John's Vale,
Along the smooth unpathway'd plain,
By sheep-track or through cottage lane,
Where no disturbance comes to intrude
Upon the pensive solitude,
Her unsuspecting eye, perchance,
With the rude Shepherd's favour'd glance,
Beholds the Faeries in array,
Whose party-coloured garments gay
The silent company betray;
Red, green, and blue; a moment's sight!
For Skiddaw-top with rosy light
Is touch'd—and all the band take flight
—Fly also, Muse! and from the dell
Mount to the ridge of Nathdale Fell;
Thence look thou forth o'er wood and lawn
Hoar with the frost-like dews of dawn;
Across yon meadowy bottom look,
Where close fogs hide their parent brook;

---

604 Gimmer-crag,] Gimmer-crag*, *1820–1832* Ghimmer-crag*, *1836– but MS, 1832/36 as 1832* twin-brother,] twin brother, *1832–*
604 *note* *The crag of the ewe lamb. *1820–*
606 rambling on] while she roves *1827–*
607 unpathway'd] unpathwayed *1820–*
608 sheep-track] sheep-track, *then comma del and* stet *written in margin* (*WW*) *MS. 1836/45*
612 Shepherd's] shepherd's *1836–* favour'd] favoured *1820–*
613 Faeries] faeries *1836–*
615 betray;] betray: *1836– but MS. 1832/36 as 1832*
618 touch'd—] touched—*1820–* flight] flight. *1820–*
621 Thence] Thence, *1820–*

---

604 Gimmer Crag is probably the rock called Fisher Crag, directly south of Raven Crag on the western side of Thirlmere. According to de Selincourt, WW probably was indebted for this passage to the Ambleside artist William Green's *A Description of Sixty Studies from Nature*, 1810 (see *PW*, II, 502).

606 The Vale of St. John's extends from the northern end of Thirlmere north toward Threlkeld.

617 Skiddaw, the second highest peak in the Lake District, is directly north of Keswick.

620 Nathdale Fell is doubtless Naddle, southwest of Threlkeld.

Of Castrigg does the vapour creep,
Neither melting nor dividing,
Ever high and higher gliding,
Glorious as at first it show'd
Winding with the winding road:
If you never saw or heard
Of such object, take my word
That the Waggon, the dull care
Of good Benjamin, is there;
And there, though hidden by the gleam,
Benjamin is with his Team,
[Faithful still whate'er] betide
Whether Follower or Guide;
And with him goes his Sailor friend
Now almost at their journey's end

---

615 Castlerigg Fell, southeast of Keswick.

And see, beyond that hamlet small,
The ruined towers of Threlkeld-hall
Lurking in a double shade,
By trees and lingering twilight made!
There, at Blencathara's rugged feet,
Sir Lancelot gave a safe retreat
To noble Clifford; from annoy
Concealed the persecuted Boy,
Well pleased in rustic garb to feed
His flock, and pipe on Shepherd's reed;
Among this multitude of hills,
Crags, woodlands, waterfalls, and rills;
Which soon the morning shall enfold,
From east to west, in ample vest
Of massy gloom and radiance bold.

The mists, that o'er the streamlet's bed
Hung low, begin to rise and spread;
Even while I speak, their skirts of grey
Are smitten by a silver ray;
And lo!—up Castrigg's naked steep
(Where smoothly urged the vapours sweep
Along—and scatter and divide
Like fleecy clouds self-multiplied)
The stately Waggon is ascending
With faithful Benjamin attending,
Apparent now beside his team—
Now lost amid a glittering steam.
[628] And with him goes his Sailor Friend,
By this time near their journey's end,

---

626 Threlkeld-hall] Threlkeld-hall, *1820–*
632 Boy,] boy, *1836–*
634 Shepherd's] shepherd's *1836–* reed;] reed *1840–*
640 streamlet's] Streamlet's *1827–1832*
645 (Where . . . urged] (Where, . . . urged, *1820–*
646 divide] divide, *1832–*
648 Waggon] waggon *1836–* ascending] ascending, *1832–*
651 lost amid a] hidden by the *1836–1840 underlined with note in margin* See alteration *MS. 1832/36*: *see also transcription of Quillinan MS., below* steam.] steam: *1836–*
652 Sailor Friend,] Sailor-friend, *1836–*
653 end,] end; *1836–*

625–626 Both the small village of Threlkeld and Threlkeld Hall are situated along the River Greta, at the foot of Blencathra or Saddleback. The Wordsworths were distantly related to the Threlkeld family of Threlkeld Hall.

629–634 See Wordsworth's *Song at the Feast of Brougham Castle* for this story.

And after their high-minded riot
Sickening into [thoughtful] quiet
As if the morning's happy hour
Had for their joys a killing power.

They are drooping, weak and dull,
But the Horses stretch and pull,
With encreasing vigour climb
Eager to repair lost time.
Whether by their own desert,
Knowing that there's cause for shame,
They are labouring to avert
At least a little of the blame
Which full surely will alight
Upon his head whom in despite
Of all his faults they love the best—
Whether for him they are distress'd,
Or by length of fasting rous'd
Are impatient to be hous'd,

And, after their high-minded riot,
Sickening into thoughtful quiet;
As if the morning's pleasant hour
Had for their joys a killing power.

They are drooping, weak, and dull;
But the horses stretch and pull,
With increasing vigour climb,
Eager to repair lost time;
Whether, by their own desert,
Knowing that there's cause for shame,
They are labouring to avert
At least a portion of the blame
Which full surely will alight
Upon his head, whom, in despite
Of all his faults, they love the best;
Whether for him they are distrest;
Or, by length of fasting rous'd,
Are impatient to be housed;

655–657 *see transcriptions of MS. 1832/36 and Quillinan MS., below*
656 hour] hour, *1836–*
657/658
Say more: for by that power a vein
Seems opened of brow-saddening pain:
As if their hearts by notes were stung
From out the lowly hedge-rows flung;
As if the warbler lost in light
Reproved their soarings of the night;
In strains of rapture pure and holy
Upbraided their distempered folly. *end of verse paragraph 1836– but*
And, sooth, for Benjamin a vein [1–2]
Is opened of still deeper pain *1845–*
[2] pain] pain, *1849* [3] their hearts] his heart *1845–* [6] their] his *1845–* night;] night, *1845–* [8] their] his *1845–*
658 Drooping are they, and weak and dull;—*1836–1840 but* weak, . . . dull; *MS. 1832/36* Drooping is he, his step is dull; *1845–*
659 pull,] pull; *1820–*
663 that there's] there is *1827–1832* what cause there is *1836–*
664 They are] They now are *1836–1840 but MS. 1832/36 as 1832*
665 At least a portion] (Kind creatures!) something *1836–1840 but MS. 1832/36 as 1832* As much as may be *1845–* blame] blame, *1820–*
666 Which full surely will] Which, they foresee, must soon *1836– but MS. 1832/36 as 1832*
667–668 *see transcriptions of MS. 1832/36 and Quillinan MS., below*
667 his] *in italics 1820–*
668 faults, they love the best;] failings, they love best; *1836–*
669 distrest;] distrest *1847*
670 rous'd,] roused, *1820–*
671 housed;] housed: *1836– but MS. 1832/36 as 1832*

Up against the hill they strain,
Tugging at the iron chain,
Tugging all with might and main,
Last and foremost, every Horse
To the utmost of his force.
And the smoke and respiration
Rises like an exhalation
Which the merry, merry sun
Takes delight to play upon.

Up against the hill they strain—
Tugging at the iron chain—
[650] Tugging all with might and main—
Last and foremost, every horse
To the utmost of his force!
And the smoke and respiration
[654] Rising like an exhalation,
Blends with the mist,—a moving shroud
To form—an undissolving cloud;
Which with slant ray the merry sun
[656] Takes delight to play upon.

---

672 strain—] strain *1836– but* strain, *MS. 1832/36*
673 chain—] chain, *1836–*
674 main—] main, *1836–*
677 respiration] respiration, *1836–*
679 Blends] Blend *1836–* mist,—] mist—*1832– but* mist, *MS. 1832/36* shroud] shroud, *1832*
680 form—] form, *1836–*
681 Which . . . ray] Which, . . . ray, *1820–*

Never, surely, old Apollo,
He or other God as old
Of whom in story we are told,
Who had a favourite to follow
Through a battle or elsewhere,
Round the object of his care
In a time of peril threw
Veil of such celestial hue,
Interpos'd so bright a screen
Him and his enemies between.

Alas! what boots it—who can hide
When the malicious Fates are bent
On working out an ill intent?
Can destiny be turned aside?
No—sad progress of my Story,

Never, surely, old Apollo,
He, or other God as old,
Of whom in story we are told,
Who had a favourite to follow
Through a battle or elsewhere,
Round the object of his care,
In a time of peril, threw
Veil of such celestial hue;
Interposed so bright a screen
Him and his enemies between!

Alas, what boots it?—who can hide
When the malicious Fates are bent
On working out an ill intent?
Can destiny be turned aside?
No—sad progress of my story!

683–689
Never Venus or Apollo,
Pleased a favourite chief to follow
Through accidents of peace or war,
In a time of peril threw,
Round the object of his care, *1832*; *see transcriptions of MS. 1832/36, of Cornell MS. fragment 1836, and of Quillinan MS., below*
Never golden-haired Apollo,
Nor blue-eyed Pallas, nor the Idalian Queen,
When each was pleased some favourite chief to follow
Through accidents of peace or war, [4]
In a perilous moment threw
Around the object of celestial care *1836–1840 but* [3] When each was *del and* Pleased *MS. 1836/45* [4] war *1840* [6] celestial *del to* their (*WW*) *then alt* Round each object of their care *MS. 1836/45*
Never Venus or {A / apollo}
Intent some favorite Chief to follow
Tho{r} ough {accidents of peace or war / accidents of peace or war}
Round the object of that care
In a time of [?pererl] threw *alt version MS. 1836/45*
Never golden-haired Apollo,
Pleased some favourite chief to follow
Through accidents of peace or war,
In a perilous moment threw
Around the object of his care *1845–*
690 A veil so rich to mortal view, *1836–1840 but MS. 1832/36 as 1832 and* [?Wiel] . . . hue *then alt* V[?e]il . . . hue *MS. 1836/45*
691 screen] screen—*1836–but MS. 1832/36 as 1832*
693 Alas,] Alas! *1832–* hide] hide, *1836–*

Benjamin! this outward glory
Cannot shield thee from thy Master
Who from Keswick has prick'd forth,
Sour and surly as the North,
And in fear of some disaster
Comes to give what help he may
Or to hear what thou canst say
If, as he needs must forebode,
Thou hast loitered on the road.

He is waiting on the height
Of Castrigg, sees the vapour bright.
Soon as he beheld he knew it
And the Waggon glimmering through it—
Glad sight, and yet it rather hath
Stirr'd him up to livelier wrath
Which he stifles, moody Man,
With all the patience that he can,
To the end that at your meeting
He may give thee decent greeting.
There he is resolved to stop
Till the Waggon gains the top,
But stop he cannot, must advance,
And Ben espies him by good chance.
In a moment he is ready,
Self-collected, poiz'd and steady,
And to be the better seen
Issues forth from out his cloud,
From his close attending shroud,
With careless air and open mien.

---

673 The Waggoner's master resided in Keswick. "K[night] is responsible for the current error which identifies Benjamin with Jackson, Southey's landlord at Greta Hall. Jackson was not the hero of W.'s poem, but was Benjamin's employer" (*PW*, II, 497). Dr Carol Landon has suggested to me, however, that by this time Jackson had been succeeded by John I'Anson, the innkeeper of the Royal Oak, from which many Keswick coaches and waggons originated.

Benjamin, this outward glory
Cannot shield thee from thy Master,
Who from Keswick has prick'd forth,
[675] Sour and surly as the north;
And, in fear of some disaster,
Comes to give what help he may,
Or to hear what thou canst say;
If, as needs he must forebode,
[680] Thou hast loitered on the road!
His doubts—his fears may now take flight—
The wish'd-for object is in sight;
Yet, trust the Muse, it rather hath
[686] Stirr'd him up to livelier wrath;
Which he stifles, moody man!
With all the patience that he can;
To the end that at your meeting,
[690] He may give thee decent greeting.

There he is—resolved to stop,
Till the Waggon gains the top;
But stop he cannot—must advance:
Him Benjamin, with lucky glance,
Espies—and instantly is ready,
[696] Self-collected, poised, and steady;
And, to be the better seen,
Issues from his radiant shroud,
From his close-attending cloud,
[700] With careless air and open mien.

697–698 *see transcription of Quillinan MS., below*
698 Benjamin,] Benjamin *1827*
699 Cannot] Fails to *1836–1840 but MS. 1832/36 as 1832*
700 prick'd] pricked *1820–*
703–707 *see transcription of Quillinan MS., below*
704 Or] And *1836– but MS. 1832/36 as 1832*
705 needs he must] he cannot but *1836–1840 but MS. 1832/36 as 1832*
706 loitered] been loitering *1836– but MS. 1832/36 as 1832*
707 doubts—his fears] fears, his doubts *1836– but* doubts, his fears, *MS. 1832/36 and* doubts, *1845–* flight—] flight: *MS. 1832/36*
708 wish'd-for] wished-for *1820–*
710 Stirr'd] Stirred *1820–*
713 that] that, *1832–*
716 Waggon] waggon *1836–*
718 with] by *1836–1840*
720 steady;] steady: *1836–*

---

700 pricked: ridden (an archaic word used by Spenser).

[?Firm] his port, [?erect] his going
[As] yon Cock that now is crowing,
And the morning light in grace
Crimsons o'er his lifted face,
And some sober thoughts arise
To steal the wandering from his eyes.
But what can all avail to clear him,
Or what need of explanation,
Parley or interrogation?
For the Master sees, alas!
That unhappy Figure near him
Limping o'er the dewy grass
Where the road it fringes, sweet,
Soft and cool to way-worn feet,
And, oh! indiginity! an Ass
By his noble Mastiff's side
Tethered to this Waggon's tail,
And the Ship in all her pride
Following after in full sail,
Not to speak of Babe and Mother
Who, contented with each other
And as snug as birds in arbour,
Find within a blessed harbour.

With eager eyes the Master pries,
Looks in and out and through and through,
Says nothing till at last he spies
A wound upon the Mastiff's head,
A wound where plainly might be read
What feats an Ass's [?hoof] can do.
But drop the rest and give the sense,
The sum of all the consequence.
'Twas briefly, that this provocation,
This complicated aggravation,
A hoard of grievances unseal'd,

Erect his port, and firm his going;
So struts yon Cock that now is crowing;
[703] And the morning light in grace
Strikes upon his lifted face,
Hurrying the pallid hue away
That might his trespasses betray.
[707] But what can all avail to clear him,
Or what need of explanation,
Parley, or interrogation?
[710] For the Master sees, alas!
That unhappy Figure near him,
Limping o'er the dewy grass,
Where the road it fringes, sweet,
Soft and cool to way-worn feet;
[715] And, O indignity! an Ass,
By his noble Mastiff's side,
Tether'd to the Waggon's tail;
And the Ship, in all her pride,
Following after in full sail!
[720] Not to speak of Babe and Mother;
Who, contented with each other,
And snug as birds in leafy arbour,
Find, within, a blessed harbour!

With eager eyes the Master pries;
[725] Looks in and out—and through and through;
Says nothing—till at last he spies
A wound upon the Mastiff's head,
A wound—where plainly might be read
[729] What feats an Ass's hoof can do!
But drop the rest:—this aggravation,
This complicated provocation,
[734] A hoard of grievances unseal'd;

---

726 Cock] cock *1836–* crowing;] crowing, *1849 (7 vols.) some copies*
733 Parley,] Parley *1832–*
741 Tether'd] Tethered *1820–* Waggon's tail;] Waggon's tail: *1820–1832* waggon's tail: *1836–*
742 Ship,] ship, *1836–*
744 Babe . . . Mother] babe . . . mother *1836–*
745 each other] each each other *1819*
749 out—] out, *1836–*
751 Mastiff's] *made lowercase, then marked* stet *MS. 1832/36*
752 wound—] wound, *1836–*
756 unseal'd;] unsealed;] *1820–*

All past forgiveness it repeal'd.
And thus, and through distemper'd blood
On both sides, Benjamin the good,
The patient and the tender-hearted,
Was from his Team and Waggon parted—
When duty of that day was o'er
Laid down his Whip and serv'd no more.
Nor could the Waggon's self survive
The want of Benjamin to drive;
Each steep, unmanageable hill
Call'd for his patience or his skill.
It linger'd on a Month or so;
What came of it I do not know,
But sure it is that through that night
And what the morning brought to light
Two losses had we to sustain:
We lost both Waggoner and Wain.

A [?sad] Catastrophe, say you—
Adventure never worth a song?
Be free to think so, for I too

[735] All past forgiveness it repeal'd;—
And thus, and through distemper'd blood
On both sides, Benjamin the good,
The patient, and the tender-hearted,
Was from his Team and Waggon parted;
[740] When duty of that day was o'er,
Laid down his whip—and served no more.—
Nor could the Waggon long survive
Which Benjamin had ceas'd to drive:
It lingered on;—Guide after Guide
Ambitiously the office tried;
[744] But each unmanageable hill
[745] Call'd for *his* patience, and *his* skill;—
[748] And sure it is, that through this night,
And what the morning brought to light,
[750] Two losses had we to sustain,
[751] We lost both WAGGONER and WAIN!

Accept, O Friend, for praise or blame,
The gift of this adventurous Song;
A record which I dared to frame,
Though timid scruples check'd me long;
They check'd me—and I left the theme
Untouch'd—in spite of many a gleam

---

757 repeal'd;—] repealed;—*1820–1832* repealed; *1836–*
758 distemper'd] distempered *1820–*
761 Team . . . Waggon] team . . . waggon *1836–*
764 Waggon . . . survive] waggon . . . survive, *1836–*
765 ceas'd] ceased *1820–*
766 Guide after Guide] guide after guide *1836–*
769 Call'd] Called *1820–* patience,] patience *1827–*
773/774 *thick and thin rules*] *thin rule 1827–1847; rule omitted 1849*
775 Song;] song; *1832–*
777 check'd] checked *1820–*
778 check'd] checked *1820–*
779 Untouch'd—] Untouched—*1827–1832* Untouched;—*1836–*

---

775 See *Paradise Lost* I, 13: "Invoke thy aid to my advent'rous song."

Have thought so many times and long.
But what I have and what I miss
I sing of these, it makes my bliss.
Nor is it I who play the part,
But a shy spirit in my heart
That comes and goes, will sometimes leap
From hiding-places ten years deep.
Sometimes, as in the present case,
Will shew a more familiar face,
Returning like a Ghost unlaid
Until the debt I owe be paid.
Forgive me, then, for I had been
On friendly terms with this Machine.
In him a Chieftain of his race,
A living Almanack, had we;
We had a speaking Diary
Which in this uneventful place
Gave every day a mark and name
By which we knew it when it came.
Yes I, and all about me here,
Through all the changes of the year
Had seen him through the mountains g[?o]
In pomp of mist or pomp of snow,
Majestically huge and slow—
Or with a milder grace adorning
The Landscape of a summer's morning
When Grasmere smooth'd her liquid plain

---

757 I sing of these: one of many epic conventions parodied in the poem.

Of fancy which thereon was shed,
Like pleasant sun-beams shifting still
Upon the side of a distant hill.
But Nature might not be gainsaid;
[756] For what I have and what I miss
I sing of these—it makes my bliss!
Nor is it I who play the part,
But a shy spirit in my heart,
[760] That comes and goes—will sometimes leap
From hiding-places ten years deep;
Sometimes, as in the present case,
Will show a more familiar face;
Returning, like a ghost unlaid,
[765] Until the debt I owe be paid.
Forgive me, then; for I had been
[767] On friendly terms with this Machine:
In him, while he was wont to trace
Our roads, through many a long year's space,
[769] A living Almanack had we;
We had a speaking Diary,
That, in this uneventful place,
Gave to the days a mark and name
By which we knew them when they came.
—Yes, I, and all about me here,
[775] Through all the changes of the year,
Had seen him through the mountains go,
In pomp of mist or pomp of snow,
Majestically huge and slow:
Or with a milder grace adorning
[780] The Landscape of a summer's morning;
While Grasmere smooth'd her liquid plain

---

781 sun-beams] sunbeams *1827–*
782 hill.] hill: *1827–*
785 these—] these;—*1836–*
789 years] years' *1819–1840*
790–791
Or, proud all rivalship to chase,
Will haunt me with familiar face; *1820, becomes*
Or haunts me with familiar face—*1827– but* face—] face, *1836–*
798 Almanack] almanack *1836–*
799 Diary,] diary, *1836–*
800 That,] That *1840–*
808 Or] Or, *1820–* with a] with *1832–1840*
809 Landscape] landscape *1836–*
810 smooth'd] smoothed *1820–*

The moving image to detain
And mighty Fairfield with a chime
Of echoes to its march kept time,
When little other business stirr'd
And little other sound was heard,
In that delicious hour of balm,
Stillness, solitude and calm,
While yet the Valley is array'd
On this side with a sober shade,
On that, is prodigally bright,
Crag, lawn and wood, with rosy light.
But most of all, thou lordly Wain,
I wish to have thee here again
When windows flap and chimney roars
And all is dismal out of doors,
And sitting by my fire I see
Eight sorry Carts, no less a train!
Unworthy Successors of thee
Come straggling through the wind and ra[?in],
And oft as they pass slowly on
Beneath my window one by one
See perch'd upon the naked height,
The summit of a cumb'rous freight,
A single Traveller, and there
Another, then perhaps a pair,
The lame, the sickly and the old,
Men, Women heartless with the cold
And Babes in wet and starvling plight
Which once, be weather as it might,

783 Dove Cottage is at the foot of Fairfield, which is east of Grasmere.
808 heartless: depressed.

The moving image to detain;
And mighty Fairfield, with a chime
Of echoes, to his march kept time;
When little other business stirr'd,
And little other sound was heard;
In that delicious hour of balm,
Stillness, solitude, and calm,
While yet the Valley is arrayed,
On this side, with a sober shade;
On that is prodigally bright—
Crag, lawn, and wood, with rosy light.—
But most of all, thou lordly Wain!
I wish to have thee here again,
When windows flap and chimney roars,
And all is dismal out of doors;
And, sitting by my fire, I see
Eight sorry Carts, no less a train!
Unworthy Successors of thee,
Come straggling through the wind and rain:
And oft, as they pass slowly on,
Beneath my window—one by one—
See, perch'd upon the naked height
The summit of a cumbrous freight,
A single Traveller—and, there,
Another—then perhaps a Pair—
The lame, the sickly, and the old;
Men, Women, heartless with the cold;
And Babes in wet and starv'ling plight;
Which once, be weather as it might,

---

814 stirr'd] stirred *1820–*
818 Valley] valley *1836–*
819 side,] side *1820–*
821 wood,] wood—*1820–* light.—] light. *1836– but MS. 1832/36 as 1832*
822 But]—But *1836– but MS. 1832/36 as 1832*
824 flap] flap, *1820*
827 Carts,] carts, *1836–*
828 Successors] successors *1836–*
831 window—one by one—] windows, one by one, *1836– but* window, *MS. 1832/36*
832 perch'd] perched *1820–*
834 Traveller—] traveller—*1836–* and, there,] and there *1827–*
835 Another— . . . Pair—] Another; . . . pair—*1836–*
837 Women,] women, *1836–*
838 Babes] babes *1836–* starv'ling] starvl'ing *1819* starveling *1820–*
839 once] *in italics 1820*

Had still a nest within a nest,
Thy shelter and their Mother's breast—
Then most of all, then far the most
Do I regret what we have lost,
Am grieved for that unhappy sin
Which robbed us of good Benjamin
And of his stately charge which none
Could keep alive when he was gone.

Had still a nest within a nest,
Thy shelter—and their Mother's breast!
Then most of all, then far the most,
Do I regret what we have lost;
[815] Am grieved for that unhappy sin
Which robbed us of good Benjamin;—
And of his stately Charge, which none
[818] Could keep alive when He was gone!

---

841 Mother's] mother's *1836–*

845 Benjamin;—] Benjamin:—*1820*

847 He] he 1827–1840 1805. *added below line in right margin 1836– but* Grasmere *entered before date (WW) MS. 1836/45* 1805 *1841–1843, 1846*

Subtitle NOTES. [*short rule*] / 1.] Notes. 1.st *Quillinan MS., sheet 1 (1^{r})* Print the following, at the *end* of the Waggoner, as a close to the Volume. / Notes. / [double short rule] / 1. *Quillinan MS., sheet 2 (2^{v})* The Waggoner: *above subtitle (EQ) MS. 1836/45* Page 131. / '*The Waggoner.*' *1845, 1849 but* Page 68. *1849*

NOTES.

1.

SEVERAL years after the event that forms the subject of the foregoing poem, in company with my friend, the late Mr. Coleridge, I happened to fall in with the person to whom the name of Benjamin is given. Upon our expressing regret that we had not, for a long time, seen upon the road either him or his waggon, he said:—"They could not do without me: and as to the man who was put in my place, no good could come out of him; he was a man of no *ideas.*"

The fact of my discarded hero's getting the horses out of a great difficulty with a word, as related in the poem, was told me by an eye-witness.

2.

The Dor-hawk, solitary bird.

When the Poem was first written the note of the bird was thus described:—

The Night-hawk is singing his frog-like tune,
Twirling his watchman's rattle about—

1–2 the foregoing poem,] this poem, *del to* the foregoing poem, *Quillinan MS., sheet 2* (1^r) the Poem, *1845, 1849*

2 in company with my friend, the late Mr. Coleridge, I] my friend the late Mr. Coleridge & I *Quillinan MS., sheet 2* (1^r *and* 2^v) *but* &] and 2^v *hyphen missing when* Cole-ridge *is broken between lines, some copies 1836*

3–4 the person to whom the name Benjamin is given] our hero. *del to* the person to whom I have given the name of Benjamin *Quillinan MS., sheet 2* (1^r *and* 2^v) *but corrected reading only in* 2^v

4 not,] not *Quillinan MS., sheet 2*(1^r) time,] time *Quillinan MS., sheet 2* (1^r)

5–6 said:—] said: *Quillinan MS., sheet 2* (1^r *and* 2^v) could not] couldn't *Quillinan MS., sheet 2* (1^r *and* 2^v) me:] me; *1840–*

7 *ideas.*"] ideas." *Quillinan MS., sheet 2* (1^r *and* 2^v)

8 hero's] Waggoner's *del to* hero's *Quillinan MS., sheet 2* (1^r)

9 word] single word *del to* word *Quillinan MS., sheet 2* (2^r)

10/11 2.] Page 277. Line 3 *MS. 1836/45* Page 131 *1845* Page 68. *1849*

11 *enclosed in single quotation marks MS. 1836/45* 'The buzzing Dor-hawk, round and round is wheeling, '—*1845–but in italics with comma following* round *and dash inside final quotation mark 1845, 1849*

14 The] 'The *1845–* Night-hawk] Nightengale *del by John Carter to* Nighthawk *MS. 1836/45*

15 about—] about—' *1845–*

but from unwillingness to startle the reader at the outset by so bold a mode of expression, the passage was altered as it now stands.

3.

After the line, Page 293, *Can any mortal clog come to her* [l. 470], followed in the MS. an incident which has been kept back. Part of the suppressed verses shall here be given as a gratification of private feeling, which the well-disposed reader will find no difficulty in excusing. They are now printed for the first time.

Can any mortal clog come to her?
It can: * * *
* * * * *
But Benjamin, in his vexation,
Possesses inward consolation;
He knows his ground, and hopes to find
A spot with all things to his mind,
An upright mural block of stone,
Moist with pure water trickling down.
A slender spring; but kind to man
It is, a true Samaritan;
Close to the highway, pouring out
Its offering from a chink or spout;
Whence all, howe'er athirst, or drooping
With toil, may drink, and without stooping.

Cries Benjamin, "Where is it, where?
Voice it hath none, but must be near."
—A star, declining towards the west,

17/18 3.] Print the following at the end of the Waggoner as a close to the volume / 2. *Quillinan MS., sheet 2 (3^{r}); del MS. 1836/45* Page 136. *1845* Page 82. *1849*

18–43 *see transcription of Cornell manuscript fragment, 1836, below*

18 A[?fter] *del preceding the line Quillinan MS., sheet 2 (3^{r}), and line not indented* Page 293,] page‸ *Quillinan MS., sheet 2 (3^{r})* Page 296, *1840, 1846; omitted 1845, 1849* Can] '*Can 1845–* *her,*] *her,*! *1845–*

19 MS.] M.S. *Quillinan MS., sheet 2 (3^{r})*

22 They are now printed for the first time.] *not present in Quillinan MS., sheet 2 (3^{r})*

23 Can] 'Can *1845–*

31 spring;] spring, *Quillinan MS., sheet 2 (3^{r})*

33 highway,] high-way, *Quillinan MS., sheet 2 (3^{r})*

35 athirst,] athirst *Quillinan MS., sheet 2 (3^{r})*

36 drink,] drink *Quillinan MS., sheet 2 (3^{r})*

36/37 *no extra space Quillinan MS., sheet 2 (3^{r})*

37 *line not indented, corrected to indented Quillinan MS., sheet 2 (3^{r})* "Where] 'Where *Quillinan MS., sheet 2 (3^{r})*

38 near."] here. *del to* near. *Quillinan MS., sheet 2 (3^{r})*

39 —A] A *corrected to*—A *Quillinan MS., sheet 2 (3^{r})* star, . . . west,] star . . . west *Quillinan MS., sheet 2 (3^{r})*

Upon the watery surface threw
Its image tremulously imprest,
That just marked out the object and withdrew:
Right welcome service! * *
* * * * *

ROCK OF NAMES!

Light is the strain, but not unjust
To Thee and thy memorial-trust,
That once seemed only to express
Love that was love in idleness;
Tokens, as year hath followed year,
How changed, alas, in character!
For they were graven on thy smooth breast
By hands of those my soul loved best;
Meek women, men as true and brave
As ever went to a hopeful grave:
Their hands and mine, when side by side
With kindred zeal and mutual pride,
We worked until the Initials took
Shapes that defied a scornful look.—
Long as for us a genial feeling
Survives, or one in need of healing,
The power, dear Rock, around thee cast,
Thy monumental power, shall last
For me and mine! O thought of pain,
That would impair it or profane!
Take all in kindness then, as said
With a staid heart but playful head;
And fail not Thou, loved Rock! to keep
Thy charge when we are laid asleep.

---

44 Ro *indented normally del to* ROCK OF NAMES *flush right, del in turn to* ROCK OF NAMES! *in right margin Quillinan MS., sheet 2 (3r)*

46 Thee . . . trust,] Thee, . . . trust *1840–*

48 love in idleness;] Love in Idleness; *del to* love in idleness; *Quillinan MS., sheet 2 (3r)* love in idleness—*MS. 1836/45*

49 year,] year *1840–*

55 mine, when] mine went *del to* mine, when *Quillinan MS., sheet 2 (3r)*

57 Initials] initials *del to* Initials *Quillinan MS., sheet 2 (3r)*

61 Rock] *underlined MS. 1836/45*

62 power] *underlined MS. 1836/45*

63 mine! mine: *Quillinan MS., sheet 2 (3v)* mine.—*MS. 1836/45*

68 asleep.] asleep.' *1845–* End. *added below center of line Quillinan MS., sheet 2 (3v)*

Transcriptions

Fragments, with Facing Photographic Reproductions

Lines from Dove Cottage MS. 44 (1802)

DC MS. 44, called MS. Verse 25 before the recent chronological renumbering of the 1785–1814 Dove Cottage papers, is also referred to as MS. M, since it includes MS. M of *The Prelude*. It also contains MS. M of *The Ruined Cottage*, MS. 4 of *Peter Bell*, and a number of shorter poems. The manuscript is homemade, and is composed of sheets of laid paper watermarked with Britannia (with a shield containing the letter H) over 1802, within a crowned oval medallion, and countermarked C HALE. The leaves measure 10.70 by 16.90 centimeters, with chain lines at intervals of 2.65 centimeters. This manuscript was expressly prepared so that Coleridge could have it with him in Malta, and he had it bound there or in Italy. For a fuller account of MS. 44 and a list of its contents, see *Chronology*: *MY*, pages 619–624, 636–637, and elsewhere; see also *RC and Pedlar*, pages 378–379.

"The Owl as if," on leaf 82ᵛ, is the final entry in the section of short poems preceding *Peter Bell* MS. 4., and is written in ink in Mary Wordsworth's hand. In the transcription that follows, line numbers in the left margin are keyed to the reading text of MS. 1.

Thou art to me but as a wave
Of the wild sea; and I would have
Some claim upon thee if I could,
Though but of common neighbourhood.
What joy to hear and to see!
Thy elder Brother I would be,
Thy Father, any thing to thee.

Now thanks to heaven that of its grace
Hath led me to this lonely place.
Joy have I had, and going hence
I bear away my recompence.
In spots like these it is we prize
Our memory, feel that she hath eyes.
Then why should I be loth to stir?
I feel this place is made for her;
To give new pleasure like the past,
Continued long as life shall last.
Nor am I loth, though pleas'd at heart,
Sweet highland Girl, from thee to part;
For I, methinks, till I grow old
As fair before me shall behold,
As I do now the Cabin small,
The Lake, the Bay, the Waterfall,
And Thee the spirit of them all.

To fill up the blank

The Owl as if he had learn'd his cheer
On the banks of Windermere
In his Tower is making merry
Mocking the Man who keeps the ferry
Hallooing from an open throat
Like one shouting for a Boat

To fill up the blank

The Owl as if he had learn'd his cheer
On the banks of Windermere
In his Tower is making merry
Mocking the Man who keeps the ferry
Hallooing from an open throat
Like one shouting for a Boat

Lines from Dove Cottage MS. 28 (1806)

DC MS. 28, earlier called MS. Verse 43, contains MS. R of *Home at Grasmere*. It is composed of three surviving gatherings (K, L, and M) of an interleaved copy of Coleridge's *Poems*, 1796. The leaves from the original volume are of wove paper watermarked J WHATMAN; the interleaves are of laid paper watermarked with Britannia in a crowned circular medallion, and countermarked COLES/1795. The leaves from the original volume measure 10.2 to 10.5 by 16.1 to 16.7 centimeters; the interleaves measure 10.5 by 17.0 centimeters, with chain lines at intervals of 2.4 centimeters. For further information about this manuscript, see *H at G*, pages 139–141. Two other interleaved gatherings (D and E) of *Poems*, 1796, have survived and form DC MS. 30. The other gatherings, together with whatever manuscript material they may have contained, have been lost.

Both *Benjamin the Waggoner* passages were written in ink by William Wordsworth. Lines 413–416 were hastily written at the top of leaf 1^r (*Poems*, p. 131, gathering K^2), and probably constitute a draft addition to lines on the verso of the once preceding, but now absent, interleaf. Lines 424–437 were more carefully written on leaf 2^r (the first interleaf), and probably represent Wordsworth's copy of an earlier draft. In the transcription that follows, line numbers in the left margin are keyed to the reading text of MS. 1.

My mind went to and fro, and waver'd long;
At length I've choſen (Samuel thinks me wrong)
That, around whoſe azure rim
Silver figures ſeem to ſwim,
Like fleece-white clouds, that on the ſkiey Blue,
Wak'd by no breeze, the ſelf-ſame ſhapes retain;
Or ocean Nymphs with limbs of ſnowy hue
Slow-floating o'er the calm cerulean plain.

Juſt ſuch a one, *mon cher ami*
(The finger ſhield of induſtry)
Th' inventive Gods, I deem, to Pallas gave
What time the vain Arachne, madly brave,
Challeng'd the blue-eyed Virgin of the ſky
A duel in embroider'd work to try.
And hence the thimbled Finger of grave Pallas
To th' erring Needle's point was more than callous.

K 2

[131]

{a
413 A bowl {of bowl of [?double] measure
414 Cries Benjamin a draft of length
ll Britains
415 We drink to Englands pride and treasure
416 Her bulwark & her tower of strength

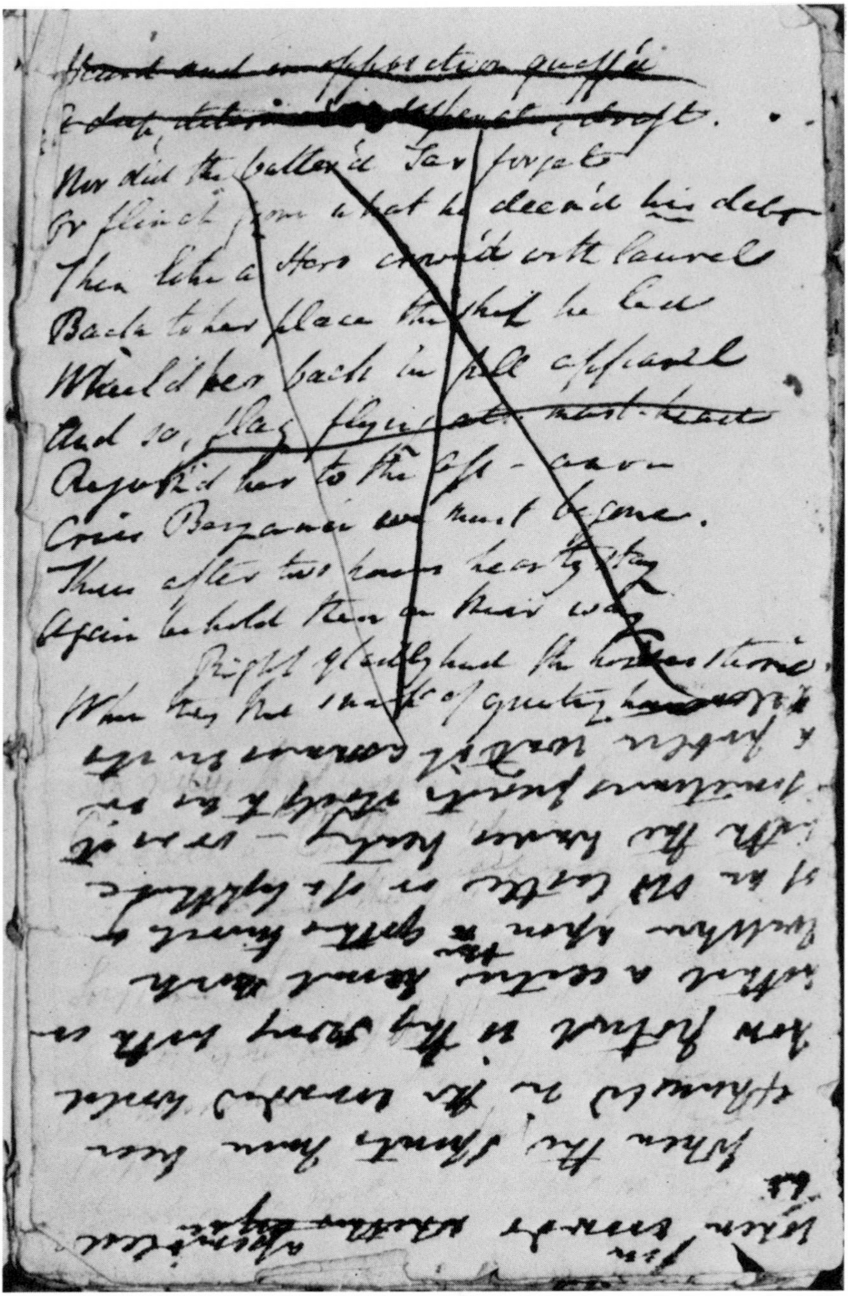

[132/133i^r]

~~Heard and in opposition quaff'd~~
~~A deep, determin'd, desperate, draft.~~
Nor did the batter'd Tar forget
Or flinch from what he deem'd his debt
Then like a Hero crown'd with laurel
Back to her place the ship he led
Wheel'd her back in full apparel
And so, flag flying at ~~mast-head~~
Reyok'd her to the Ass—anon
Cries Benjamin we must be gone.
Thus after two hours hearty stay
Again behold them on their way
        Right gladly had the horses stirr'd
When they the smack of greeting heard

Lines from Dove Cottage MS. 47 (1806)

DC MS. 47, earlier called MS. Verse 28, contains *Prelude* MS. X and *Excursion* MS. X. The leaves, which measure 9.6 by 15.3 centimeters, are of laid paper watermarked F D or F, with chain lines at intervals of 2.65 centimeters; similar paper appears in DC MSS. 38 (*Prelude* MS. W), 48 (*Prelude* MS. Y), and 70, and the Green Family Account Book. The notebook is bound in green paper boards and contains fifty surviving leaves (or stubs) of perhaps sixty-two. For a further account of this manuscript, see *Chronology: MY*, page 645; see also *Prelude*, page xxxi.

Lines 651–657 of *Benjamin the Waggoner* were written in ink by William Wordsworth on the otherwise blank recto of leaf 11; this leaf is preceded by five stubs, two full leaves, one stub, and two more full leaves. The "Waggoner" in pencil is in a modern hand. In the transcription that follows, line numbers in the left margin are keyed to the reading text of MS. 1.

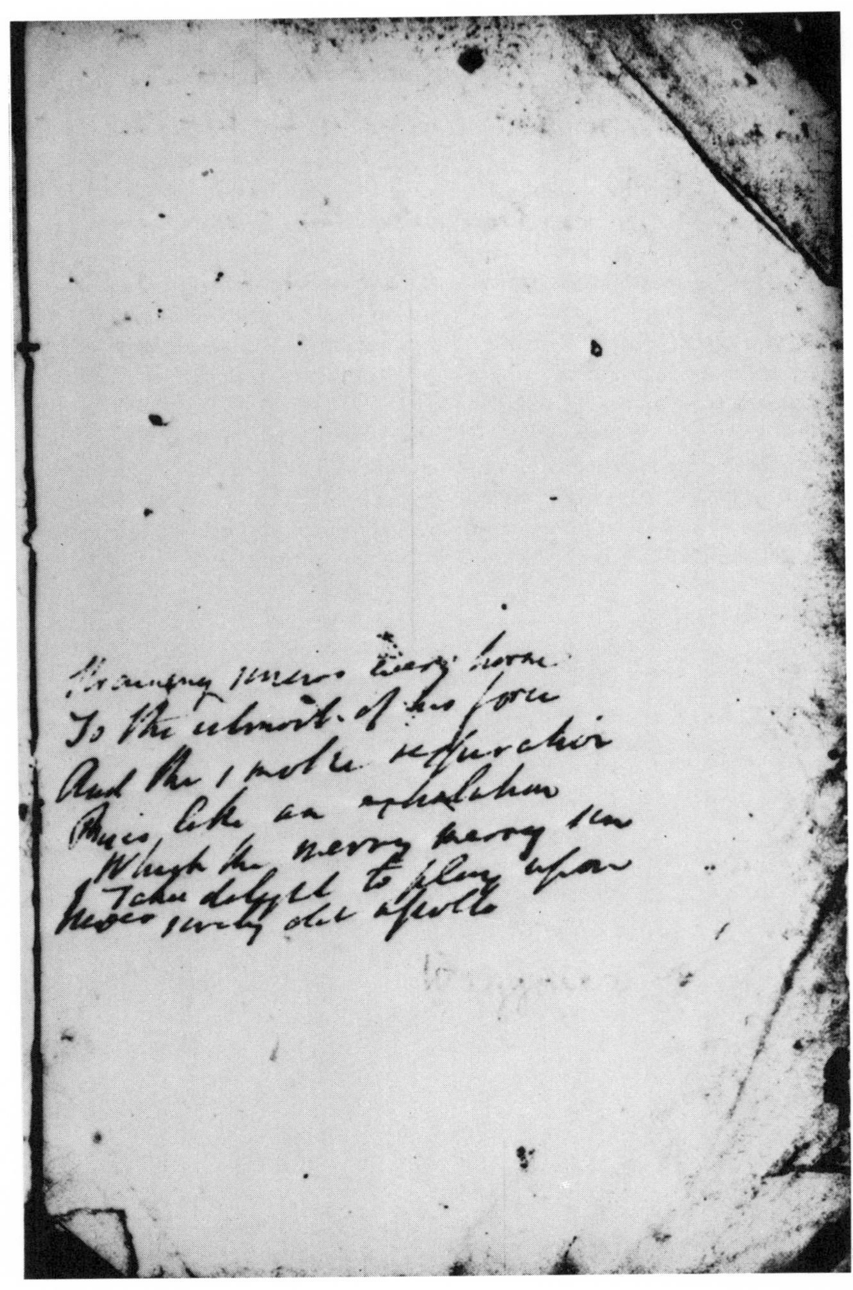

Straining sinews every horse
To the utmost of his force
And the smoke respiration
Rises like an exhalation
Which the merry merry sun
Takes delight to play upon
Never surely old Apollo

[11r]

Straining sinews every horse
To the utmost of his force
And the smoke respiration
Rises like an exhalation
   Which the merry merry sun
   Takes delight to play upon
Never surely old Apollo

Lines from Dove Cottage MS. 60 (1812)

DC MS. 60, earlier called MS. Verse 35, contains *Peter Bell* MS. 5. The leaves of this homemade notebook measure on average 11.5 by 18.7 centimeters, with chain lines at intervals of 2.3 centimeters. They are of laid paper watermarked with a hunting horn in crowned shield and countermarked "1798." The same paper occurs in *Benjamin the Waggoner* MSS. 1 and 2 (see headnote to the MS. 2 transcription) and a number of other manuscripts and letters of this period. Some questions remain about the use of the hunting horn/1798 paper, but for a valuable discussion of this complex matter see *Chronology*: *MY*, pages 697–699 and notes on 189 and 312–313. The leaves of the manuscript, in gatherings of two, were bound in a piece of parchment cut from an old legal document; *Benjamin the Waggoner* MS. 1 was similarly bound.

Both *Benjamin the Waggoner* passages were entered in ink on leaf 1^r: the first page of *Peter Bell* MS. 5. Lines 480–483, in the blank space left at the top of the page, are in William Wordsworth's hand; lines [471]–473, surrounding the title, are in Sara Hutchinson's hand. The first words in Sara Hutchinson's hand, "No not," seem related to line 471 of the first edition:

> No notion have they—not a thought,

In the transcription that follows, line numbers in the left margin are keyed to the reading text of the first edition, *The Waggoner* (1819). Lines 480–483 do not appear at all in MS. 1, occur in the form of drafts on leaves 23^v and 24^r of MS. 2, and were carefully entered by Sara Hutchinson in MS. 3 between lines 566 and 567, after the fair copy had been transcribed. Lines [471]–473 are loosely related to lines [516]–518 of MS. 1 and correspond closely to lines [556]–558 of MS. 3, where Sara Hutchinson carefully corrected the earlier fair-copy reading.

Earth sparkles sky & lake serene
[illegible] all – a scene
[illegible]
[illegible] creature

Peter Bell

Prologue

[illegible]

There's something in a flying horse,
There's something in a huge balloon,
But through the clouds I'll never float
Until I have a little Boat
~~For~~ [Whose] shape ~~just~~ [is] like the crescent moon

And now I have a little Boat
In shape ~~just like the~~ [a very] crescent moon;
Fast through the clouds my Boat can sail
But if perchance your faith should fail,
Look up and you shall see me soon.

The woods my Friends, are round you roaring
The woods are roaring like a sea
The noise of danger's in your ears.

[1^r]

480 Earth spangled sky & lake serene
481 Involved & restless all—a scene
a
482 Pregnant with rare img} gination
483 Rich change & multiplied
creation

[?471] *No not*

{from brought
472 *that is {not joyless region*
473 *They while they coast*
the silent lake

Benjamin the Waggoner MS. 2 (1806)

Transcriptions with Facing Photographic Reproductions
and Variant Readings of MS. 1
in an *Apparatus Criticus*

Benjamin the Waggoner MS. 2 (1806)

Benjamin the Waggoner MS. 1 (DC MS. 56) and MS. 2 (BL Ashley 4637) are in small, homemade notebooks containing only this poem. The leaves of both vary slightly in size, but average about 11.5 by 18.7 centimeters, with chain lines at intervals of 2.3 centimeters. The paper, which is laid, is watermarked with a hunting horn in crowned shield and countermarked "1798." Similar paper appears in such manuscripts of the period as DC MS. 57, DC MS. 60 (*Peter Bell* MS. 5), parts of *Prelude* MSS. A and B, and parts of BL Add. MS. 47,864 (printer's copy for *Poems in Two Volumes*). The watermark also appears on a slip inserted in booklet I of DC Journal 12 (*Recollections* MS. D), on which is written a memorandum concluding "Re transcribed & finished Feby 21st 1806"; it occurs as well in family letters written between late 1805 and early 1808, and again (though generally on paper of a heavier texture) in 1810 and somewhat later. (See *Chronology*: *MY*, pp. 697–699 and notes on 189 and 312–313.) The leaves of MSS. 1 and 2, in gatherings of two, were almost certainly sewn into their homemade bindings after the initial transcriptions were complete, and (as the needle holes suggest) perhaps after a few corrections had been made. MS. 1 is bound in a piece of parchment cut from an old legal document dated "Fourth Day of Augt. 1743." MS. 2 is bound in a folded piece of mottled cardboard. In both manuscripts, the fair-copy transcriptions are in the hand of Mary Wordsworth; a close examination of her sister's often very similar handwriting reveals that the traditional attribution to Sara Hutchinson by de Selincourt and others is incorrect.

In the transcription of MS. 2 that follows, line numbers in the left margin are keyed to the reading text of MS. 1. In transcriptions of drafts, the range of roughly corresponding line numbers is shown within brackets at the upper right of the page. On pages that contain no fair copy, original lines of draft (including alternate drafts) are set in large type so that they can be easily distinguished from later revisions to these lines.

The *apparatus criticus* of MS. 1 readings records all variants from the original fair-copy lines of MS. 2 (except for single-letter miswritings corrected by the copyist) and all revisions added in MS. 1. In-line revisions, shown in the *apparatus criticus* with a brace, are by Mary Wordsworth unless otherwise noted; all other revisions are by William Wordsworth unless otherwise noted. Unlike MS. 2, MS. 1 has generally not been complicated by the addition of messy passages of draft; photographs of the only major exception are given below in Appendix I: "Coleridge and *Benjamin the Waggoner*." The opening page of MS. 1 (leaf 1^r), p. 40, is offered primarily for illustration. The photographs facing the transcriptions show all pages of MS. 2 that contain writing (one recto and eleven versos are blank). The MS. 2 photographs (BL Ashley 4637, folios 1–37) are reproduced by permission of the British Library.

This Poem was at first ~~and~~ thrown
off ~~from~~ under a lively impulse of feeling,
~~in~~ during the first fortnight of the month
of Janry 1806 and has since
at several times been carefully revised
and with the Authors best efforts, inspirited

W Wordsworth

Benjamin the Waggoner &c

[1r]

This Poem was at first ~~writ~~ thrown
under {of
off ~~from~~ a lively impulse {, feeling
during
~~in~~ the first fortnight of the month
of Janry 180 and has since
at several times been carefully revised
retouched &
and with the Author's best efforts, inspirited
W Wordsworth

Benjamin the Waggoner &c

The crossed-out page numbers were entered by T. J. Wise; the leaf numbers that replace them were entered at the British Museum.

The final digit of the date was left blank by WW (probably in 1836) and supplied by T. J. Wise; see Appendix II.

And the silence makes it sweet
Hush, there is some One on the stir!
'Tis Benjamin the Waggoner
Who long hath trod this ~~mountain~~ toilsome way
Companion of the night or day.
That far-off tinkling's drowsy cheer,
Mix'd with a faint yet grating sound
In a moment lost and found,
The Wain announces by whose side
Along the banks of Rydale there
He paces on, a trusty Guide;
Listen! you can hardly hear
Hither, he is weary is bending
Now he leaves the lower ground &c
And up the craggy hill ascending
Many a stop and stay he makes
Many a breathing fit he takes.
Steep the way and wearisome,
Yet all the while is whip is dumb

The Horses &c

[1v] [25–33]

‸And the silence makes it sweet
!   !
Hush { there is some One on the stir, } B
—Tis Benjamin the Waggoner:
                                   toilsome
Who long hath trod this ~~mountain~~ way
Companion of the night or day.
That far-off tinkling's drowsy chear,
Mix'd with a faint yet grating sound
In a moment lost and found,
The Wain announces by whose side
Along the banks of Rydale Mere
                              G
He paces on, a trusty g}uide;
Listen! you can hardly hear.
—Hither he is course is bending
Now he leaves the lower ground
And up the craggy hill ascending
Many a stop and stay he makes
Many a breathing fit he takes.
Steep the way and wearisome,
Yet all the while is whip is dumb

The Horses &c

For the significance of the large B in upper right corner, see WW's note on 4r.

This is the beginning.

First part – this burning day of June

Its very twilight is gone out

The night-hawk is singing his frog-like tune

While restlessly he wheels about

That solitary bird &c

Tis spent – this burning day of June

Tis spent this [illegible] day

Its very twilight is gone out

As restlessly he wheels about

That solitary bird

Is all that can be heard

Such forge as their bright lamps would be

For they come in company

And shine in quietness secure

On the mossy bank by the cottage door

As safe as on the loneliest moor

In the sky &c

[2^v] [1–13]

This is the Beginning.

Tis spent—this burning day of June
Its very Twilight is gone out
The Night-hawk is singing his froglike tune
While restlessly he wheels about
That solitary Bird &c.
Is all that &c
~~Tis Spent—this burning~~ day of June

this
Spent is ~~this loitering~~ day

very
It ~~lingering~~ twilight is gone out
As restlessly she wheels about
That solitary bird
Is all that can be heard

That never-resting

The Cottage
And the [?little]

nothing dread
⊗Rich prize as their bright lamps would be

e
Forth they comp} in company
⊗And shine in quietness secure
On the mossy bank by the cottage door
A safe as on the loneliest moor
In the sky &c

The three faintly visible lines in mid-page, beginning "That never-resting," are in pencil; the first of them revises l. 5, the other two are related to ll. 9–12, all on 3^r. Also on 3^r is a crossed-out asterisk corresponding to the symbol visible here. The lines following it here were probably entered first, to be inserted after l. 11; they were then prefaced by the lines marked by the circled X (and the asterisks were deleted), which corresponds to an identical symbol at l. 10 on 3^r. All five of the full lines to be added were entered first in pencil (but with "Cottage" capitalized), then overwritten in ink.

'Tis spent — this burning day of June
...
The Night-hawk is singing his frog-like tune
As restlessly he wheels about
That solitary Bird
Is all that can be heard

Benjamin the Waggoner &c

Canto 1st

'Tis spent &c see opposite page

At last this loitering day of June
This long long day is going out,
The Night-hawk is singing his frog-like tune
Twirling his Watchman's rattle about
That new creature bird
Is all that can be heard
In silence deeper far, than that of deepest noon.

Now that the Children are abed
The little Glow-worms nothing dread
Such prize as their bright lamp would be
Forth they come in company

In the sky and on the hill
Every thing is hush'd and still
The clouds show here and there a spot
Of a star that twinkles not
The air is like a Lion's den
Close and hot, and now and then
Comes a tired and sultry breeze

[3^r]

[?glow] [?lamps] [?beams]
Tis spent—this burning day of June
{r
last {[?]emain ~~are~~ going
Its ~~very twilight is gone~~ out
The Night-hawk is singing his froglike tune
As restlessly he wheels about
That solitary Bird
Is all that can be heard

Benjamin the Waggoner &c

Canto 1.st

Tis spent &c see opposite page
1 *At last this loitering day of June*
2 *This long long day is going out,*
3 *The Night-hawk is singing his frog-like tune*
4 *Twirling his Watchman's rattle about*
never-resting
5 *That ~~busy, busy~~ Bird*
6 *Is all that can be heard*
7 *In silence deeper far, than that of deepest noon.*
~~abed~~
{ abed
8 *Now that the Children are* {*in their Beds*
{s dread
9 *The little Glow-worm* { *nothing ~~dreads~~*
⊗ Rich prize as their bright lamps would be
10 ~~*Pretty playthings as they would be*~~
11 *Forth they come in company*
12 ✱~~*And lift their fearless heads*~~ }
13 *In the sky and on the hill*
14 *Every thing is hush'd and still*
15 *The clouds shew here and there a spot*
16 *Of a star that twinkles not*
17 *The air is like a Lion's den*
18 *Close and hot, and now and then*
And [?now] & [?then]
19 *Comes a tired and sultry breeze*

---

canto heading not present
2 This long] This long, *with* long, *in pencil (WW), then ink (MW)* out,] out
4 watchman's
5,7 *no commas*
8 in their Beds *del to* abed
10 *first four words del to* Rich prize as their bright lamps
12 *del to* And shine in quietness secure
on the mossy bank by the cottage door
As safe as on the loneliest moor

7/8 In pencil; underwriting below was erased.
9 The "s" of "dreads" was deleted by erasure.
10, 12 The symbols in margin are repeated on 2^v.
12 The "ir" of "their" and the "s" of "heads" were first deleted by erasure.
18 Line number includes revisions on 2^v: deletions in pencil.
18/19 In pencil.

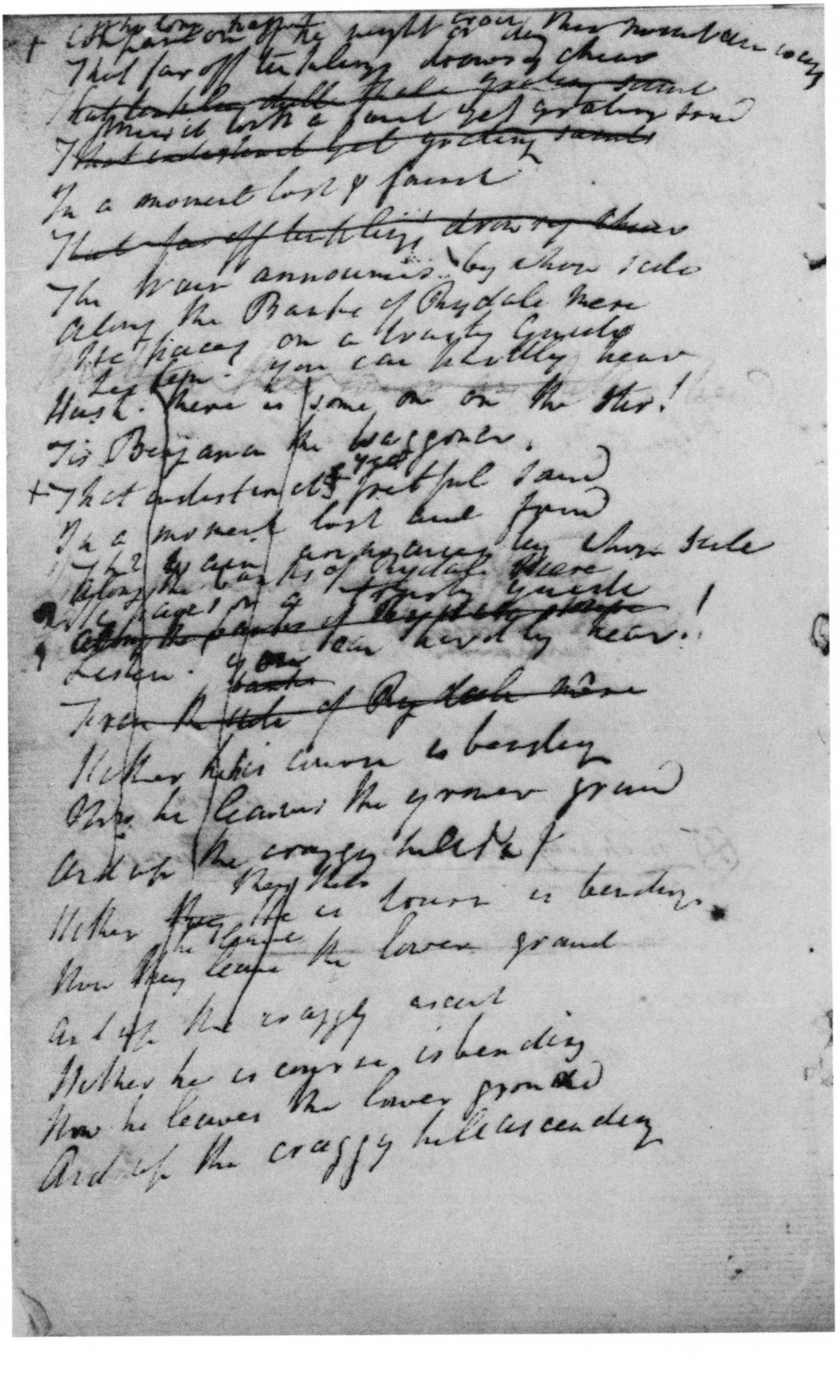

[3v] [26–33]

[?~~They~~]
[?~~Harken~~] ~~their course are hither~~ bending

In a moment lost & found
Listen you can hardly hear

Who long hath trod this mountain way
×Companion of the night or day
That far off tinklings drowsy chear
~~That tinkling dull that grating sound~~
Mix'd with a faint yet grating sound
~~That indistinct yet grating sound~~
In a moment lost & found
~~That far off tinkling's drowsy chear~~
The Wain announces by whose side
Along the Banks of Rydale Mere
He paces on a trusty Guide
Listen! you can hardly hear
Hush! there is some one on the stir!
Tis Benjamin the Waggoner.

yet
+That indistinct ~~&~~ fretful sound
In a moment lost and found
The Wain announces by whose side
Along the banks of Rydale Mere
He paces on a trusty guide
~~Along the banks of Rydale Mere~~

ou
Listen! y[?] can hardly hear!
~~banks~~
~~From the side of Rydale Mere~~

h
Hither he is course is bending
Now he leaves the greener grond
And up the craggy hill &c &

they their
Hither ~~they~~ He is Cours is bending
he leave
Now they leave the lower grond
And up the craggy [?ascent]
Hither he is course is bending
nd
Now he leaves the lower gron d
And up the craggy hill ascending

Three underlying pencil lines, faintly visible in the photograph, are separately transcribed above the ink lines.

The two crosses in the left margin are related to X's in the right margin of 4r, which indicate where insertions were to be made.

In the next-to-last ink line, the original "n" was made to serve as "u" by the revision.

With a haunting, and a panting
Like the stifling of disease
The mountains seem of wondrous height
And in the heavens there is a weight
But the dews allay the heat
And the silence makes it sweet.
Hush, there is some one on the stir
'Tis Benjamin the Waggoner
From the side of Rydale mere
Hither he his course is bending
With a faint and fretful sound
Listen! you can hardly hear
Now he's on the lower ground
And up the craggy hill ascending
Many a stop and stay he makes
Many a breathing fit he takes
Steep the way and wearisome
Yet all the while his whip is dumb

The Horses have worked with right good will
And now are up at the top of the hill
He was patient they were strong
And now they smoothly glide along
Gathering breath and pleased to win
The praises of good Benjamin
Heaven shield him and from ill defend
For he is their Father and their Friend

[4r]

With a haunting, and a panting
                                    is
Like the stifling of d[?~~es~~]} *ease*
                     seem
The mountains ~~*are*~~ *of wondrous height*
And in the heavens there is a weight
But the dews allay the heat
And the silence makes it sweet. (turn back
[?seem]   to 1st leaf
in this book
markd B

Hush
~~*Hush*~~*! there is some one on the stir*
1st   T}   2nd The dark night's Fellow traveller
'T}*is Benjamin the Waggoner*
Long hath he trod this × mountain way ×
~~*From the side of Rydale mere*~~
~~*Hither he his course is bending*~~
~~*With a faint and fretful sound*~~
~~In a moment lost and found~~
[? ? ?]
~~[?*Such as marks the*] *listening ear*~~
~~Listen! you can hardly hear~~
~~*Now he leaves the lower ground*~~
~~*And up the craggy hill*~~ *ascending*
Many a stop and stay he makes
Many a breathing fit he takes
Steep the way and wearisome
Yet all the while his whip is dumb

---

20 *no comma; here marginal line numbers in ink (MW) begin and run by 20s through 380*
21 disease
are }
22 [?seem]}
25 *no period*
26 Hush! *del in pencil, with traces of erased pencil above line*
31 ⊗ Such as marks the listening ear *del in pencil;* × *in pencil indicates insertion of lines written by WW on facing 2r*

In a moment lost & found
Listen! you can hardly hear

31 then del in ink and same 2 lines entered in ink, 30/31 and 31/32, without !
37 dumb] dumb.

---

21 Deletion by erasure.
22 The "seem" is in pencil overwritten in ink.
25/26 The "seem" is in pencil.
27 The "1st" and "2nd" were intended to reverse the order of the lines.
28 The X's correspond to crosses on 3v.
31 Deleted in pencil, then erased in favor of the two added lines.

With a haunting, and a panting
Like the stifling of disease
The mountains seem of wondrous height
And in the heavens there is a weight
But the dews allay the heat
And the silence makes it sweet

Turn back to 1st leaf in the book marked B

Hush there is some one on the stir
'Tis Benjamin the Waggoner
From the side of Rydale mere
Hither he his course is bending
With a faint and fretful sound
In a moment lost and found
Listen you can hardly hear
Now he leaves the lower ground
And up the craggy hill ascending
Many a stop and stay he makes
Many a breathing fit he takes
Steep the way and wearisome
Yet all the while his whip is dumb

The Horses have worked with right good will
And now are up at the top of the hill
He was patient they were strong
And now they smoothly glide along
Gathering breath and pleased to win
The praises of good Benjamin
Heaven shield him and from ill defend
For he is their Father and their Friend

The Horses have worked with right good will
And now are up at the top of the hill
He was patient they were strong
And now they smoothly glide along
Gathering breath and pleased to win
The praises of good Benjamin
Heaven shield him and from ill defend
For he is their Father and their Friend

---

45 father . . . friend

\+ Why need our travellers then, (though freed
~~Then why need Benjamin~~ (though freed
His best resolves) be on his guard

[4^v] [61]

+ *Why need our Traveller then, (though frail*
~~Then why need Benjamin~~, (though frail
His best resolves) be on his guard

5

From all mishap and every snare!
But why so early with this prayer?
Is it for threatenings in the sky
Or for some other danger nigh
No, none is near him yet, though he
Be one of much infirmity
For at the bottom of the Brow
Where once the Dove and Olive-bough
Offered a greeting of good Ale
To all who entered Grasmere Vale
And tempted him who must depart
To leave it with a jovial heart
There where the Dove and Olive-bough
Once hung, a Poet harbours now
A simple water-drinking Bard
Why need our Traveller then (Though free
~~Then why need Ben~~ be on his guard?
His best resolves) be
He marches by secure and bold
Yet thinking on the times of old
It seems that all looks wond'rous cold
He shrugs his shoulders shakes his head
And for the honest Folks within
It is a doubt with Benjamin
Whether they be alive or dead

No danger's here, no none at all
Beyond his wish is He secure
But pass a mile and then for trial
Then for the pride of self denial
If he resist that tempting door

[5r]

F{
F{*rom all mishap and every snare*{!
But why so early with this prayer{?
Is it for threatenings in the sky
Or for some other danger nigh
No, none is near him yet, though he
Be one of much infirmity
For at the bottom of the Brow 60
Where once the Dove and Olive-bough
Offered a greeting of good Ale
To all who entered Grasmere Vale
And tempted him who must depart
To leave it with a jovial heart
There where the Dove and Olive-bough
Once hung, a Poet harbours now
A simple water-drinking Bard
Why need our Traveller then (Though frail
+ ~~*Then why need Ben*~~ *be on his guard*{?
His best resolves)^
He marches by secure and bold
Yet thinking on the times of old
It seems that all looks wond'rous cold
He shrugs his shoulders shakes his head
And for the honest Folks within
It is a doubt with Benjamin
Whether they be alive or dead

No danger's here, no none at all
{He
Beyond his wish is {*Ben secure*
But pass a mile and then for trial 80
Then for the pride of self-denial
he
he *If* ~~*thou*~~ *resist that tempting door*

---

50 *no commas*

57 jo{via / yfu}l

60 *no hyphen* Bard.

62 [?amb]l{march / es}

70 {He / Ben

73–76 *For STC's suggested revisions to these lines, and WW's drafts in response to them, both on 3v, see Appendix I. Fair-copy variants and revisions on 4v are given both here and in Appendix I.*

73 thou *del in pencil to* he

---

52 WW's line number takes account of revisions carried out on 4r and 3v, where eight lines were dropped and fourteen added.

71 WW's line number includes revisions on this page.

73 The "he" in the margin is in pencil.

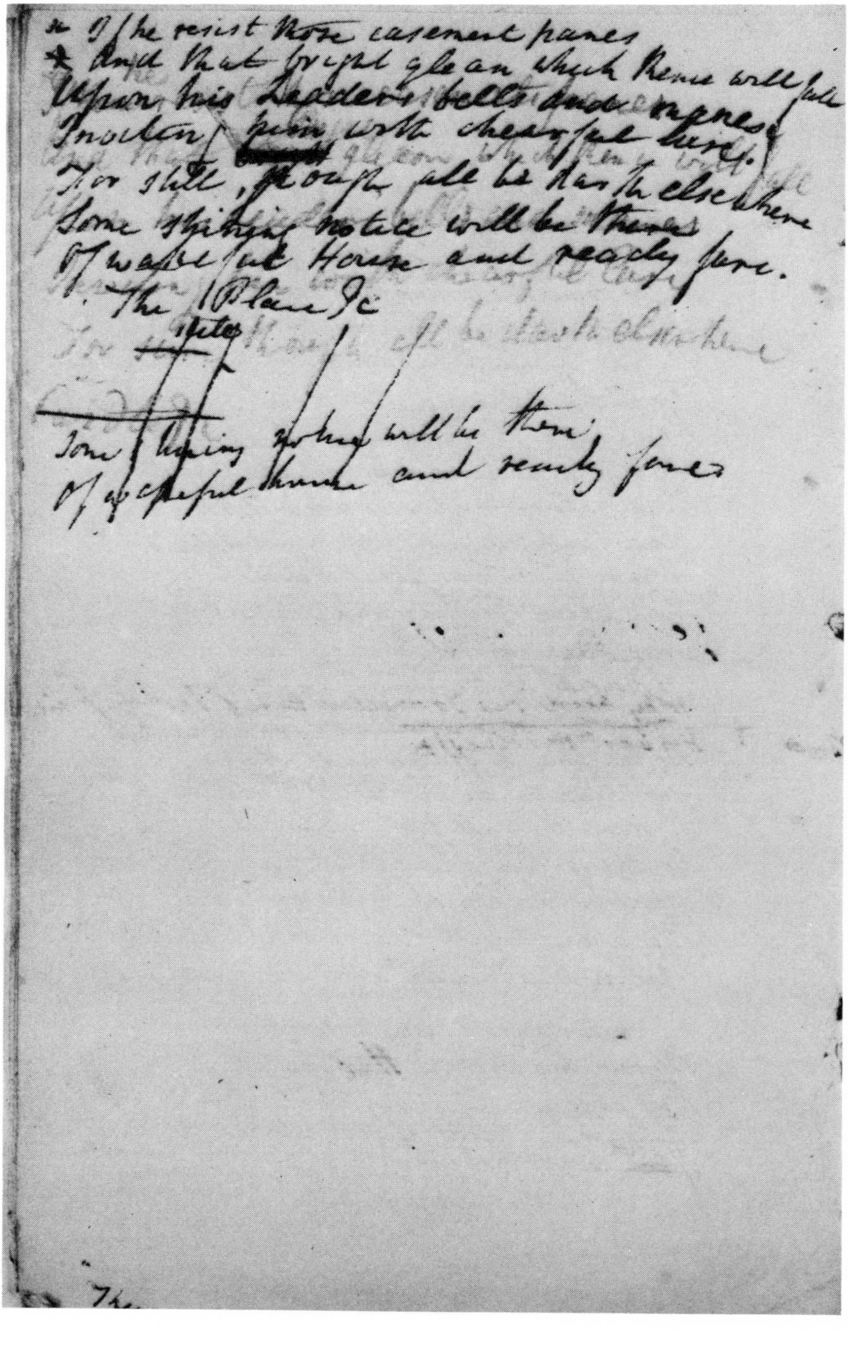

[5v] [75–78]

he
If ~~thou~~ resist those casement panes
Bright
bright
And that ~~bright~~ [?clear] gleam which thence will fall
Upon his Leaders' bells and manes
Inviting him with chearful lure
still
For ~~sure~~ ^ though all be dark elsewhere
~~Candle &c~~

* If he resist those casement panes
* And that bright gleam which thence will fall
Upon his Leaders bells and manes[?~~e~~]
Inviting him with chearful lure.
For still, though all be dark elsewhere
Some shining notice will be there
Of wakeful House and ready fare.
The Place &c

Some shining notice will be there
Of wakeful house and ready fare.

Th[?is]

The underlying pencil lines, visible in the photograph, are separately transcribed at the top of the page. In this passage, "still" was added in ink to replace "sure," deleted in ink. In the second line the word "bright" is in ink. Symbols in ink in the left margin, below, correspond to symbols on 6r. In the third ink line, the deletion was by erasure.

X 6

Which with such friendly voice will call
~~Look at thee with so bright a lure~~
~~For surely if no other where~~
~~Candle or Lamp is burning there.~~

The place to Benjamin full well
Is known and for as strong a spell
As used to be that Sign of love
And hope the Olive-bough and Dove
He knows it to his cost good Man!
Who does not know the famous Swan?
Uncouth although the object be
An image of perplexity
Yet not the less ~~But what of that~~ it is our boast
For it was painted by the Host
His own conceit the figure plann'd
'Twas coloured all by his own hand
And Ben with self-dissatisfaction
Could tell long tales of its attraction.

Well! that is past and in despite
Of open door and shining light
And now soon Benjamin essays
The long ascent of Dunmail-raise
And with his team is gentle here
As when he crossed from Rydale mere
And when they do not dread his voice
They only hear it to rejoice
Their efforts and their time they measure

[6[r]]

Which with such friendly voice will call X
+ ~~*Look at thee with so bright a lure*~~
~~*For surely if no other where*~~
Candle or Lamp is burning there.

The place to Benjamin full well
Is known and for as strong a spell
As used to be that Sign of love
And hope the Olive-bough and Dove
He knows it to his cost, good Man!
Who does not know the famous Swan?
Uncouth although the object be
An image of perplexity
Yet not the less
~~*But what of that*~~ *it is our boast*
For it was painted by the Host 100
His own conceit the figure plann'd
'Twas coloured all by his own hand
And Ben with self-dissatisfaction
Could tell long tales of its attraction.

Well! that is past, and in despite
Of open door and shining light
And now good Benjamin essays
The long ascent of Dunmal-raise
And with his Team is gentle here
As when he clomb from Rydale-Mere
His whip they do not dread: his voice
They only hear it to~~o~~ rejoice
Their efforts and their time they measure

---

75 *Penciled X's by STC at beginning and end of line indicate placement of his revisions on facing verso* Look at *alt* Meet *in pencil above line* thee *del in pencil and pen to* him *in pencil above line* Will [?meet] thee *in pencil, del, below line*
76 *del in pencil to* For sure though all be dark elsewhere
77 lamp *no period*
80 sign
82 *no comma*
89 coloure / [?painte] d
91 *no period*
97 Rydale mere
99 to

---

74 The symbols, in pencil on the left, in ink on the right, show where the insertions of lines drafted on 5[v] were to be made.
87 WW's line number incorporates revisions on this page, by which three lines were dropped and seven added.
99 Deletion by erasure.

8 Will work for nobody but me
Let Simon flog and Arthur curse
He knows they only make bad worse.
Good proof of this the Country gain'd
One day when ye were vex'd and strained
Entrusted then to other's care
And forc'd unworthy stripes to bear.
Here was it, on this rugged spot
Which now contented with our lot
We climb, that piteously abused
Ye plung'd in anger & confused
As chance would have it, passing by,
I saw you in your jeopardy;
A word from me was like a charm
The ranks were taken with one mind
And your huge burthen safe from harm
Moved like a vessel in the wind.
— Yes without me up hills so high
'Tis vain to strive for mastery
Let force and flattery both be tried
This Monster at our heels must lie
Midway upon the bleak Fell-side
As dead as Bowder-stone—to stir
— No more till Ben be Waggoner
Grieve not &c

[6^v^]

⊗ Will work for nobody but me
                og   Ar
Let Simon fl{[?ay]} and ar}thur curse
He knows they only make bad worse.
Good proof of this the country gain'd
One day when ye were vex'd and strained
Entrusted then to other's care
And forc'd unworthy stripes to bear.
Here was it, on this rugged spot
Which now contented with our lot
We climb, that piteously abused
Ye plung'd in anger & confused.
As chance would have it, passing by,
I saw you in your jeopardy;
A word from me was like a charm
The ranks were taken with one mind
And your huge burthen safe from harm
Moved like a vessel in the wind.
—Yes, without me up hills so high
'Tis vain to strive for mastery
⊗ ~~Let Simon flog and Arthur curse,~~
   ~~it only~~ [?~~leads~~ to]
~~He knows, they only make bad worse~~
   Yes
~~That without me up hills so high~~
~~Tis vain to strive for mastery~~
Let force and flattery both be tried
This Monster at our heels must lie
                              ~~bleak steep~~ [?~~dark~~] ~~bleak~~
                                                  {F
~~Midway upon the huge~~^{~~fell-side~~
~~As dead &c~~
Midway upon the bleak ~~feel~~ Fell-side
                                    {;—
As dead as Bowder Stone{; to stir
—No more till Ben be Waggoner
        grieve not &c

These lines develop drafts on 36^v^ and the inside back cover of the notebook.
The symbol in the margin at the top of the page corresponds to a symbol on 7^r^.
The underlying pencil lines, faintly visible in the photograph, appear to be identical to seven lines on the bottom third of the page, in ink, beginning "Let Simon flog . . ."; the eighth pencil line reads: "As dead as Bowder stone—to stir."
The line number, 140, of course includes the revision.

~~13~~ 7

To stand or go is at their pleasure
He knows that each will do his best
And while they strain and while they rest
He thus pursues his thoughts at leisure

Now am I fairly safe tonight
And never was my heart more light
I've been a sinner I avow
But better times are coming now
A sinner lately worse than ever
But God will bless a good endeavour
And to my soul's delight I find
The evil One is cast behind
Yes, let my Master fume and fret
I'm here and with my Horses yet
~~When I was gone he felt his lack~~
~~[illegible]~~
~~And was right glad to have me back~~
~~[illegible] without me~~
My jolly team he finds that ye
Will work for nobody but me
see opp: page ~~That without [illegible] up hills so high~~
~~[illegible]~~
~~[illegible]~~
As dead as Bowder-stone, to stir
No more, till Ben be Waggoner.
~~When I was gone he felt his lack~~
~~And was right glad to have me back~~
Then grieve not jolly Team! though tough
Our road be sometimes steep and rough

[7r]

To stand or go is at their pleasure
He knows that each will do his best
And while they strain and while they rest
He thus pursues his thoughts at leisure

Now am I fairly safe tonight
And never was my heart more light
I've been a sinner I avow
But better times are coming now
A sinner, lately worse than ever
But God will bless a good endeavour
And to my soul's delight I find
The evil One is cast behind
Yes, let my Master fume and fret
I'm here and with my Horses yet
When I was gone he felt his lack
~~*He makes a mighty noise about me*~~
And was right glad to have me back
~~*And yet he cannot do without*~~ *me*
See *My jolly Team he finds that ye*
Will work for nobody but me
⊛ ~~That without me up hills~~ so *high*
See opp: page ~~Tis vain to strive for mastery~~
~~*This Monster at our heels must lie,*~~
{ As dead as Bowder-stone, to {stir [?stir]} }
{ *Dead as a cheese upon a shelf* }
○ { No more till Ben be Waggoner. }
{ *Or fairly learn to draw itself* }
~~*When I was gone he felt his lack*~~
~~*And was right glad to have me back*~~
Then grieve not jolly Team! though tough
Our road be sometimes steep and rough

---

105 tonight] to night
109 *no comma*
115–124 *For STC's suggested revisions to these lines, and WW's draft in response to them, both on 5v see Appendix I. Fair-copy variants and revisions on 6r are given both here and in Appendix I.*
115–116 *del to* When I was gone he felt his lack
And was right glad to have me back
119–124 *del in ink*
119 Finds that with hills so steep and high
121–122
Dead as a cheese upon a shelf
Or fairly learn to draw {itself [?a shelf]} *underwriting erased; lines del in pencil to*
As dead as Bowder-stone—to stir
No more till Ben be Waggoner
121/122, 122/123 *Penciled marks by STC indicate placement of revisions on facing verso*
123 {felt [?knew]}

---

119 The erased line was probably the reading of MS. 1.
121/122 The circle in margin is in pencil.
121—122 Erased, as well as overwritten.

For though full oft they make you strain
And halt for breath and halt again
Yet to their sturdiness 'tis owing
That side by side we thus are going

[7v]

[132–133]

For though full oft they make you fecht
Your breath with many a weary strecht
you
For they strain to the full
With many a slowly weary
Yet to their sturdiness
~~To them & their good grace~~ tis owing
That side by side we yet are going

strain
For though full oft they make you ^ ~~fetch~~
~~Breath spent~~
~~Your breath with many a weary stretch~~
And halt for breath & halt again
Yet to their sturdiness tis owing
That side by side we now are going
⊗For though full oft they make you strain
And halt for breath and halt again

Yet to their stur{d / [?t]}iness 'tis owing
That side by side we thus are going.

The symbol in the left margin matches a symbol on 8r.

~~14~~ 8

But take your time, no more I ask
I know you're equal to your task
And for us all I'll sing the praise
Of our good friend here Dunmal-raise
And of his brother Banks and Braes
For [illegible] they form the tether
By which we have been kept together

While Benjamin in earnest mood
His meditations thus pursued
A storm which had been smothered long
Was growing inwardly more strong
And in its struggles to get free
Was busily employ'd as he
The Thunder had begun to growl
He heard not too intent of soul
The air was now without a breath
He mark'd not that 'twas still as death
But now some drops upon his head
Fell with the weight of drops of lead
He starts, and at the admonition
Takes a survey of his condition
The road is black before his eyes
Glimmering faintly where it lies
Black is the sky, and every hill
Up to the sky, is blacker still
A huge and melancholy room
Hung round and overhung with gloom

[8[r]]

But take your time, no more I ask
I know you're equal to your task
And for us all I'll sing the praise
Of our good friend here Dunmal-raise
And of his brother {B [?~~b~~]*anks and* {Br [?~~br~~]*aes*
⊗*For plain it is* {, ~~*that*~~ *they'*~~*re*~~ ^form *the tether*
By which we have been kept together

While Benjamin in earnest mood
His meditations thus pursued
A storm which had been smothered long
Was growing inwardly more strong
And in its struggles to get free
Was busily employ'd as he
The Thunder had begun to growl
He heard not too intent of soul
The air was now without a breath
He mark'd not that 'twas still as death
But now some drops upon his head
Fell, with the weight of drops of lead
He starts, and at the admonition
Takes a survey of his condition
The road is black before his eyes
Glimmering faintly where it lies
Black is the sky, and every hill
Up to the sky, is blacker still
A huge and melancholy room
Hung round and overhung with gloom

---

127 *no comma*
131 Banks . . . Braes
132 they're *del to* they form
140 Thunder] thunder
150 *no comma*
151 *no comma*

130, 148 WW's line numbers here, as in the remainder of the manuscript, appear to incorporate his revisions. See notes to 5[r] and 6[r].
131 Deletion by erasure.
132 The comma, the horizontal deletions, and the added "form" were all in pencil, overwritten in ink.

9

Save that above a single height
Is to be seen a lurid light
Above Helmcrag, a streak half dead
A burning of a sullen red
And near that lurid light full well
The Astrologer dread Sydrophel
Where at his desk and book he sits
Puzzling on high his wicked wits
He who from Quarter in the North
For mischief looks or sends it forth
Sharing his wild domain in common
With southern neighbour the old Woman
A pair that spite of wind and weather
Still sit upon Helmcrag together.

The Astrologer was not unseen
By solitary Benjamin
But total darkness came anon
And he and every thing was gone
The rain rush'd down, the road was batter'd
As with the weight of billows shatter'd
The Horses are dismay'd nor know
Whether they should stand or go
And Benjamin is groping near them
Sees nothing and can scarcely hear them
He is astounded wonder not
With such a charge in such a spot
Astounded in the mountain gap

[9[r]]

Save that above a single height
Is to be seen a lurid light
Above Helm-crag, a streak half dead
A burning of a sullen red
And near that lurid light full well
o
Th' Astr[?l] { *loger dread Sydrophel*
Where at his desk and book he sits
{, on high, his
Puzzling { ~~*his wicked*~~ *wicked wits*
He who from Quarter in the North
For mischief looks or sends it forth
Sharing his wild domain in common
With southern neighbor the old Woman
A pair that spite of wind and weather
Still sit upon Helm-crag together.

The Astrologer was not unseen
By solitary Benjamin
But total darkness came anon
And he and every thing was gone
The rain rush'd down, the road was batter'd
As with the weight of billows shatter'd
are dismay'd nor
The Horses ~~*scarcely seem to*~~ *know*
Whether they should stand or go
is
And Benjamin ~~*though*~~ *groping near them*
Sees nothing and can scarcely hear them
He is astounded, wonder not
With such a charge in such a spot
Astounded in the mountain gap

---

158 light,
159 Astrologer Sydro {phel / fel}
161 his wicked,
162 Quarter] quarter
165 neighbor] Neighbor
166 spite of *over erasure*
167 *no period*
172 *no comma*
174 seem'd *with* 'd *erased*
175 should *with* sho *del in pencil*
176 {And / For} though *del in pencil to* is

And sullen motions long & slow
That to a drooping darkness go

Darkness and silence deep & then

[9v] [185–189]

And sullen motions long and slow
That to a dreary distance go
~~Till breaking in upon the dying strain~~
Darkness and silence deep and then
A rending oer his head begins the fray
again
Darkness and silence deep—& then
A rending oer his head begins the fray
again

All entries are in pencil.

By peals of thunder clap on clap
With now and then a dismal flash
And somewhere as it seems a crash
Among the rocks; with weight of rain
And sullen motions long & slow
That to a dreary distance go
Till breaking in upon the dying strain
A rending o'er his head begins the fray again

Meanwhile uncertain what to do
And oftentimes compell'd to halt
The Horses cautiously pursue
Their way without mishap or fault
And now have reach'd that pile of Stones
Heap'd over brave King Dunmail's bones
He who had once supreme command
Last King of rocky Cumberland
His bones and those of all his Power
Slain here in a disastrous hour

When passing through this stony strait
('Tis little wider than a gate)
Benjamin can faintly hear
A voice that comes from some one near
A female voice a voice of fear
"Stop" says the Voice "whoe'er you be
Stop, stop good Friend and pity me"

[10ʳ]

181 *By peals of thunder clap on clap*
182 *With now and then a dismal flash*
~~vivid~~ vivid
~~[?Whose][?] [?light] glare reveals his team~~
it seems
183 *And somewhere as ~~it seems~~ a crash*
~~he thinks~~
{;
184 *Among the rocks*{ *with weight of rain*
{ And sullen motions long & slow }
185 { *~~And echoes long and violent~~* }
{ That to a dreary distance go }
186 { *~~That when the thunder's force is spent~~* }
{ Till breaking in upon the dying strain }
187 { *~~Yell and yell from Fell to Fell~~* }
{ A rending oer his head begins the }
188 { *~~As if they would with might and main~~* }
{ fray again }
189 { *~~Provoke it to begin again~~* }

190 *Meanwhile uncertain what to do*
191 *And oftentimes compell'd to halt*
192 *The* [?~~ir~~] *Horses cautiously pursue*
193 *Their way without mishap or fault*

By }
181 [?With]}
where }
183 some [?place]}
185–189

And echoes long and violent
That when the thunder's force is spent
Yell and yell from Fell to Fell
As if they would with might and main
Provoke it to begin again

del in pencil by MW to lines on facing 7ᵛ

And sullen motions long & slow
That to a dreary distance go
Till breaking in upon the dying strain [3]
A rending oer his head begins the fray again

ll. 3–4 then del in pencil by WW to

Darkness, & silence deep: & then
A rending oer his head begins the fray again

original ll. 185–189 then del in ink by MW to final version entered directly below

And sullen motions long and slow
That to a dreary distance go
!}
Darkness and silence deep;} and then
A rending o'er his head begins the fray again

192 The

185–189 Deletion by erasure.
192 Deletion by erasure.

By peals of thunder clap on clap
With now and then a dismal flash
And somewhere as it seems a crash
Among the rocks; with weight of rain
And sullen motions long & slow
That to a dreary distance go
Till breaking in upon the dying strain
A rending o'er his head begins the fray again

Meanwhile uncertain what to do
And oftentimes compell'd to halt
The Horses cautiously pursue
Their way without mishap or fault
And now have reach'd that pile of Stones
Heap'd over brave King Dunmail's bones
He who had once supreme command
Last King of rocky Cumberland
His bones and those of all his Power
Slain here in a disastrous hour

When passing through this stony strait
('Tis little wider than a gate)
Benjamin can faintly hear
A voice that comes from some one near
A female voice a voice of fear
"Stop" says the Voice "whoe'er you be
Stop, stop good Friend and pity me"

194 *And now have reach'd that pile of Stones*
brave
195 *Heap'd over ~~good~~ King Dunmal's bones*
196 *He who had once supreme command*
{~~Last K~~} Last King of
197 {~~*Our K*~~} ~~*ing in*~~ ^ *rocky Cumberland*
198 *His bones and those of all his Power*
199 *Slain here in a disastrous hour*

200 *When passing through this stony strait*
201 *('Tis little wider than a gate)*
202 *Benjamin can faintly hear*
A voice that comes from some one near
203 *A female voice a voice of fear*
204 *"Stop" says the Voice "whoe'er you be*
205 *Stop, stop good Friend and pity me"*

---

194 stones
202/203 *crowded in between lines*
203 Voice, a
204 *no quotation marks* ye

---

197 The overwritten "Last" was entered first in pencil, then in ink.

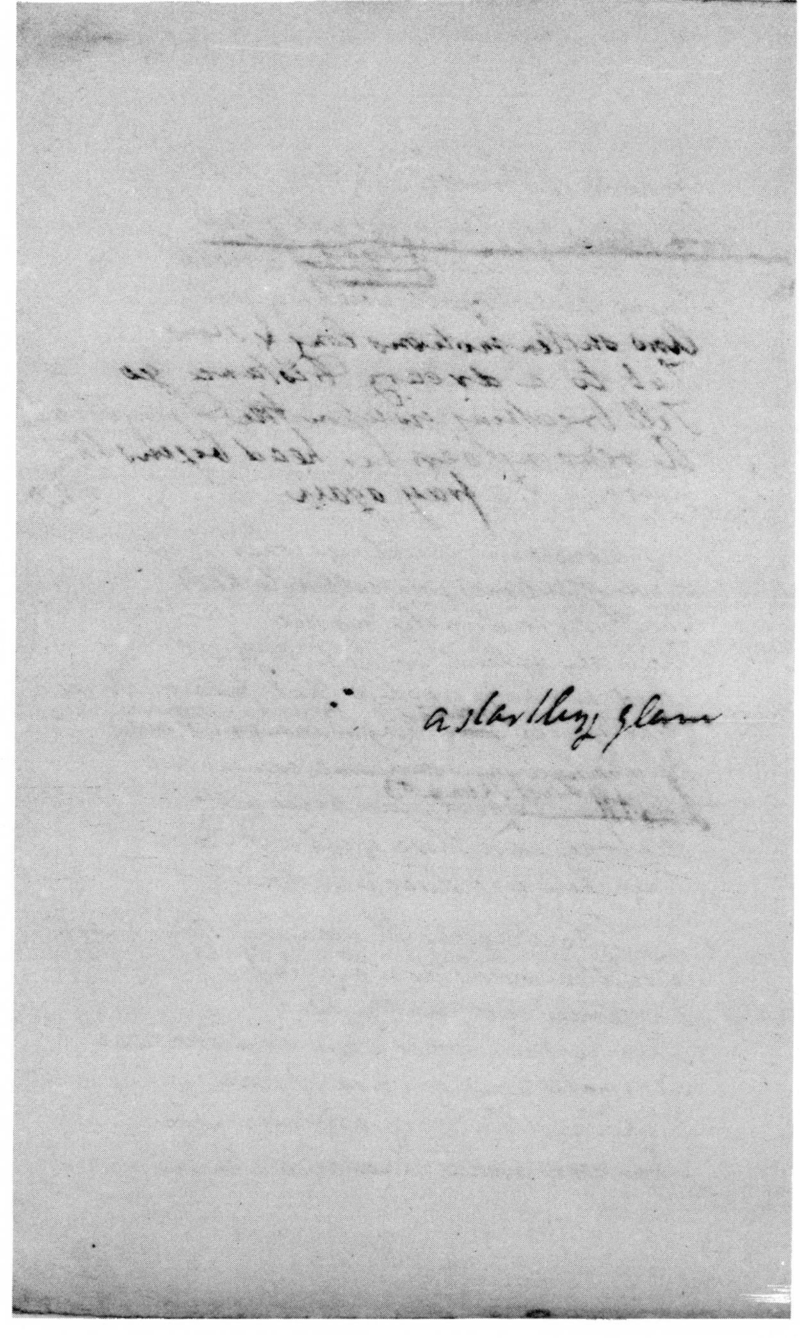

[10^{v}] [219]

a startling glare

And less in pity than in wonder
Amid the darkness and the thunder
Good Benjamin with prompt command
Summons his Horses to a stand

"Now tell" says he "in honest deed
Who you are, and what you need"
Careless of this adjuration
The Voice to move commiseration
Still prolong'd its supplication
"This storm that beats so furiously
This dreadful Place! oh pity me!"

While this was said with sobs between
And many tears by one unseen
There came a flash a [illegible] glare
And all Seat-Sandal was laid bare
[illegible]
'Twas not a time for nice suggestion
And Benjamin without further question
Taking her for some way-worn Rover
Said "mount and get you under cover".

Another Voice that was as hoarse
As brook with steep and stony course
Cried out "good Brother why so fast?
I've had a glimpse of you, avast!
Let go, or since you must be civil
Take her at once for good and evil".

[11r]

206 *And less in pity than in wonder*
207 *Amid the darkness and the thunder*
208 *Good Benjamin with prompt command*
209 *Summons his Horses to a stand*

210 *"Now tell" says he "in honest deed*
211 *Who you are, and what you need"*
212 *Careless of this adjuration*
213 *The Voice to move commiseration*
214 *Still prolong'd its supplication*
215 *"This storm that beats so furiously*
216 *This dreadful Place! oh pity me!"*

217 *While this was said with sobs between*
218 *And many tears by one unseen*
a ~~dismal~~ glare
219 [?in] *There came a flash* ~~*and held the candle*~~
And all Seat-Sandal was laid bare
220 ~~*To the whole bosom of Seat Sandal*~~
And all Seat Sandal was laid bare
221 *'Twas not a time for nice suggestion*
222 *And Benjamin without further question*
223 *Taking her for some way-worn Rover*
224 *Said "mount and get you under cover."*

225 *Another Voice that was as hoarse*
226 *As brook with steep and stony course*
227 *Cried out "good Brother why so fast?*
228 *I've had a glimpse of you, avast!*
229 *Let go, or since you must be civil*
230 *Take her at once for good and evil."*

---

211 *no comma* your *with* r *erased*
212 adjuration
214 prolonged
216 place!
217–218 said, . . . tears, *both commas added, probably by WW*
219 *last four words del to* a dismal glare
220 *first five words del to* And all *and* was laid bare *added at end of line*
224 Said, Y{ou/e} *no period*
226 Brook
227 *no question mark*
230 {and/or} *no period*

---

219 The revision, entered first in pencil, then in ink (as was the deletion line), was itself revised on 10v.
220/221 In pencil.

~~23~~ 12

"It is my Husband" softly said
The Woman, as if half afraid
By this time she was snug within
Through help of honest Benjamin
She and her Babe for Babe she had
No wonder then if ~~she~~ her heart was glad
And now the same strong Voice more near
Said cordially "my Friend what cheer?
Rough doings these! as God's my judge
The sky owes somebody a grudge
We've had in half an hour, or less
A twelvemonth's terror and distress
But Kate give thanks for this and ride
In quiet and be pacified

Then Benjamin entreats the Man
Would mount too, quickly as he can
The Sailor, Sailor now no more
But such he had been heretofore.
To courteous Benjamin replied
"Go you your way and mind not me
For I must have, whate'er betide
My Ass and fifty things beside
Go, and I'll follow speedily."

The Waggon moves, and with its load
Descends along the sloping road
And to a little tent hard by
Turns the Sailor instantly

[12r]

"It is my Husband" softly said
The Woman, as if half afraid
By this time she was snug within
Through help of honest Benjamin
She and her Babe for Babe she had
her heart
No wonder then if ~~she~~ ^ was glad
And now the same strong Voice more near
Said cordially "my Friend what cheer?
Rough doings these! as God's my judge
The sky owes somebody a grudge
We've had in half an hour, or less
A twelvemonth's terror and distress
But Kate give thanks for this and ride
In quiet and be pacified

Then Benjamin entreats the Man
Would mount too, quickly as he can
The Sailor, Sailor now no more
But such he had been heretofore
To courteous Benjamin replied
"Go you your way and mind not me
For I must have, whate'er betide
My Ass and fifty things beside
Go, and I'll follow speedily."

The Waggon moves, and with its load
Descends along the sloping road
And to a little tent hard by
Turns the Sailor instantly

---

236 ~~she~~ {r heart / ^was}
238 *no question mark*
240 ows *alt to* owes
242 terr{or / [? or an]} *underwriting erased*
244 pacified"
249 Benjamin
250 you] your *with* r *erased* way,
252 Ass, besig{d / e}
253 {Go, and / [?Haste—]} *no period*
254 *no comma*

---

236 The revision was written in pencil and overwritten in ink.

~~15~~ 13

For when at closing-in of day
The Family had come that way
Green pasture and the soft warm air
Had tempted them to settle there
Green is the grass for Beast to graze
Around the stones of Dunmal-raise

The Sailor gathers up his Bed
Takes down the canvas overhead
And after farewell to the Place
A parting word though not of grace
Pursues, with Ass and all his store 301
The way the Waggon went before.

Canto 2d

If Wytheburn's lowly House of Prayer
As lowly as the lowliest dwelling
Had, with its Belfrey's humble stock
A little Pair, that hang in air
Been Mistress also of a Clock
(And one too not in crazy plight)
Twelve strokes that Clock would have been telling
Under the brow of old Helvellyn

[13r]

For when at closing-in of day
The Family had come that way
Green pasture and the soft warm air
Had tempted them to settle there
Green is the grass for Beast to graze
Around the stones of Dunmal-raise

The Sailor gathers up his Bed
Takes down the Canvas overhead
And after farewell to the Place
A parting word though not of grace
Pursues, with Ass and all his store
The way the Waggon went before. 301

Canto 2.[d]

If Wytheburn's lowly House of Prayer
As lowly as the lowliest dwelling
Had, with its Belfrey's humble stock
A little Pair, that hang in air
Been Mistress also of a Clock
(And one too not in crazy plight)
Twelve strokes that Clock would have been telling
brow
Under the ~~nose~~ of old Helvellyn

---

258 when,
259 th{at / is}
264 Bed] bed
265 canvas
266 Place] place
267 word,
268 *no comma*
269/270 Canto 2.[d]] Second Part
270 lone{w / ly}
277 nose *del in ink*; brow *penciled in margin and above* nose *with caret*

Its dead-cole of midnight
Then, when the Hero of my Tale
Was passing by and down the Vale
(The Vale now silent hush'd I ween
As if a storm had never been)
Proceeding with an easy mind
And little thought of Him behind
Who having used his utmost haste
Gain'd ground upon the Waggon fast
And now is almost at its heels
And gives another lusty cheer
For spite of rumbling of the wheels
A welcome greeting he can hear
It is a fiddle in its glee
Dinning from the Cherry Tree

Hence the sound the light is there
As Benjamin is now aware
Who neither saw nor heard no more
Then if he had been deaf and blind
Till rouz'd up by the Sailor's roar
He hears the sound and sees the light
And in a moment calls to mind
That 'tis the Village merry-night

Although before in no dejection
He gladdens at the recollection
His heart with sudden joy is filled

[14[r]]

278 *Its bead-roll of midnight*
279 *Then, when the Hero of my Tale*
280 *Was passing by, and down the Vale*
281 *(The Vale now silent hush'd I ween*
282 *As if a storm had never been)*
283 *Proceeding with an easy mind*
284 *And little thought of Him behind*
285 *Who having used his utmost haste*
286 *Gain'd ground upon the Waggon fast*
287 *And now is almost at its heels*
288 *And gives another lusty cheer*
289 *For spite of rumbling of the wheels*
290 *A welcome greeting he can hear*
291 *It is a fiddle in its glee*
292 *Dinning from the Cherry Tree*

293 *Thence the sound the light is there*
294 *As Benjamin is now aware*
295 *Who neither saw nor heard* {— *no more*
296 *Then if he had been deaf and blind*
297 *'Till rouz'd up by the Sailor's roar*
298 *He hears the sound and sees the light*
299 *And in a moment calls to mind*
300 *That 'tis the Village merry-night*

301 *Although before in no dejection*
302 *He gladdens at the recollection*
His heart with sudden joy is filled

---

280 *no comma*
281 silent,
lus
288 [?hear]}ty
292 Tree.
295 *dash added*
297 Till
300 merry-night.
s
302 gladden{'d

15

His ears are by the music thrilled
His eyes take pleasure in the road
Glittering before him bright and broad
And Benjamin is wet and cold
And there are reasons manifold
That make the good tow'rds which he's yearning
Look fairly like an honest earning

Nor has thought time to come and go
To vibrate between yes and no.
For cries the Sailor "glorious chance
That blew us hither, — dance Boys, dance
Rare luck for us! my honest Soul
I'll treat thee with a friendly Bowl"
He draws him to the door "come in
Come, come" cries he to Benjamin,
And Benjamin — ah woe is me!
Gave the word, the Horses heard
And halted, though reluctantly

Blithe souls and lightsome hearts have we
Feasting at the Cherry Tree
This was the outside proclamation
This was the inside salutation
What bustling jostling high and low
A universal overflow
What tankards foaming from the tap
What store of Cakes in every lap

[15r]

His ears are by the music thrilled
His eyes take pleasure in the road
Glittering before him bright and broad
{*And*
303 {*For Benjamin is wet and cold*
304 *And there are reasons manifold*
305 *That* ~~*makes*~~ *make the good tow'rds which he's yearning*
306 *Look fairly like an honest* ~~*y*~~*earning*

307 *Nor has thought time to come and go*
308 *To vibrate between yes and no.*
309 *For cries the Sailor "glorious chance*
{—dance Boys dance}
310 *That blew us hither,* {*lucky dance!*}
311 Rare luck for us! my honest Soul
312 *I'll treat thee with a friendly Bowl"*
313 *He draws him to the door "come in*
314 *Come, come" cries he to Benjamin*
315 *And Benjamin—ah woe is me!*
316 *Gave the word, the Horses heard*
317 *And halted, though reluctantly*

Souls }
318 *Blithe hearts*} *and lightsome hearts have we*
319 *Feasting at the Cherry Tree*
320 *This was the outside proclamation*
321 *This was the inside salutation*
322 *What bustling jostling high and low*
323 *A universal overflow*
324 *What tankards foaming from the tap*
325 *What store of Cakes in every lap*

302/303 *asterisk indicates insertion of lines in MW's hand on facing 12v*

*His heart with sudden joy is filled
{re
His ears a{s by the music thrill'd
His eyes take pleasure in the road
Glittering before him bright & broad

,}
good towr{rds}
305 make good for
306 yearning. *with* y *erased*
308 *no period*
310 hither, lucky dance *with* lucky dance *del in pencil; asterisk indicates insertion of penciled words in WW's hand on facing 12v* Dance! boys, dance! *MW then del in ink* lucky *and added*! Boys, dance! *to complete revision of original fair-copy line* hither, dance! Boys, dance!

my honest }
311 *The final form of WW's penciled line on facing 12v* Brave luck for us, ~~good natured~~} Soul *has been entered in one-line space without comma by MW*
313 door,
315 ah!
317 reluctantly.
318 Blithe Souls
324 Tap

305,306 Deletions by erasure.
310 WW apparently preserved the exclamation point, to follow "Boys."
311 MW left a blank in transcription, as also in MS. 1, which WW filled, writing the first four words in pencil before overwriting in ink.
318 The overwritten "hearts" was erased.

~~21~~ 16

What thumping stumping overhead
The Thunder had not been more busy
With such a stir you would have said
This little Place may well be dizzy
'Tis who can dance with greatest vigour
'Tis what can be most prompt and eager
As if it heard the fiddle's call
The Pewter clatters on the wall
The very Bacon shews its feeling
Swinging from the smoky ceiling

A steaming Bowl, a blazing Fire
What greater good can heart desire
Twere worth a wise Man's while to try
The utmost anger of the sky
To <u>seek</u> even thoughts of painful cast
If such be the amends at last
Now should you think I judge amiss
The Cherry Tree shews proof of this
For soon of all the happy there
Our Travellers are the happiest pair
All care with Benjamin is gone
A Cæsar past the Rubicon
He thinks not of his long long strife
The Sailor Man by nature gay
Hath no resolves to throw away
And he has now forgot his Wife
Hath quite forgotten her or may be

[16r]

What thumping, stumping overhead
The Thunder had not been more busy
With such a stir you would have said
This little Place may well be dizzy
'Tis who can dance with greatest vigour
'Tis what can be most prompt and eager
As if it heard the fiddle's call
The Pewter clatters on the wall
The very Bacon shews its feeling
Swinging from the smoky ceiling

A steaming Bowl, a blazing Fire
What greater good can heart desire
'Twere worth a wise Man's while to try
The utmost {anger / rigour} of the sky
To seek even thoughts of painful cast
If such be the amends at last
Now should you think I judge amiss
The Cherry Tree shews proof of this
For soon of all the happy there
Our Travellers are the happiest pair
All care with Benjamin is gone
in *A Cæsar past the Rubicon*
He thinks not of his long long strife—
The Sailor Man by nature gay
Ha{th / s} no resolves to throw away
And he has now forgot his Wife
Hath quite forgotten her or may be

---

330 'T{is / was}
333 clatter{s / 'd}
334 shew{s / 'd}
336 *no comma* fire
339 anger
340 *no underlining*
341/342 *lines 344–346 entered prematurely by MW, then del; 345 ends* there *rather than* pair
347 Ca{æ / e}sar

---

339 The overwritten "rigour" was erased.
347 What looks like WW's "in" in the margin is in pencil.
350 Overwriting in pencil.

~~38~~ 17

Knows ~~what is~~ the very truth I wis
That she is better where she is
Under cover
Terror over
Sleeping by her sleeping Baby

With bowl in hand
(It may not stand)
Gladdest of the gladsome band
Amid their own delight and fun
They hear when every dance is done
They hear when every fit is o'er
The fiddle's squeak that call to bliss
Ever followed by a kiss
They envy not the happy lot
But enjoy their own the more:

While thus they sit and thus they fare
Up springs the Tailor from his chair
Limps (for I might have told before
That he was lame) across the floor
Is gone, returns, and with a prize
With what? a Ship of lusty size
A Vessel following at his heels
Upon a frame that goes by wheels
A gallant stately Man of War
Gliding on a sliding car
Surprize to all but most surprize

[17r]

very
Knows ~~what is~~ the^truth I wis
That she is better where she is
Under cover
Terror over
Sleeping by her sleeping Baby

With Bowl in hand
(It may not stand)
Gladdest of the gladsome band
Amid their own delight and fun
They hear when every dance is done
They hear when every fit is o'er
The fiddle's squeak that call to bliss
Ever followed by a kiss
They envy not the happy lot
But enjoy their own the more.

While thus they sit and thus they fare
Up springs the Sailor from his chair
Limps (for I might have told before
That he was lame) across the floor
Is gone, returns, and with a prize
With what? a Ship of lusty size
A Vessel following at his heels
Upon a frame that goes by wheels
A gallant stately Man of War
Sliding on a sliding car
Surprize to all but most surprize

---

357 *period added*
358–359 *not indented*
365 follow'd
367 *period added*
370 Limps, might / [?should]
372 returns,] returns

---

353 The revision may be over erased pencil; the deletion line was drawn in pencil, then in ink.

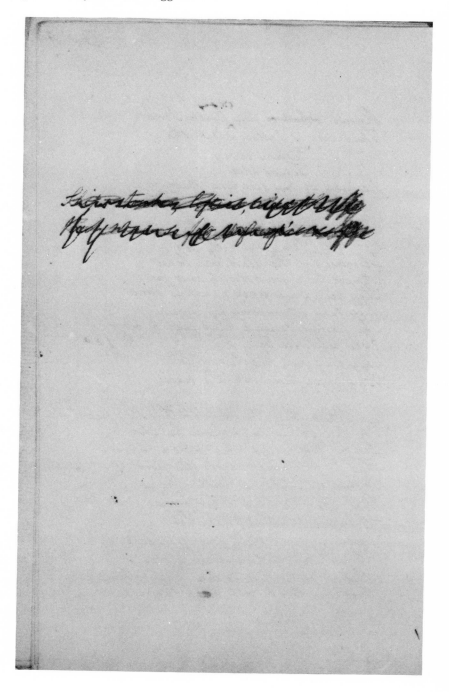

[17v]

[384/385]

~~*Ships stouter, loftier, ride the Sea*~~
~~*But none so far renown'd as She*~~

18

To Benjamin who rubs his eyes
Not knowing that he had befriended
A Man so gloriously attended.

"This" cries the Sailor "a third Rate is;
Stand back and you shall see her gratis;
This was the Flag Ship at the Nile,
The Vanguard; you may smirk and smile,
But, pretty Maid! if you look near
You'll find you've much in little here:
A nobler Ship did never swim
And you shall have her in full trim;
I'll set, my Friends, to do you honour
Set every inch of sail upon her"
So said, so done; and masts, sails, yards
He names them all and interlards
His speech with uncouth terms of art
Accomplish'd in the Showman's part
And then as from a sudden check
Cries out "'tis there the Quarter deck
On which brave Admiral Nelson stood
A sight that would have roused your blood
One eye he had which bright as ten
Burnt like a fire among his men.
Let this be Land and that be Sea
Here lay the French and thus came we."
—Hush'd was by this the fiddle's sound

[18r]

379 *To Benjamin who rubs his eyes*
380 *Not knowing that he had befriended*
381 *A Man so gloriously attended.*

third}
382 "*This*" *cries the Sailor* "*a first*} *Rate is;*
[?~~see~~] see
~~view~~} {:
383 *Stand back and you shall see*}^*her gratis*{,
——×——×——×——×——×—— ×
384 *This was the Flag Ship at the Nile,*
385 *The Vanguard; you may smirk and smile,*
386 *But, pretty Maid! if you look near*
387 *You'll find you've much in little here:*
388 *A nobler Ship did never swim*
389 *And you shall have her in full trim;*
390 *I'll set, my Friends, to do you honour*
391 *Set every inch of sail upon her*"
392 *So said, so done; and masts, sails, yards*
393 *He names them all and interlards*
394 *His speech, with uncouth terms of art*
395 *Accomplish'd in the Showman's part*
396 *And then as from a sudden check*
397 *Cries out* "'*tis there the Quarter deck*
398 *On which brave Admiral Nelson stood*
rouz'd r bl}
399 *A sight that would have* ~~*done*~~ *you*^ *g*}*ood*
400 *One eye he had which bright as ten*

---

381 *no period*
382 rate *semicolon added*
383 back, *with comma added* *colon added*
384 *comma added*
{;
385 Vanguard{,
386 *comma added*
387 *colon added*
389 *no semicolon*
392 done,
397 *quotation marks probably added*
398–405 The lines were crowded by MW into lower margin of 16r and upper margin of 17r; also 402–403 were reversed, and immediately corrected. Narrative sense, together with the secondary but in itself inconclusive evidence of marginal spacing and MS. 2 fair-copy sequence, indicates that both the omission and the reversal were made in error.
ten}
400 stood}

382/383 The deleted "see" is in pencil.
383/384 On the facing verso, MW wrote out two lines for insertion here. They are deleted, in pencil and in pen, and are not included in WW's line count at l. 385. The row of X's here is also lined out in pencil.

To Benjamin who rubs his eyes
Not knowing that he had befriended
A Man so gloriously attended.

"This" cries the Sailor "a third Rate is;
Stand back and you shall see her gratis;
This was the Flag Ship at the Nile,
The Vanguard; you may smirk and smile,
But, pretty Maid! if you look near
You'll find you've much in little here:
A nobler Ship did never swim
And you shall have her in full trim;
I'll set, my Friends, to do you honour
Set every inch of sail upon her"
So said, so done; and masts, sails, yards
He names them all and interlards
His speech with uncouth terms of art
Accomplish'd in the Showman's part
And then as from a sudden check
Cries out "'tis there the Quarter deck
On which brave Admiral Nelson stood
A sight that would have roused your blood
One eye he had which bright as ten
Burnt like a fire among his men.
Let this be Land and that be Sea
Here lay the French and thus came we."
—Hush'd was by this the fiddler's sound

401 *Burnt like a fire among his men* {

403 *Let th* {*is* / ~~*at*~~} *be Land and that be Sea*
402 *Here lay the French and thus came we."*
404 *—Hush'd was by this the fiddle's sound*

403–402

Here lay the French and thus came we
Let this be Land and that be Sea"

erased and overwritten

Let th {at / is} be Land and that be Sea
Here lay the French and thus came we"—

404 *no dash* Hush'd was *over erasure*

---

403 The "at" in "that" was deleted by erasure.

The Dancers all were gather'd round
And such the stillness of the house
You might have heard a nibbling mouse
While borrowing helps where'er he may
The Sailor through the story runs
Of Ships to Ships and Guns to Guns
And does his utmost to display
The dismal conflict and the might
And terror of that wondrous night
"A Bowl, a Bowl of double measure"
Cries Benjamin "a draught of length
To Nelson, Englands pride and treasure
Her bulwark and her tower of strength!"
When Benjamin had seized the bowl
The Mastiff gave a warning growl
The Mastiff from beneath the Waggon
Where he lay watchful as a Dragon
Rattled his chain, 'twas all in vain
For Benjamin triumphant Soul!
He heard the monitory growl
Heard, and in opposition quaff'd
A deep, determined, desperate draught
Nor did the batter'd Tar forget
Or flinch from what he deem'd his debt
Then like a Hero crown'd with laurel
Back to her place the Ship he led

[19^r]

405 *The Dancers all were gather'd round* 140
406 *And such the stillness of the house*
You You}
407 *One*{ *might have heard a nibbling mouse*
408 *While borrowing helps where'er he may*
409 *The Sailor through the Story runs*
410 *Of Ships to Ships and Guns to Guns*
411 *And does his utmost to display*
The dismal conflict and the might
And terror *of that wond'rous night*
"A Bowl, a Bowl of double measure"
413 *"A Bowl a Bowl of double measure"*
{ *ught of length*}
414 *Cries Benjamin "a dra*{*ft of length*}
415 *To Nelson, England's pride and treasure*
416 *Her bulwark and her tower of strength!"*
417 *When Benjamin had seized the bowl*
418 *The Mastiff gave a warning growl*
419 *The Mastiff from beneath the Waggon*
420 *Where he lay watchful as a Dragon*
421 *Rattled his chain, 'twas all in vain*
422 *For Benjamin triumphant Soul!*
423 *He heard the monitory growl*
424 *Heard, and in opposition quaff'd* 160
425 *A deep, determined, desperate draught*
426 *Nor did the batter'd Tar forget*
427 *Or flinch from what he deem'd his debt*
428 *Then like a Hero crown'd with laurel*
429 *Back to her place the Ship he led*

The Dancers all were }
405 [? Then all the Dancers]}
{One
407 {[?You]
409 story
411/413 *over erasure of* [?The history of that wondrous day]. *A draft of these lines in WW's hand, erased, is on the opposite page.* wond'rous] wondrous
413 bowl a bowl measure"] measure
416 *no exclamation point*
417 seiz'd *with* 420 *in right margin begin WW's penciled line numbers; they run by 20s to end of MS*
421 *no comma*
or }
423 monit[?]}y
424 *no comma*
{ught
425 determin'd, dra{ft
428 hero

---

407 The "You" in margin is in pencil.
408 Deletion in pencil.
411/413 The erased word was probably "conflict," copied by mistake from the line above.

~~3~~ 20

Wheel'd her back in full apparel
And so Flag flying at mast head
Re-yoked her to the Ass, anon
~~Cries~~ Says Benjamin we must be gone
Thus after two hours hearty stay
Again behold them on their way 171

Canto 3^d

Right gladly had the Horses stirr'd
When they the smack of greeting heard
The smack of greeting from the door
The sign that they might move once more
You think these doings must have bred
In them disheartening doubts and dread
No, not a Horse of all the eight
Although it be a moonless night
Fears either for himself or freight
For this they know and know full well
And this in pleasure I may tell
That Benjamin with half his brains
Is worth the best with all their pains

[20r]

430 *Wheel'd her back in full apparel*
431 *And so Flag flying at mast head*
432 *Re-yoked her to the Ass, anon*
Says
~~Cries~~ }
433 *Says* } *Benjamin we must be gone*
434 *Thus after two hours hearty stay*
435 *Again behold them on their way* 171

Canto 3.d

stirr'd }
436 *Right gladly had the Horses heard* }
437 *When they the smack of greeting heard*
438 *The smack of greeting from the door*
439 *The sign that they might move once more*
440 *You think these doings must have bred*
441 *In them disheartening doubts and dread*
{ ,
442 *No* { *not a Horse of all the eight*
443 *Although it be a moonless night*
444 *Fears either for himself or freight*
445 *For this they know and know full well*
446 *And this in pleasure I may tell*
447 *That Benjamin with half his brains*
448 *Is worth the best with all their pains*

---

fl }
431 [?Fl] } ag
Re- }
432 [?He] } yoked *no comma*
Says }
433 Cries }
Again }
435 [?Once more] } way.
435/436 Canto 3.d] Third Part
436 stirr'd
440 Your *with* r *erased*
442 *no comma*
in }
446 [?with] }

---

433 The deletion line and the added "Says" are in pencil.

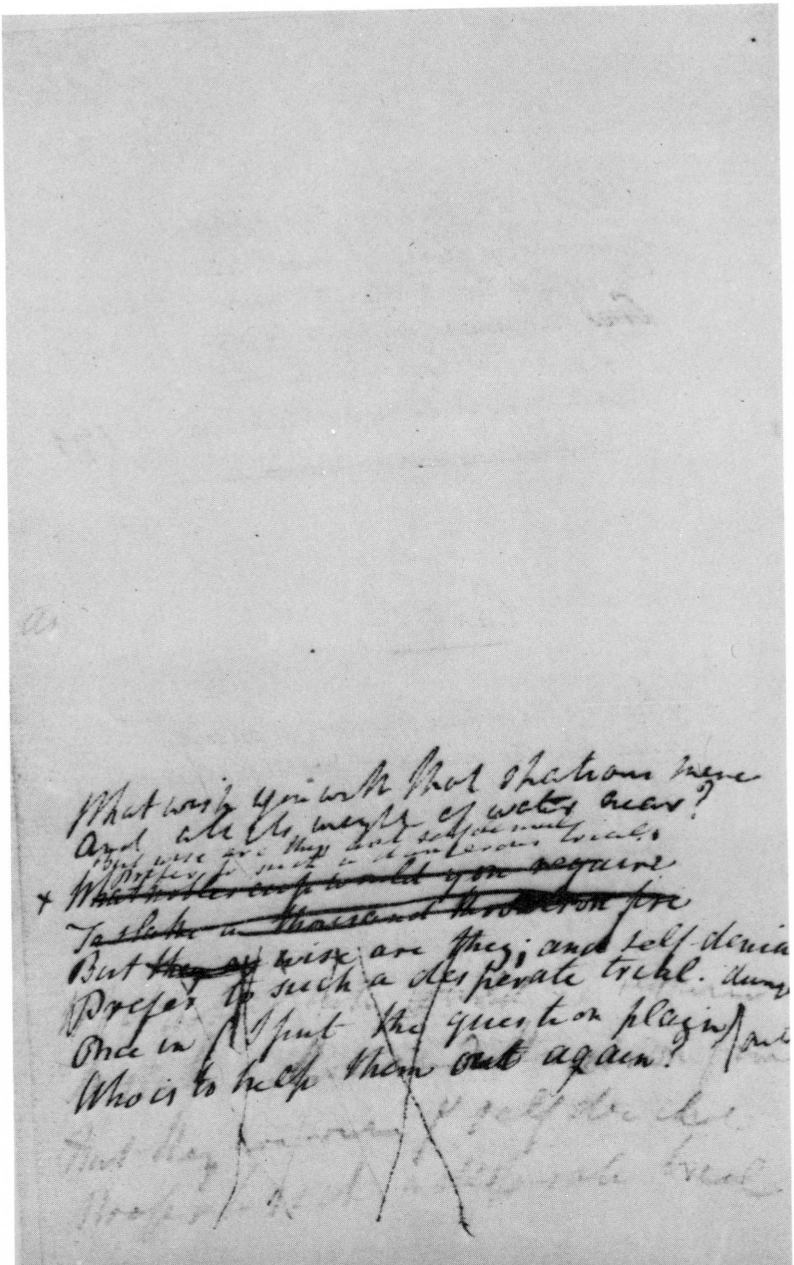

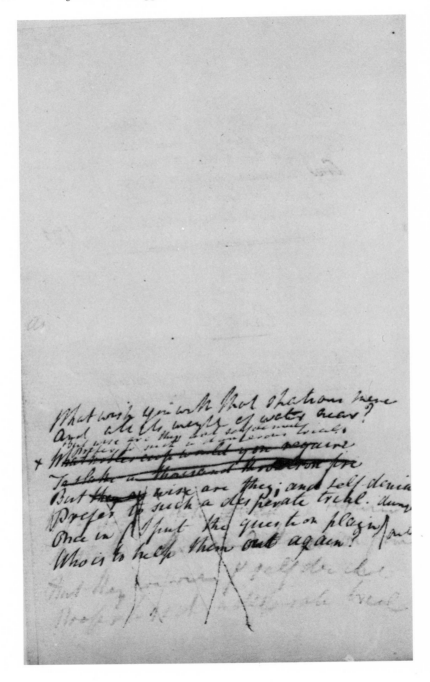

[20v] [468–473]

A[?n]

What nobler cup would you require
To slake a thousand throats on fire
But they are wise & self denial
Prefer to such a desperate trial

What wish you with that spatious mere
And all its weight of water near?
But wise are they and self denial
Prefer to such a dangerous trial.
× ~~What nobler cup would you require~~
~~To slake a thousand throats on fire~~
But ~~they ar~~ wise are they; and self-denial
Prefer to such a desperate trial. dangerous
Once in (I put the question plain)
out
Who is to help them out again?

The underlying pencil lines, one of them an isolated false start, are separately transcribed above the ink lines.

The X in the margin corresponds to an X on 21r. The undeleted lines above it were added later, and were incorporated in MS. 3.

21

And if they had a prayer to make
The prayer would be that they might take
With him whatever comes in course
The better fortune or the worse
That no one else may have business near them
And drunk or sober he should steer them
 So forth in dauntless mood they fare
And with them goes the guardian pair.
 Now Heroes for the true commotion
The blessing of your late devotion
Can aught on earth impede delight
Still mounting to a higher height
And higher still a greedy flight
Can any low-born care pursue her
Can any mortal clog come to her
It can—if chance a strong desire
Such as did soon lay hold of these
Should rise and set the throat on fire
And nothing by to give us ease.
× [illegible]
[illegible]
[illegible]
[illegible]
[illegible]
[illegible]

[21r]

And if they had a prayer to make
The prayer would be that they might take
With him whatever comes in course
The better fortune or the worse
That no one else may have business near them
And drunk or sober he should steer them

So forth in dauntless mood they fare 20
And with them goes the guardian pair

Now Heroes for the true commotion
The blessing of your late devotion
—Can aught on earth impede delight
Still mounting to a higher height
And higher still, a greedy flight
Can any low-born care pursue her
Can any mortal clog come to her
It can—if chance a strong desire
Such as did soon lay hold of these
Should rise and set the throat on fire

And nothing by to give us ease {.}
× ~~*What wish you with that spacious mere*~~
~~*And all its weight of water near*~~
~~*What nobler cup would Ye be at*~~

~~*No, no, they are to*{o *wise for that*~~
~~*Once in, I put the question plain*~~
~~*Who is to help them out again?*~~

---

452 or } with
453 else *inserted above line*
457 commotion
461 *no comma*
468–471 *del; X indicates insertion of lines in WW's hand on facing 17v*

What nobler cup would ye desire
To slake a thousand throats on fire
But wise are they—and self-denial
Prefer to such a desperate trial.

470 ye
471 *no commas* too
472 *no comma*
473 *no question mark*

---

457 The erased word may have been "devotion," a copyist's error.

468 The X in margin shows where the lines drafted on 20v, most of them then deleted, were to be inserted. A faint pencil line also runs down the left margin from l. 457 (or perhaps 459) to l. 473.

Cries Benjamin where is it where
Once [illegible] but must I be [illegible]
Cries Benjamin, "Where is it? where?
Once it hath [illegible] but must be near."
A Star

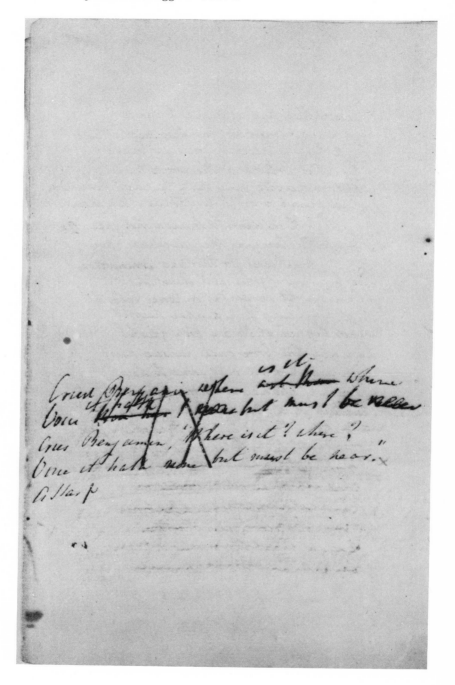

[21v] [484–486]

Cried Benjamin where ~~art thou~~ is it where
Voice ~~thou hast~~ it hath none but must be near
Cries Benjamin, "Where is it? where?
Voice it hath none but must be near."
A Star &

The X visible in the photograph following the fourth line is blotted through from the other side of the leaf.

~~45~~. 22

But Benjamin in his vexation
Possesses inward consolation
He knows his ground and hopes to find
A spot with all things to his mind
An upright monumental Stone
With purest water trickling down
A spring that doth but faintly bleed
And yet sufficient for their need
A slender Spring yet kind to Man
A cordial true Samaritan
Close to the highway pouring out
Its offering from a chink or spout
Whence all however tired and drooping
May drink at leisure without stooping

Cries Benjamin where is it, where?
Voice it hath none but must be near.
~~I know my beverage must be near~~
—A star declining to the west
Its image faintly had impress'd
Upon the smooth and dewy block
The surface of the upright rock
And he espies it by this sign
And both there take a draught divine
Could happier more convenient place
Be given in fortunes utmost grace.
They have a comfort in their madness
And feel that this is sober gladness

[22^r]

this cross a mistake the lines are to be inserted

474 *But Benjamin in* <u>*his*</u> *vexation*
475 *Possesses inward consolation*
476 *He knows his ground and hopes to find*
477 *A Spot with all things to his mind*
An upright monumental Stone
With purest water trickling down
in *A spring that doth but faintly bleed*
And yet sufficient for {*their* / [?~~our~~]} *need*
478 *A slender Spring yet kind to Man*
479 *A cordial true Samaritan*
480 *Close to the highway pouring out*
481 *Its offering from a chink or spout*
482 *Whence all however tired and drooping*
483 *May drink at leisure without stooping*

484 *Cries Benjamin "where is it* {' / } *where?*
X Voice it hath none but must be near.
485 ~~*I know my treasure must be near*~~
— }
486 — } *A star declining to the west*
487 *Its image faintly had impress'd*
488 *Upon the smooth and dewy block*
489 *The surface of the upright rock*
490 *And he espies it by this sign*
491 *And both there take a draught divine*
492 *Could happier more convenient place*
493 *Be given in fortune's utmost grace*
494 *They have a comfort in their madness*
495 *And feel that this is sober gladness*

477/478 *inserted later*
485 near."
486 *dash added in margin* Star
488 Upon] Upom *mistake in transcription*
491 dra {ught divine / ft divine} *with rewritten* vine *over erased word in pencil by WW*

A faint pencil line runs down the entire left margin, and ll. 474–483 were deleted with a faint pencil X, as well as the ink X visible in the photograph.
477/478 Deletion by erasure.
485 The X apparently points to the deleted draft on 21^v.
486 The dash was added, probably by WW, in pencil and in ink.

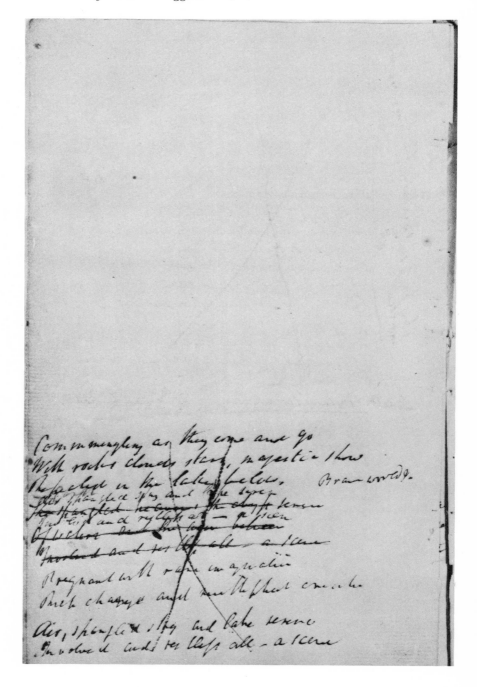

Commingling as they come and go
With rocks clouds stars, majestic show
Reflected in the lake below.

Pregnant with rare imagination
Rich change and multiplied creation

Air, spangled sky and lake serene
Involved and reflects all — a scene

[22v] [519–520]

Commingling as they come and go
With rocks clouds stars, majestic show
Repeated in the lake below. Brave world &.
—Earth
Air spangled sky and lake serene
~~The spangled heavens the abyss serene~~
Involv'd and restless all—a scene
~~Of waters and the air between~~
~~Involved and restless all—a scene~~
Pregnant with rare imagination
Rich change and multiplied creation

Air, spangled sky and lake serene
Involved and restless all—a scene

"Earth" under the third line is in pencil.

23

Ah! dearest Spot! dear Rock of Names
From which the Pair thus slaked their flames
Ah! deem not this light strain unjust
To thee and to thy precious trust
That file which gentle, brave and good
The near in friendship and in blood
The hands of those I love the best
Committed to thy faithful breast
Their hands and mine dear Rock! when we
Have rested by the side of thee
So long as life a genial feeling
Or one that stands in need of healing
Thy powers shall last—oh thought of pain
That would impair it or profane!
Take all in kindness then as said
With a fond heart though playful head
And thou thy record duly keep
Long after we are laid asleep.

As winds by pausing do grow stronger
How fierce when they can pause no longer.
So back again the tempest rush'd
That for a moment had been hush'd
No notions have they not a thought
No one that is not highly wrought
Beside the ~~loud~~ shining and silent Lake
Their inspiration I partake
Share their empyreal spirits—yea
Behold the rack and imagery
The [illegible] pictures, and the gleams
Of colours bright as feverish dreams
[illegible] as they come and go
With towers, clouds, stars, majestic shapes

[illegible]

[23r]

Checks I think the interest and stops the progress therefore better out, do as you think best, Let ~~the~~ the lines however be ~~inserted~~ put in the Margin

496 *Ah! dearest Spot! dear Rock of Names*
497 *From which the Pair thus slaked their flames*
498 *Ah! deem not this light strain unjust*
499 *To thee and to thy precious trust*
500 *That file which gentle, brave and good*
501 *The near in friendship and in blood*
502 *The hands of those I love the best*
503 *Committed to thy faithful breast*
Their hands and mine dear Rock! wh en we
Have rested by the side of thee
504 *No, long as I've a genial feeling*
505 *Or one that stands in need of healing*
Thy power shall last—oh thought of pain
That would impair it or profane!
508 *Take all in kindness then as said*
509 *With a fond heart though playful head*
510 *And thou thy record duly keep*
511 *Long after we are laid asleep*

---

497 the] our
500 *no comma*
501 ne [?de] ar
503/504 *inserted later* Rock whe {n / re}
505/508

X [I will preserve thy rightful power
Inviolate till life's final hour

del in ink; penciled line and X in left margin indicate insertion of WW's penciled lines on facing 20v

*
Thy power shall last: oh! thought of pain,
That would impair it or profane!

508 A {Take all in kind / [?ll take with kind]} ness
509 playfull
511 they we asleep.

WW's indecision about the "Rock of Names" passage is reflected by a faint penciled X (visible in the photograph) through that passage; a fainter X crosses the first four or five lines that follow. SH, in preparing MS. 3, followed WW's instruction by relegating the passage to the bottom margin, in tiny handwriting.

503/504 The partially erased word was probably "where."
505/508 The erased lines were probably the MS. 1 reading.

23

Ah! dearest Spot! dear Rock of Names
From which the Pair thus slaked their flames
Ah! deem not this light strain unjust
To thee and to thy precious trust
That file which gentle, brave and good
The near in friendship and in blood
The hands of those I love the best
Committed to thy faithful breast
Their hands and mine dear Rock! when we
Have rested by the side of thee
So long as I've a genial feeling
Or one that stands in need of healing
Thy power shall last— Oh thought of pain
That would impair it or profane!
Take all in kindness then as said
With a fond heart though playful head
And thou thy record duly keep
Long after we are laid asleep.

As winds by pausing do grow stronger
How fierce when they can pause no longer
So back again the tempest rush'd
That for a moment had been hush'd
So riotous have they not a thought
No one that is not highly wrought
Beside the ~~lonely~~ strong and silent Lake
Their inspiration I partake
Share their empyreal spirits—yea
Behold the vast and imagery
The moving pictures, and the gleams
Of colours bright as feverish dreams
Are imprisoning as they come and go
With rocks, clouds, stars, majestic show

512 *As winds by pausing do grow stronger*
513 *How fierce when they can pause no longer!*
So back again the tempest rush'd
That for a moment had been hush'd
516 *No notions have they not a thought*
517 *Not one that is not highly wrought*
spring
518 *Beside the ~~spring~~ and silent Lake*
519 *Their inspiration I partake*

Share their empyreal Spirits—yea
Behold the radiant imagery
The moving pictures, and the gleams
Of Colour bright as feverish dreams
Commingling as they come and go
With rocks, clouds, stars, majestic show

512–515 *WW wrote drafting for these lines on facing* 20^{v} *in pencil, now erased; but line 512 begins with* like

512 do *inserted with caret*

514–515

So now the tempest of delight
Broke forth with [?aggravated m]ight

del by erasure to

So back again the tempest rush'd
That for a moment had been hush'd

518 Spring

519 inspiration *over erasure* *asterisk indicates insertion below line of lines in MW's hand on facing* 20^{v}

*Share their empyreal spirits, yea
Behold the radiant imagery,
The moving pictures, & the gleams
Of colours bright as feverish dreams;
Oh! what

deletion by erasure

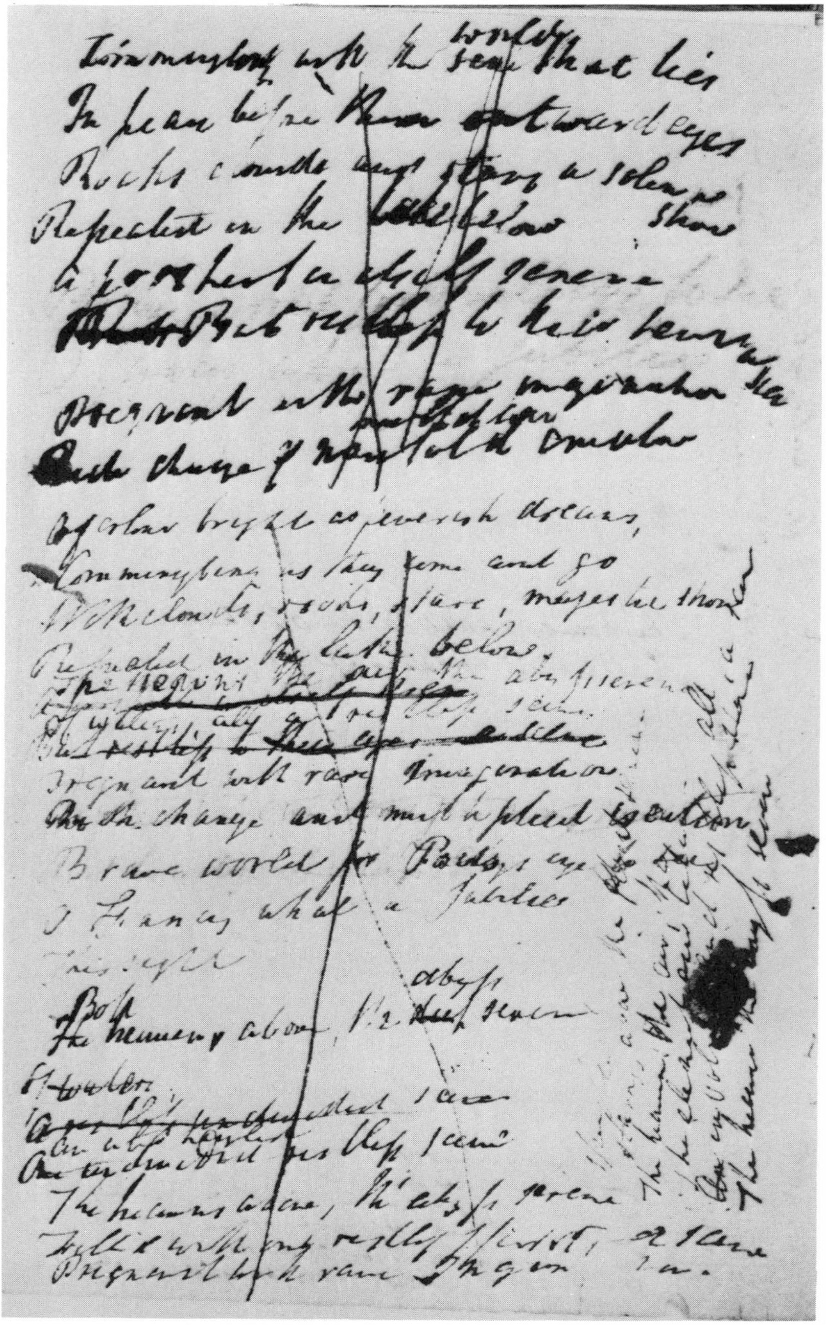

[23v] [519/520; 520–522]

Brave world for Poets eye to see
O fancy what a jubilee

Com} {ing world
[?Is]} mingl {ed with the ~~scene~~ that lies
In peace before their outward eyes
Rocks clouds and stars a solemn
show
Repeated in the lake below
A prospect in itself serene
[?And] }
[?But]} But restless to their hearts a scene
Pregnant with rare imagination
R } multiplied
[?]} ich change & manifold creation
Of colour bright as feverish dreams,
Commingling as they come and go
With clouds, rocks, stars, majestic show
Repeated in the lake below.
The Heavns the air the abyss serene
~~A prospect in itself serene~~
Of waters, all a restless scene
~~But restless to their eyes—a scene~~
I}
Pregnant with rare i} magination
R }
[?]} ich change and multiplied creation
{Poet's
Brave world for {Fancy's eye to see
O Fancy what a Jubilee
This sight

Both abyss
~~The~~ heavens above, the ~~deep~~ serene
Of waters
~~A restless undivided scene~~
An [?intermingled]
One undivided restless scene
The heavens above, th' abyss serene
Fill'd with one restless Spirit,—a scene
Pregnant with rare Imagination.

spangled
star[?ry] above the {[?flood] / ab[?yss]} serene
the}
The heavens [?]} air, the
The element [?and] between
all, a scene
~~An~~ involved and restless ~~scene~~
ab}
The heavens the [?]} yss serene

Underneath the fifth, sixth, and seventh lines are two lines of pencil draft, transcribed separately at the top of the page. Below the middle of the page, the two lines beginning "Rich change . . ." were written over two deleted pencil lines of draft—probably for the same lines.

~~Repeated in the lake below~~ ~~41~~ 24

Share their empyreal spirits, yea
Behold the radiant imagery,
The moving pictures and the gleams
Of colour bright as feverish dreams;
Brave work for Poet's eye to see
O Fancy what a Jubilee.
This sight to see the Muse imparts
And then what kindness in their hearts
What tears of rapture what vow-making
Profound entreaties and hand-shaking
What solemn vacant interlacing
As if they'd fall asleep embracing
Then in the turbulence of glee
And in the excess of amity
Cries Benjamin "that Ass of thine
He spoils thy sport and hinders mine
If he were tethered to the Waggon
He'd drag as well what he is dragging
And we, as brother should with Brother,
Might trudge it along-side each other"
So to the Waggon's skirts they tied
The Creature by the Mastiff's side
(The Mastiff not well-pleased to be
So very near such company)
And staggering to the Rock once more
They drank as deeply as before
Their burning faces they bedewed

[24ʳ]

Repeated in the lake below

~~Share their empyreal spirits, yea~~
~~Behold the radiant imagery,~~
~~The moving pictures and the gleams~~
~~Of colour bright as feverish dreams;~~
X world
{Brave ^ for Poet's eye to see
520 {*Oh! what a jubilee of fancy!*
{O Fancy what a jubilee.
521 {*A braver world no Poet can see*
522 *This sight to me the Muse imparts*
523 *And then what kindness in their hearts*
524 *What tears of rapture what vow-making*
525 *Profound entreaties and hand-shaking*
526 *What solemn vacant interlacing*
527 *As if they'd fall asleep embracing*
528 *Then in the turbulence of glee*
529 *And in the excess of amity*
530 *Cries Benjamin "that Ass of thine*
531 *He spoils thy sport and hinders mine*
534 *If he were tethered to the Waggon*
{*d*
535 *He'd drag as well what he is* {*gragging*
536 *And we, as Brother should with Brother,*
537 *~~Might~~ trudge it along-side each other"*
538 *——So to the Waggon's skirts they tied*
Th}
539 *On*{*e Creature by the Mastiff's side*
540 *(The Mastiff not well pleased to be*
541 *So very near such company)*
umbling
542 *And st~~aggering~~ to the Rock once more*
543 *They drank as deeply as before*
544 *Their burning faces they bedew'd*

spangled
~~The heavens above the abyss serene~~
Of waters & ~~the air between~~
Involved and restless all—a scene

---

520 *no exclamation point* *WW has inserted above line*

Brave world as Poets eye can see

what a jubilee of *del and* what a jubilee *added by WW at end of line*

526 vacant

531/534

Poor Beast! I know no harm is meant
But he's a sad impediment *del*

535 dragging

536 Brother,] Brother

{udge
537 tr{avel *and* it *inserted with caret*

C}
539 The c {reature

541 Company)

542 rock

The two fair-copy lines lying under WW's insertion preceding l. 522 were first deleted in pencil, then erased; they are marked by a vertical pencil line in the left margin.

537 The deletion is in pencil.

WW's drafts in the left margin are continuous with drafts in the right margin of 23ᵛ.

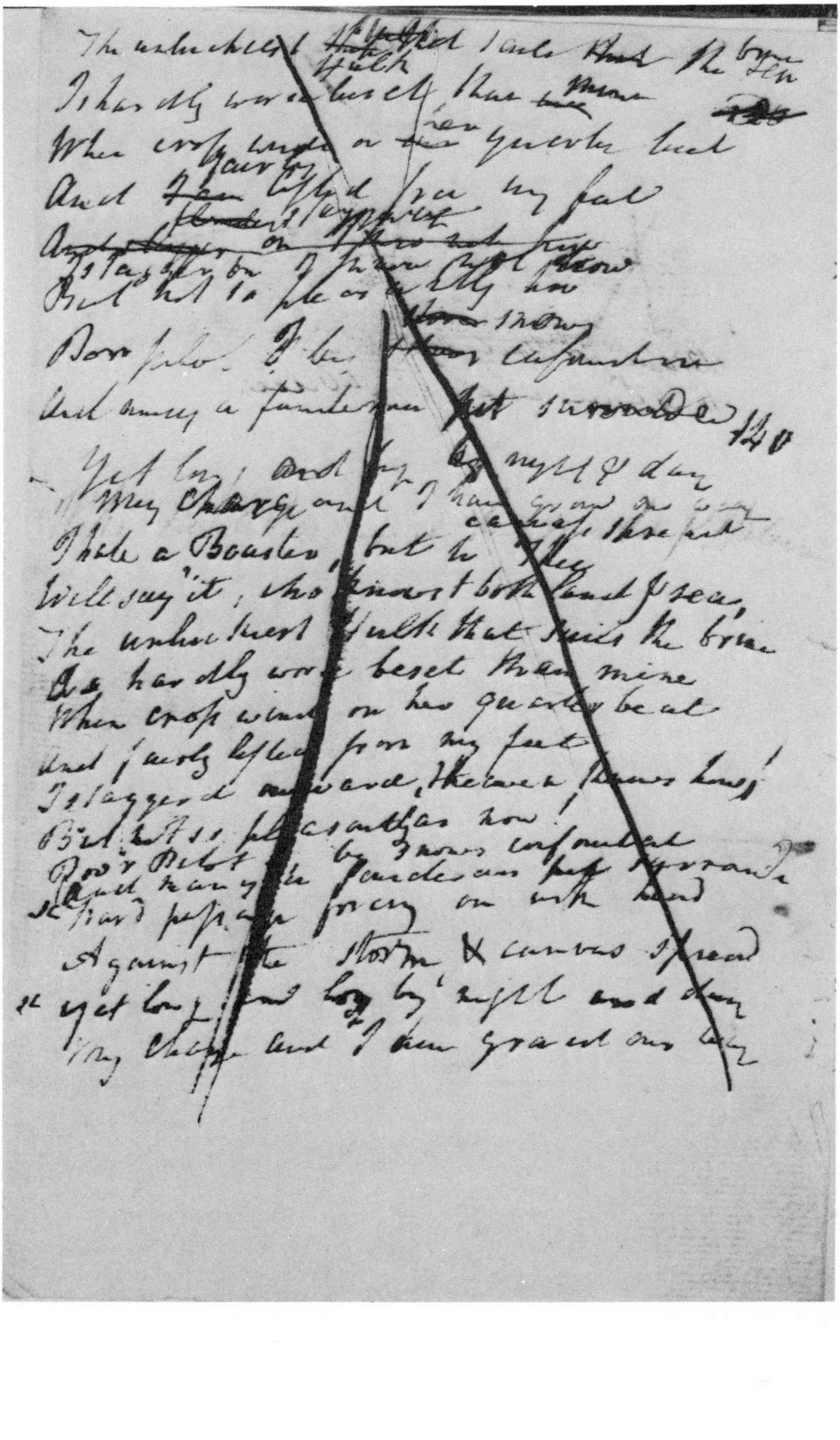

[24v] [557–558]

~~Hulk~~ brine
The unluckiest ~~Ship~~ that sails ~~that~~ the sea
Hulk mine
Is hardly worse beset than ~~me~~
her
When cross winds on ~~our~~ quarter beat
fairly
And ~~I am~~ lifted from my feet
~~flounder~~ staggering
~~And stagger on I kno not how~~
h
I stagger on I know not [?]ow
But not so pleasantly [?how.]
~~[?storms]~~ snows
Poor pilot I by [~~?storms~~] confounded
And many a founderous pit surrounded
Yet long and long by night & day
My charge and I have ground our way
canvass spread
I hate a Boaster, but to Thee
,
Will say it, who knowst both land & sea,
The unluckiest Hulk that sails the brine
Is
[?] hardly worse beset than mine
When cross wind[?s] on her quarter beat
And fairly lifted from my feet
H ,
I staggerd onward, heaven knows how!
ly
But not so pleasant as now!
Poor Pilot I, by snows confounded
And many a founderous pit surrounde
/(*Hard passage forcing on with head*
Against the storm, & canvas spread
/(Yet long and long by night and day
h
My charge and I [?]ave ground our way

The line beginning "My charge . . ." is written over a pencil line in WW's hand: "I like said Benjamin her make & [?Stature]"—l. 550 on 25r.
Lines 3 and 4 from the bottom are in DW's hand.

~~41~~ 25

And thus their journey all renew'd
~~The Vanguard following (do not blame~~
~~The Poet for the unlucky name~~
~~Nor tease him, he makes no pretence~~
~~To wit that deals in double sense)~~
The Vanguard following close behind
Sails spread as if to catch the wind
"Thy Wife and Child are snug and warm
Thy Ship will travel without harm
I like" said Benj amain her make and stature
And this of mine, this bulky creature
Of which I have the steering this,
Seen fairly, is not much amiss
We want your streamers, Friend! you know
But altogether as we go
We make a kind of handsome show
Among these hills from first to last [illegible]
We've weather'd many ~~a~~ an ~~stormy~~ angry blast +
+ Aye long and long by night and day
Together have we grouned our way
Through foul and fair our task fulfilling
And long shall be so yet, God willing."

"Plague on the whooping and the howl"
Replies the Tar of yon screech Owl"
But instantly began a fray

[25r]

545 *And thus their journey all renew'd*
~~*The Vanguard following (do not blame*~~
~~*The Poet for the unlucky name*~~
~~*Nor praise him, he makes no pretence*~~
~~*To wit that deals in double sense)*~~
546 *The Vanguard following close behind*
547 *Sails spread as if to catch the wind*

548 *"Thy Wife and Child are snug and warm*
549 *Thy Ship will travel without harm*
j} amin
550 *I like" said Ben* } ^ *"her make and stature*
551 *And this of mine, this bulky Creature*
552 *Of which I have the steering, this,*
553 *Seen fairly, is not much amiss.*
554 *We want your streamers Friend! you know*
555 *But altogether as we go* ~~*we make*~~
556 *We make a kind of handsome show*
X turn over leaf
Am }
[?*Al*]} *ong these hills from first to last*
an ~~angry~~ furious
We've weather'd many ~~*a*~~ *stormy blast* +
557 X *Aye long and long by night and day*
558 *Together have we ground our way*
559 *Through foul and fair our task fulfilling*
560 *And long shall do so yet, God willing!"*

the w }
561 *"Plague on* ~~*the*~~ } *hooping and the howl"*
562 *Replies the Tar "of yon screech Owl"*
563 *But instantly began a fray*

545/546 *asterisks indicate insertion of lines in MW's hand on facing 21v*

* The Vanguard following (do not blame
The Poet for the unlucky name
Nor praise him, he makes no pretence
To wit that deals in double sense)
The Vanguard del

546 Vanguard *inserted in gap*
547 wind.
547/548 *no extra space between verse paragraphs*
549 "Thy will travel without *over erasure*
550 said Ben "her *over erasure and* jamin *inserted by WW above line with caret overwriting his penciled* quoth [?Ben her]
553 *no period*
555 But altogether as we go
557 *del by erasure; then included in revision 557/558*
557/558
Among these hills from first to last
Weve weathered many a stormy blast
Aye}
A} long and long by night and day
561 the hooping

555, 561 Deletions by erasure.
556/557, 557 The cross and X's in margin point to drafts on 24v and 25v. The overwritten portion of "Along" was erased.

a kind of handsome show
Among these hills from first to last,
We've weather'd many a furious blast
Hard passage forcing on, with head
Against the storm and canvass spread;
[illegible]
[illegible]
[illegible]
[illegible]
I hate a Boaster — but to thee
Will say't who know'st both land & sea
The unluckiest Hulk that sails the brine
Is hardly worse beset than mine
When cross winds on her quarter beat;
And fairly lifted from my feet
I stagger onward — heaven knows how
But not so pleasantly as now!
Poor Pilot I — by snows confounded
And many a foundrous pit surrounded
[illegible]
[illegible]
[illegible]
Through foul and fair our task fulfilling
[illegible]
by night and day
Yet here we are
Grinding through rough and smooth, our way,
Through foul and fair our task fulfilling,
be so yet God willing
And long shall
Blame on the halting [illegible] turn back,

[25v] [556–561; 579–581]

[?Ben] this whip shall
lay
A Thousand if they come this way
I know that Wanton's noisy station
I know him and his occupation

a kind of handsome show
Among these hills from first to last,
We've weather'd many a furious blast
Hard passage forcing on, with head
Against the storm and canvass spread;
~~Worse handling far and sorrier plight~~
~~Then that which has been ours to night~~
~~Stemming our way—to this how slight~~
~~The hindrance we have had to night~~
I hate a Boaster—but to Thee
Will say {'t ~~it~~} who knows't both land & sea
The unluckiest Hulk that sails the brine
Is hardly worse beset than mine
When cross winds on her quarter beat;
And fairly lifted from my feet
I stagger onward—{H heaven} knows not how,
—} But not so pleasantly as now!
Poor Pilot I—b[?]{y} {snows ~~storms~~} confounded
And many a foundrous pit surrounded
~~Yet long & long by night and day~~
~~My charge and I have ground our way~~
~~Through foul and fair~~ our task fulf{[?i] ulling}
~~And long shall do~~ s[?~~et~~]{o} ~~yet God willing~~

Yet here we are by night and day
Grinding, through rough and smooth, our way,
Through foul and fair our task fulfilling
And l{ong [?]} shall ~~do~~ be so yet God willing
Plague on the hooping & {~~tur~~ ~~and~~} (turn back)

The overwritten pencil lines faintly visible toward the bottom of the page are transcribed separately before the ink lines.

26

That called their thoughts another way
The Mastiff, ill-condition'd carl
What must he do but growl and snarl
Still more and more dissatisfied
With the meek comrade at his side
Till, not incensed though put to proof,
The Ass uplifting a fore hoof,
Salutes the Mastiff on the head
And so were better manners bred
And all was calmed and quieted
"Yon Screech-Owl," cries the Sailor turning
Back to his former cause of mourning
"Yon Owl pray God that all be well
Tis worse than any funeral bell
As sure as I've the gift of sight
We shall be meeting ghosts tonight."
Said Benjamin, This Whip shall lay
A thousand if they come this way.
I know that Wanton's noisy station
I know him and his occupation
The jolly Bird hath learnt his cheer
On the banks of Windermere
Where a tribe of them make merry
Mocking the Man that keeps the Ferry
Hallooing from an open throat
Like Travellers shouting for a Boat
The tricks he learn'd at Windermere
This vagrant Owl is playing here

[26[r]]

564 *That called their thoughts another way*
565 *The Mastiff, ill-condition'd carl*
566 *What must he do but growl and snarl*
567 *Still more and more dissatisfied*
568 *With the meek comrade at his side*
569 *Till, not incensed, though put to proof*
570 *The Ass uplifting a fore hoof*
571 *Salutes the Mastiff on the head*
572 *And so were better manners bred*
573 *And all was calmed and quieted*

S} {-o}
574 *"Yon s{creech {O}wl," cries the Sailor turning*
575 *Back to his former cause of mourning*
576 *"Yon Owl! pray God that all be well*
577 *'Tis worse than any funeral bell*
578 *As sure as I've the gift of sight*
579 *We shall be meeting ghosts to-night"*

Quoth Said }
[?Said]} Benjamin, This Whip shall lay
* A Thousand if they come this way.
{I know that Wanton's noisy station
580 { *"Ps[?haw pshaw]" cries Ben "I know his station*
581 in ~~*I know him, and his occupation*~~
I know him and his occupation
582 *The jolly Bird has learnt his cheer*
583 *On the banks of Windermere*
584 *Where a tribe of them make merry*

---

565 *no comma*
568 Comrade
569 incensed,] incensed
570 *last four words over erasure*
573 quieted.
574 Sailor,
576 *no exclamation point*
579 Ghosts
579/580 *asterisk indicates insertion of WW's penciled lines on facing 22[v]*

Said Ben I have a Whip to lay
A thousand if they come our way
I know that Wanton's noisy station

transferred to recto by MW as

* Said Benjamin "my whip shall lay
A thousand if they come this way.
I know that Wanton's noisy station

cries }
580 "Pshaw pshaw" [?says]} Ben "I know his station" *del*
581 *no comma*
583 Banks

579/580 "Quoth," "[?Said]," and asterisk in pencil.
580 Partly erased.

That called their thoughts another way
The Mastiff, ill-condition'd carl
What must he do but growl and snarl
Still more and more dissatisfied
With the meek comrade at his side
Till, not incensed though put to proof,
The Ass uplifting a fore hoof,
Salutes the Mastiff on the head
And so were better manners bred
And all was calmed and quieted

"Yon Screech-Owl," cries the Sailor turning
Back to his former cause of mourning
Yon Owl pray God that all be well
Tis worse than any funeral bell
As sure as I've the gift of sight
We shall be meeting ghosts to-night
Said Benjamin, This Whip shall lay
A thousand if they come this way
I know that Wanton's noisy station
I know him and his occupation
The jolly Bird hath learnt his cheer
On the banks of Windermere
Where a tribe of them make merry
Mocking the Man that keeps the Ferry
Hallooing from an open throat
Like Traveller shouting for a Boat
The tricks he learn'd at Windermere
This vagrant Owl is playing here

Mocking the Man that keeps the Ferry
Hallooing from an open throat
Like Traveller shouting for a Boat
The tricks he learn'd at Windermere
vagrant
This ~~*lonely*~~ ^ *Owl is playing here*

---

588 trick{s
589 lonely] *alt* vagrant *in pencil by WW with* a *reinforced in ink*

---

589 The revision was written first in pencil, then in ink.

And manyful gust of ~~merry~~ social song
Breaks from them as they wind along
While to the musick from on high
Canto 4
The Echoes make a glad reply
Thus they with freaks of proud delight
Beguile the remnant of the night.
[illegible]
But the sage Muse the triumph heeds
No farther than her story needs;
Nor will she servilely attend
The loitering journey to its end.
Blithe Spirits of her own impel
The Muse who scents the morning air,
To take of this transported pair
A brief and ~~[illegible]~~ unreproved farewell
To quit the slow-pac'd waggon's side
And wander down yon hawthorn dell
With murmuring Greta for her guide
— There doth she ken the awful form
Of Raven Crag black as a storm
Glimmering through the twilight pale!
And, ~~[illegible]~~ Ghimmer-crag, his tall twin Brother
Each peering forth to greet the Other.
And ~~wandering~~ rambling on through St John's vale,
Along the smooth unpathwayed plain
By sheeptrack, or through Cottage lane

[26^{v}] [598–607]

jovial
⊗ And many a gust of ~~merry~~ song
Breaks from them as they wind along
W
Thile to the music from on high
The Echoes make a glad reply

Canto 4th
Thus they with freaks of proud delight
Beguile the remnant of the night.
⊗ And many a snatch &c see top of opposite page
But the sage Muse the~~ir~~ triumph heeds
o
N[?] farther than her story needs;
Nor will she servilely attend
The loitering journey to its end.
Blithe Spirits of her own impel,
M
The m use who scents the morning air,
To take of this transported pair
unreproved
A brief and ~~undisturbed~~ farewell
To quit the slow-pac'd Waggon's side
And wander down yon hawthorn dell
With murmuring Greta for her gude.

Benjamin among the stars
Beheld a dancing and a glancing
Such &
Canto fourth

—There doth she ken the awful form
Of Raven Crag black as a storm
Glimmering through the twilight pale!
mer
Gim~~er~~-crag
And, ~~opposite~~, his tall twin Brother
Each peering forth to greet the Other.
rambling
And ~~wandering~~ on through St John's Vale,
Along the smooth unpathway'd plain
By sheeptrack, or through Cottage Lane

The first four lines were entered after the page was started, and are therefore set apart.

The three lines and heading, in pencil, faintly visible at the middle of the page, are separately transcribed between the two verse paragraphs.

The circled X's in left margin are keyed to the draft in the top margin on 27^{r}.

And many a snatch of jovial song
Regales them as they travel along
While to the music from on high
The Echoes make a glad reply
But the sage Muse &c

Here 4 lines belong to opposite page 27

That is the worst of his employment
He's in the height of his enjoyment"

This explanation stilled the alarm
Cured the fore-boder like a charm
This, and the manner and the voice
Summon'd the Sailor to rejoice
His heart is up he fears no evil
From life or death from Man or Devil
He wheel'd, and making many stops
Brandish'd his crutch against the mountain tops
And while he talk'd of blows and scars
Benjamin among the stars
Beheld a dancing and a glancing
Such retreating and advancing
As, I ween, was never seen
In bloodiest battle since the days of Mars

Triumphant Pair, pursue your sport
~~Bath~~
radiance bold

What is yon that glitters bright
Like a cloud of Rainbow-light
Like—it is a huddle cloud
Or a rainbow-coloured shroud
Such as doth round Angels blaze
Travelling along heavenly ways
Slowly, slowly up the steep

[27^r]

And many a snatch of jovial song
Regales them as they wind along
While to the music from on high
The Echoes make a glad reply
But the sage Muse &c

These 4 lines belong to opposite page

590 *That is the worst of his employment*
591 *He's in the height of his enjoyment"*

592 *This explanation stilled the alarm*
593 *Cured the fore-boder like a charm*
594 *This, and the manner and the voice*
595 *Summon'd the Sailor to rejoice*
596 *His heart is up he fears no evil*
597 *From life or death from Man or Devil*
598 *He wheel'd, and making many stops*
599 *Brandish'd his crutch against the mountain-tops*
600 *And while he talk'd of blows and scars*
jamin
601 *Ben*^ ~~*beheld*~~ *among the stars*
Beheld— {—
602 ~~*Such*~~^*a dancing* { *and a glancing*
603 *Such retreating and advancing*
604 *As, I ween, was never seen*
605 *In bloodiest battle since the days of Mars*

End of 3^d Canto

But leave these [?to pursue their sport]
606 *Triumphant Pair! pursue your sport*
And [? ? ? ?]
607 ~~*But let us cut our Story short*~~

---

590 is the worst of *over* , [? ?], *is erased*
591 enjoyment."
592 still'd
598 *no comma*
599 Brandished
601–602 *redrafted on facing 23^v in pencil by WW*

among }
Benjamin [?] [?] } the Stars
Beheld a dancing & a glancing

601 beheld *del and* jamin *inserted above line by WW*
602 Such *del to* Beheld *by WW*
605 Mars.
606 *all but* sport *over erasure* Pair!] pair
But }
607 And } story short.

---

606 Revisions above and below the line are in pencil.

And many a snatch of jovial song
Regales them as they travel along
While to the music from on high
The Echoes make a glad reply.
~~The~~ But the savage Muse &c

Place 4 lines below to opposite page 27 ~~83~~

That is the worst of his employment
He's in the height of his enjoyment"

This explanation stilled the alarm
Cured the fore-boder like a charm
This, and the manner and the voice
Summon'd the Sailor to rejoice
His heart is up he fears no evil
From life or death from Man or Devil
He wheel'd, and making many stops
Brandish'd his crutch against the mountain tops
And while he talk'd of blows and scars
Ben~~[illegible]~~jamin among the stars
~~Saw~~ Beheld a dancing ~~and~~ a glancing
Such retreating and advancing
As, I ween, was never seen
In bloodiest battle since the days of Mars
~~[illegible]~~ [illegible]
Triumphant ~~[illegible]~~ pursue your sport
~~But let us cut our story short~~

radiance bold

What is yon that glitters bright
Like a Cloud of Rainbow-light
Like — it is a [illegible] cloud
Or a rainbow-coloured shroud
Such as doth round Angels blaze
Travelling along heavenly ways
Slowly, slowly up the steep

radiance bold
What is yon that glitters bright
Like a Cloud of Rainbow-light
Like—it is a purple cloud
Or a rainbow-coloured shroud
Such as doth round Angels blaze
Travelling along heavenly ways
Slowly, slowly up the steep

607/608 The added phrase is related to drafts for revision of this passage on 28[v].
609 cloud Rainbow-light?
610 Like—] Like!

Where no disturbance comes to intrude
Upon the pensive solitude,
Her unsuspecting eye, perchance,
With the rude Shepherd's favoured glance,
Beholds the Faeries in array,
Whose party-colour'd garments gay
The silent company betray;
Red, green, and blue; a moment's sight!
For Skiddaw-top with rosy light
Is touch'd and all the band take flight.
—Fly also Muse! and from the dell
Mount to the ridge of Nathdale Fell
Thence look thou forth o'er wood and lawn
Hoar with the frost-like dews of dawn
[illegible]
[illegible]
[illegible]
[illegible] Towers of Threlkeld hall,
Where at Blencathara's rugged feet
Sir Lancelot gave a safe retreat
To noble Clifford; from annoy
Concealed the persecuted Boy;
Well pleased in rustic garb to feed
His flock, and pipe on Shepherd's reed,

[27v] [606–607]

Where no disturbance comes to intrude
Upon the pensive solitude,
Her unsupecting eye, perchance,
With the rude Shepherd's favoured glance,
[?~~Descries~~]
Beholds the Faeries in array,
Whose party-colour'd garments gay
The silent company betray,
Red, green, and blue; a moments sight!
For Skiddaw-top with rosy light
Is touch'd and all the band take flight.
—Fly also Muse! and from the dell
Mount to the ridge of Nath-dale Fell
Thence look thou forth oer wood and lawn
see end of Mss.
Hoar with the frost-like dews of dawn
See end of Book
Across that foggy [?shadow] look
That [?closely hides] [?hides] its parent
~~Oer many a scatter'd Cottage small~~ brook
And see beyond that hamlet smal
The [?lurking]
Far as the Towers of Threlkeld hall,
The [?green marge]
Where at Blencathara's rugged feet
Sir Lancelot gave a safe retreat
To noble Clifford; from annoy
Concealed
~~Shrouded~~ the persecuted Boy;
Well pleas'd, in rustic garb, to feed
His
~~The~~ flock, and pipe on Shepherds reed,

28

Of Castrigg does the vapour creep
Neither melting nor dividing
Ever high and higher gliding
Glorious as at first it show'd
Winding with the winding road;
If you never saw or heard
Of such object take my word
That the Waggon the dull care
Of good Benjamin is there
And there though hidden by the gleam
Benjamin is with his Team
Faithful still whate'er betide
Whither follow'd as guide
And with him goes his Sailor friend
Now almost at their journey's end
And after their high-minded riot
Sickening into thoughtful quiet
As if the morning's happy hour
Had for them just a killing power

They are drooping, weak and dull
But the Horses stretch and pull
With encreasing vigour climb
Eager to repair lost time
Whether by their own desert
Knowing that there's cause for shame
They are labouring to avert
At least a little of the blame

[28r]

Of Castrigg does the vapour creep
Neither melting nor dividing
Ever high and higher gliding
Glorious as at first it show'd
Winding with the winding road:
If you never saw or heard
Of such object take my word
That the Waggon the dull care
Of good Benjamin is there
And there though hidden by the gleam
Benjamin is with his Team
Faithful still whate'er betide
Whether follower or guide
And with him goes his Sailor friend
Now almost at their journey's end
And after their high-minded riot
Sickening into thoughtful qui et
As if the morning's happy hour
Had for their joys a killing power

They are drooping, weak and dull
But the Horses stretch and pull
With encreasing vigour climb
Eager to repair lost time
Whether by their own desert
Knowing that there's cause for {*sh* ~~*b*~~*lame*}
They are labouring to avert
At least a little of the blame

---

626 *all but* betide *over erasure*
627 Follower . . . Guide
628 him *inserted with caret*
631 thoughtful *over erasure, del in pencil to* mutual *by WW; also* Mutual *in pencil in left margin*
633 power.
639–640 *no erasure*

---

631 Originally "[?] quiet."
639 Deletion by erasure.
640 Probably a copyist's error, with "blame" (l. 639) followed by l. 642, which had to be erased.

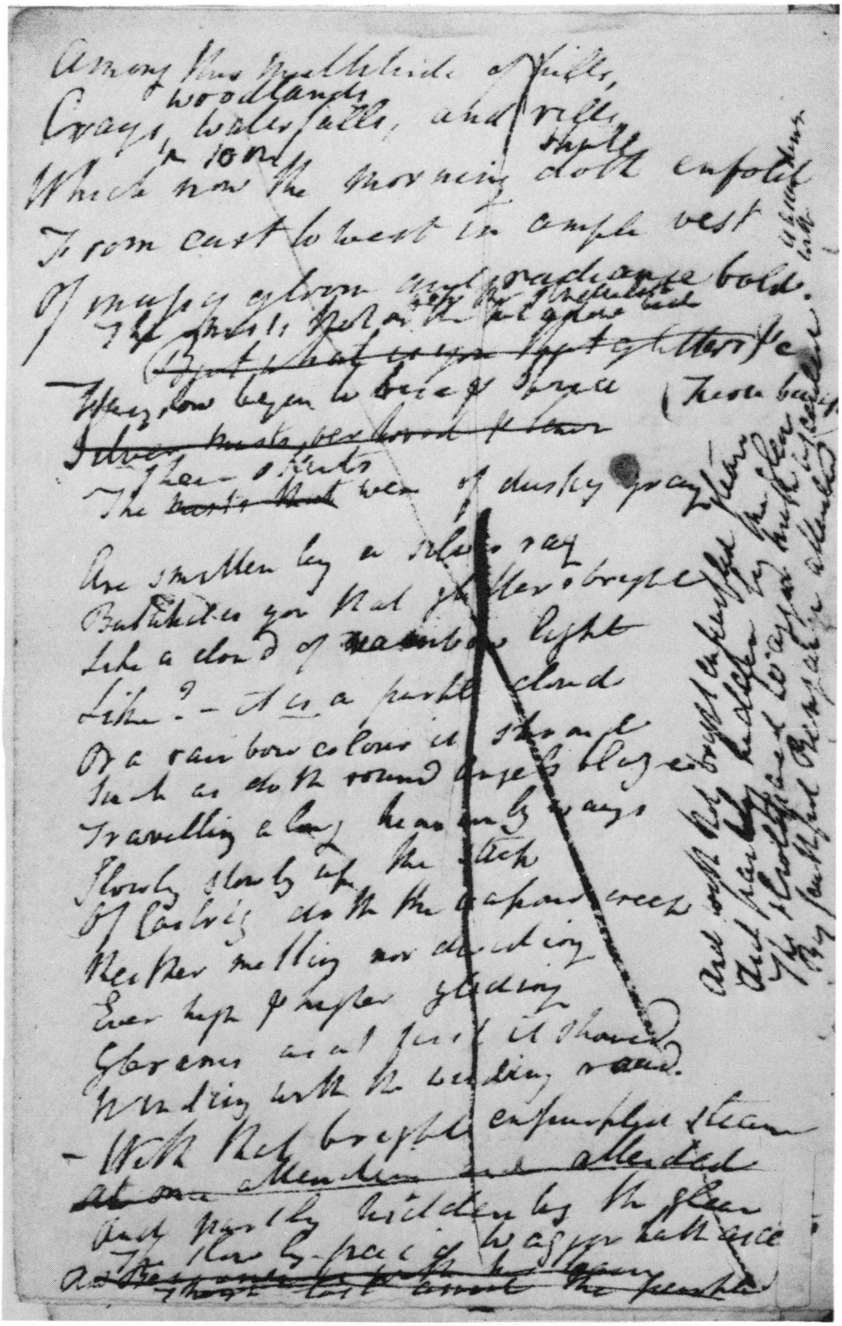

[28v]

[606–625]

woodlands
soon shall
oer the streamlets
r
Their skirts

Among this multitude of hills,
Crags,^waterfalls, and rills,
Which now the morning doth enfold
From east to west in ample vest
Of massy gloom and radiance bold.

The mists that on the meadows bed
~~But what is yon that glitters &c~~

Hung low begin to [?]}ise & spred (Turn back)
~~Silver mists oer Wood & Lawn~~
The ~~mists that~~ were of dusky gray
Are smitten by a silver ray
But what is yon that glitters bright
Like a cloud of rainbow light
Like?—it is a purple cloud
Or a rainbow colour'd shroud
Such as doth round Angels blaze
Travelling along heavenly ways
Slowly slowly up the steep
Of Castrig doth the vapour creep
Neither melting nor dividing
Ever high & higher gliding
Glorious as at first it showed
Winding with the winding road.
—With that bright enpurpled steam
~~At once attending and attended~~
And partly hidden by the gleam
The slowly-pac'd Waggon hath ascended
~~And Benjamin is with his team~~
~~Though lost amid the purple steam~~

And with that bright enpurpled steam
ly
And part}[?ing] hidden by the glea
The [?slwlo] pacd Waggon hath ascended
is ascending
with
By faithful Benjain attended

These drafts are developed on 35v and 36r. A small fold in the paper has obscured "ascended" and "steam" at the bottom of the facing photograph.

~~87~~ 29

Which full surely will alight
Upon his head whom in despite
Of all his faults they love the best
Whether for him they are distress'd
Or by length of fasting rous'd
Are impatient to be hous'd
Up against the hill they strain
Tugging at the iron chain
Tugging all with might and main
Last and foremost every Horse
To the utmost of his force
And the smoke and respiration
Rises like an exhalation
Which ~~the merry~~ with that bright merry Sun
Takes delight to play upon
Never surely old Apollo
He or other God as old
Of whom in story we are told
Who had a favourite to follow
Through a battle or elsewhere
Round the object of his care
In a time of peril threw
Veil of such celestial hue
Interpos'd so bright a screen
Him and his enemies between

Alas. what boots it, who can hide
When the malicious Fates are bent
On working out an ill intent
Can destiny be turn'd aside?

[29r]

Which full surely will alight
Upon his head whom in despite
Of all his faults they love the best
Whether for him they are distress'd
Or by length of fasting rous'd
Are impatient to be hous'd
Up against the hill they strain
Tugging at the iron chain
Tugging all with might and main
Last and foremost every Horse
To the utmost of his force
And the smoke and respiration
Rises like an exhalation
with slant ray the {S
Which ~~*the merry*~~, *merry* {*sun* ~~from the east~~
Takes delight to play upon
Never surely old Apollo
He or other God as old
Of whom in story we are told
{*d*
Who ha{*s a favourite to follow*
Through a battle or elsewhere
Round the object of his care
In a time of peril threw
Veil of such celestial hue
Interpos'd so bright a screen
Him and his enemies between

Alas! what boots it, who can hide
When the malicious Fates are bent
O{
I {*n working out an ill intent*
Can destiny be turn'd aside?

---

648 *no erasure*
651 foremost,
657 Never, surely,
667 *no comma*
669 On
670 turned

---

648 The erased word may have been "chain" from the line below.

Winding with the winding road
And with that bright empurpled steam
And partly hidden by the gleam
The slowpaced Waggon is ascending
With faithful Benjamin attending
Apparent now ~~amid~~ beside his team
Now lost amid the purple steam
And with him goes the

And Benjamin by lucky chance
Espies him
In a moment he is ready

[29v] [619–628; 694–695]

Winding with the winding road
And with that bright empurpled steam
And partly hidden by the gleam
The slow pac'd Waggon is ascending
With faithful Benjamin attending
beside
Apparent now ~~amid th~~ his team
Now lost amid the purple steam
And with him goes &c

And Benjamin by lucky chance
Espies him—
In a moment he is ready

And Benjamin by lucky chance
Espies him—
In a

The pencil lines underneath the last three lines in ink are placed after them in the transcription.

~~54~~ 30

No—sad progress of my Story
Benjamin! this outward glory
Cannot shield thee from thy Master
Who from Keswick has prick'd forth
Sour and surly as the north
And in fear of some disaster
Comes to give what help he may
Or to hear what thou canst say
If as needs he must forebode
Thou hast loitered on the road
He is waiting on the height
Of Castrigg, sees the vapour bright
Soon as he beheld he knew it
And the Waggon glimmering through it
Glad sight, and yet it rather hath
Stirr'd him up to livelier wrath
Which he stifles moody Man
With all the patience that he can
To the end that at your meeting
He may give thee decent greeting

There he is resolved to stop
Till the Waggon gains the top
But stop he cannot must advance
And Ben jamen ~~espies him~~ by luckey ~~good~~ chance.
Espies him ~~In a~~ moment he is ready
Self-collected poiz'd and steady
And to be the better seen

[30r]

No—sad progress of my Story
Benjamin! this outward glory
Cannot shield thee from thy Master
Who from Keswick has prick'd forth
Sour and surly as the north
And in fear of some disaster
Comes to give what help he may
Or to hear what thou canst say
If, as needs he must forebode
Thou hast loitered on the road
He is waiting on the height
Of Castrigg, sees the vapour bright
Soon as he beheld he knew it
And the Waggon glimmering through it
Glad sight, and yet it rather hath
Stirr'd him up to livelier wrath
Which he stifles moody Man
With all the patience that he can
To the end that at your meeting
He may give thee decent greeting

There he is resolved to stop
'Till the Waggon gains the top
But stop he cannot must advance
jamin lucky
And Ben ~~espies him~~ by ~~good~~ chance
Espies him—
In a moment he is ready
Self-collected, poiz'd and steady
And to be the better seen

---

675 North
678 w} t} hat
680/681 *vertical pencil line in right margin probably indicates no para*
682 *no comma*
685 *no comma*
691 *no para but WW has penciled* P *in margin*
692 *no apostrophe*
694 jamin *inserted above line* espies him *del* good *del to* lucky
695 Espies him—*inserted above line*
696 *no comma*

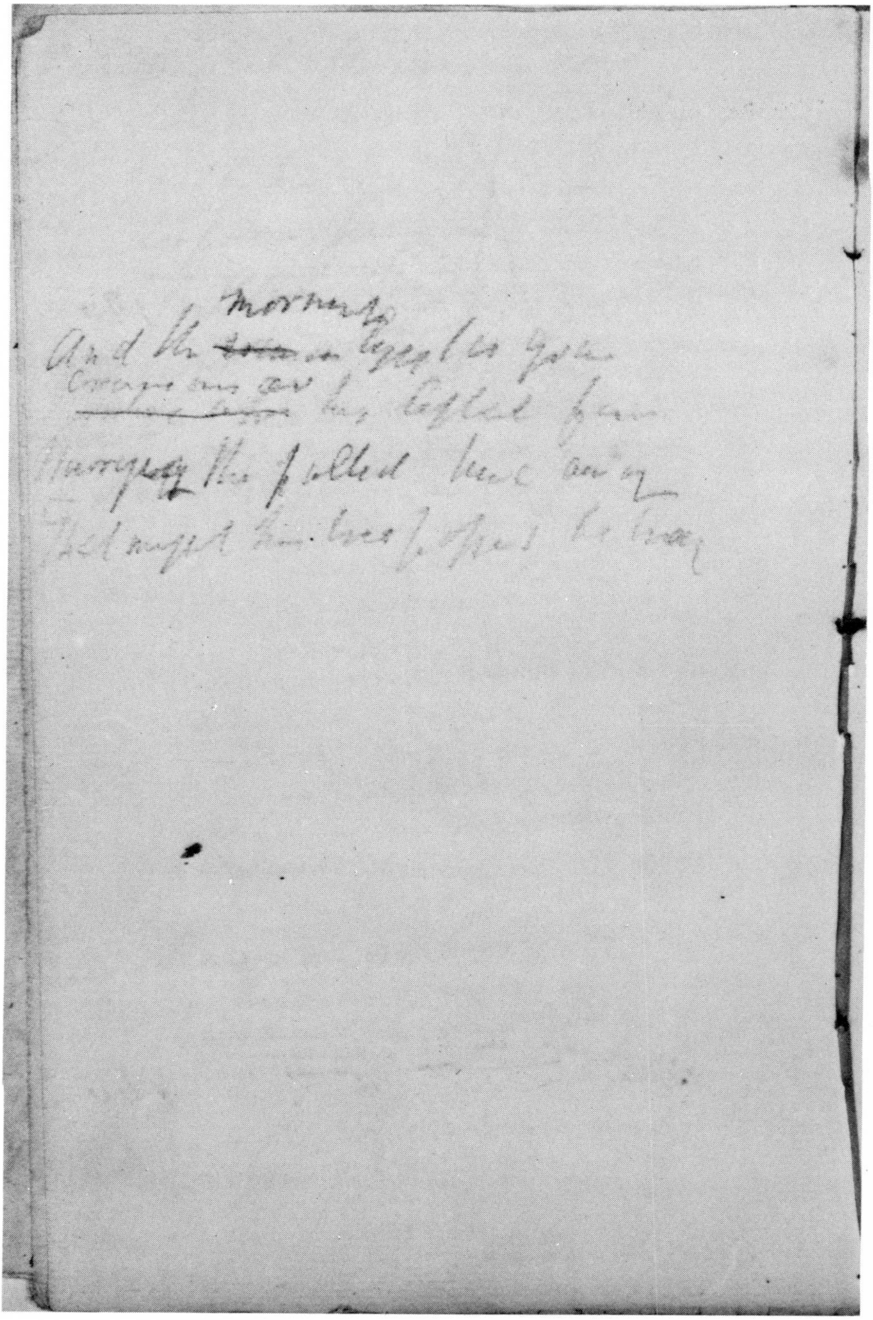

[30v] [703–706]

morning
And the ~~crimson~~ light in grace
Crimsons oer
~~Strikes upon~~ his lifted face
Hurrying the pallid hue away
That might his trespasses betray

All in pencil.

~~56~~ 31

Issues forth from out his shroud
From his close attending cloud
With careless air and open mien
Erect his port and firm his going
As yon Cock that now is crowing
And the morning light in grace
Strikes upon
~~Crimsons o'er~~ his lifted face
Hurrying the pallid hue away
~~And some little Mighty cause~~
That might his trespasses betray.
~~To steal the wandering from his eyes~~
But what can all avail to clear him
Or what need of explanation
Parley or interrogation
For the Master sees alas!
That unhappy Figure near him
Limping o'er the dewy grass
Where the road it fringes, sweet
Soft and cool to way-worn feet
And, O indignity! an Ass.
By his noble Mastiff's side
Tethered to the Waggon's tail
And the Ship in all her pride
Following after in full sail
Not to speak of Babe and Mother
Who contented with each other
And as snug as Birds in arbour
Find within a blessed harbour.

[31r]

698 *Issues forth from out his shroud*
699 *From his close attending cloud*
700 *With careless air and open mien*
701 *Erect his port and firm his going*
702 *As yon Cock that now is crowing*
703 *And the morning light in grace*
Strikes upon
704 ~~*Crimsons oer*~~ *his lifted face*
Hurrying the pallid hue away
705 ~~*And some sober thoughts arise*~~
That might his trespasses betray.
706 ~~*To steal the wandering from his eyes*~~
707 *But what can all avail to clear him*
708 *Or what need of explanation*
P
709 [?] *arley or interrogation*
710 *For the Master sees alas!*
711 *That unhappy Figure near him*
712 *Limping o'er the dewy grass*
713 *Where the road it fringes, sweet*
714 *Soft and cool to way-worn feet*
!
715 *And,* O *indignity* *an Ass* 160
716 *By his noble Mastiff's side*
717 *Tethered to the Waggon's tail*
718 *And the Ship in all her pride*
719 *Following after in full sail*
720 *Not to speak of Babe and Mother*
721 *Who contented with each other*
722 *And as snug as Birds in arbour*
723 *Find within a blessed harbour.*

---

shroud
698 cloud
cloud
699 shroud
Erect & firm
701 [?Firm] port, [?erect]
702 As *over erasure*
704 Crimsons o'er *del to* Strikes upon
705 *line del to* Hurrying the pallid hue away
is
706 h er *underwriting, probably a copyist's error, erased* *line del to* That might his trespasses betray
709 Parley
715 oh! *with*! *erased* indignity!
716 *no apostrophe*
e
717 th is
722 birds
723 *no period*

---

715 WW skipped a line in his count, probably because 140 on 30r was placed ambiguously between two lines. An erasure at the end of the line may have taken out an exclamation point.

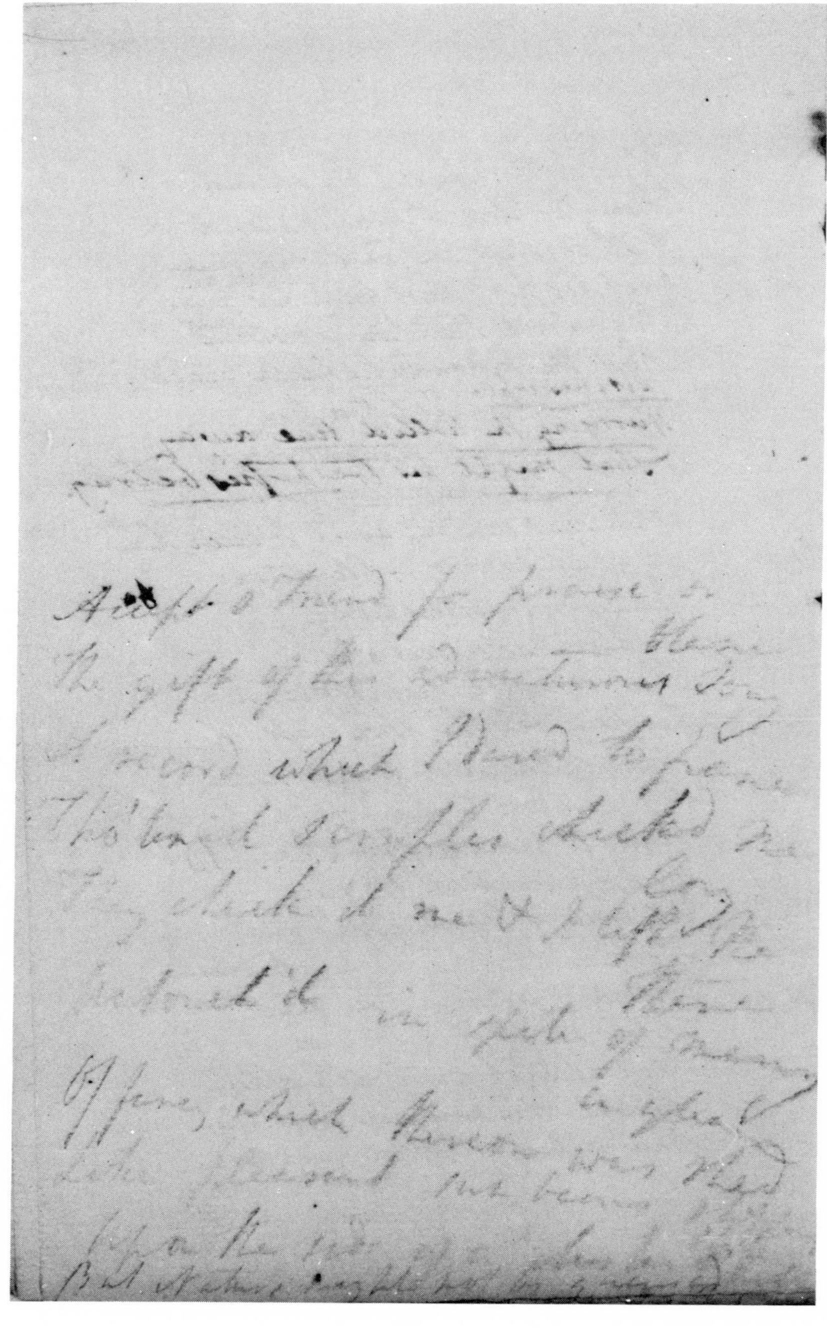

[31v] [752–755]

Accept O Friend for praise or
blame
The gift of this adventurous Song
A record which I dared to frame
Tho' timid scruples check'd me
long
They check'd me & I left the
theme
Untouch'd in spite of many
a gleam
Of fancy which thereon was shed
Like pleasant sun beams shifting
still
Upon the side of a distant hill
But Nature might not be gainsaid

All in pencil in DW's hand.

~~65~~ . 32

With eager eyes the Master pries
Looks in and out and through and through
Says nothing till at last he spies
A wound upon the Mastiff's head
A wound where plainly might be read
What feats an Ass's paw can do
But drop the rest and give the sense
The sum of all the consequence
'Twas briefly, that this aggravation
This complicated provocation
A hoard of grievances unseal'd
All past forgiveness it repeal'd
And thus, and through distemper'd blood
On both sides Benjamin the good
The patient and the tender hearted
Was from his Team and Waggon parted
When duty of that day was o'er
Laid down his Whip and serv'd no more
Nor could the Waggon's self survive
The want of Benjamin to drive
Each steep unmanageable hill
Call'd for his patience or his skill
It linger'd on a month or so
What came of it I do not know
But sure it is that through that night
And what the morning brought to light

[32r]

With eager eyes the Master pries
Looks in and out and through and through
Says nothing till at last he spies
A wound upon the Mastiff's head
A wound where plainly might be read
What feats an Ass's paw can do
But drop the rest and give the sense
The sum of all the consequence
'Twas briefly, that this aggravation
This complicated provocation
A hoard of grievances unseal'd
All past forgiveness it repeal'd
And thus, and through distemper'd blood
On both sides Benjamin the good
The patient and the tender-hearted
Was from his Team and Waggon parted
When duty of that day was o'er
Laid down his Whip and serv'd no more
Nor could the Waggon's self survive
The want of Benjamin to drive
Each steep unmanageable hill
Call'd for his patience or his skill
It linger'd on a month or so
What came of it I do not know
But sure it is that through that night
And what the morning brought to light

---

724 *false start* With eager *without paragraph indention, erased*

729 paw } [?hoof] } do.

732 aggrav } provoc } ation

733 provoca } aggrava } tion

737 *false start on facing 29v of all but final letter, erased*

746 Month

A record which I dared to frame
Though timid scruples check'd me long
They check'd me, and I left the theme
Untouch'd, in spite of many a gleam
Of fancy which thereon was shed
Like pleasant sunbeams shifting still
Upon the side of a distant hill.
But Nature might not be gainsaid
For what I have and what I miss &c

In him, while he was wont to ~~frame~~ trace
Our roads, through many a long year's space

[32v] [751–757]

A blank catastrophe [?said]
Th{'/a}adventure is ill framed for song
And [?e'en] you think so yet I {too/[?]}
[?Once] thought so oftentimes & long
said you
will [? ?] for
Thadventure is ill framed for song
[?] faith
Such Friend, your notice, and I too
[? ? ?]
[?~~Had~~] ~~thought~~ so oftentimes & long
And therefore long I left the theme
Untouch'd in spite of many a gleam
Of fancy that thereon was shed
~~gayly~~
Like {[?~~gayly~~] / [?~~shifting~~]} shifting sunbeams
spread
Like pleasant sunbeams shifting still
Upon the side of a distant hill
But Nature might not be gainsaid
For what I have and what I

⊗A record which I dared to frame
Though timid scruples check'd me long
They check'd me and I left the theme
spite of
Untouch'd, in ^ many a gleam
Of fancy which thereon was shed
Like pleasant sunbeams shifting still
Upon the side of a distant hill.
But Nature might not be gainsaid
For what I have and what I miss &c

trace
⊗In him, while he was wont to ~~pace~~
Our Roads, through many a long year's
space

The underlying pencil lines are all transcribed ahead of the two ink passages. The circled X's correspond to similar marks on 33r.

33

~~45~~

Two losses had we to sustain
We lost both Waggoner and Wain. 196
Accept O Friend for praise or blame
The gift of this adventurous song
~~[illegible]~~
~~Adventures [illegible] this song~~
~~Be free to think [illegible]~~
~~Have [illegible] many times and long~~
For ~~But what~~ I have and what I miss
I sing of these, it makes my bliss
Nor is it I who play the part
But a shy spirit in my heart
That comes and goes, will sometimes leap
From hiding-places ten years deep
Sometimes, as in the present case
Will shew a more familiar face
Returning like a Ghost unlaid
Until the debt I owe be paid
Forgive me then for I had been
On friendly terms with this Machine:
(+) ~~[illegible]~~
A Loving Almanack had we
We had a speaking Diary
Which in this uneventful Place
Gave ~~every day~~ to the days a mark and name
By which we knew ~~[illegible]~~ them as they came

[33r]

750 *Two losses had we to sustain*
751 *We lost both Waggoner and Wain.* 196

Accept O Friend! for praise or blame
The gift of this adventurous song
~~blank~~
752 ⊗ ~~*A poor Catastrophe say you*~~
753 ~~*Adventure never worth a song*~~
754 ~~*Be free to think so for I too*~~
755 ~~*Have thought so many times and long*~~
\+
For
756 ~~*But what I*~~ *have and what I miss*
757 *I sing of these, it makes my bliss*
758 *Nor is it I who play the part*
759 *But a shy spirit in my heart*
760 *That comes and goes, will sometimes leap*
761 *From hiding-places ten years deep*

752–755 *on facing 29v WW has penciled alternative drafts; the first five lines seem to have been written at the same time, the final five lines later*

Unfavorable theme for song
Dishear {tening / [?]} [?prophesy] for I too
Half thought so often times and long

But Nature [?might] not be constrained
That Conquest finally was gained

And therefore long I left the theme
Untouch'd in spite of many a {gl / dr}eam
Of Fancy that theron was shed
Like gayly shifting sunbeams spread
Upon a distant mountain's head

WW then entered in pen five lines in the space left between lines 751 and 752 on 30r and continued them with five more lines written over penciled draft on 29v

Accept O Friend for praise or blame
The gift of this adventurous song
A record which I dared to frame
Though timid scruples checked me long
They checked me and I left the theme
In spite of many a gleam
Of Fancy which thereon was shed
still
Like pleasant sunbeams shifting ~~still~~
Upon the side of a distant hill
But Nature might not be gainsaid

752 {poor / [?sad]} *with* blank *written above line by WW, then del*
756 {m / M}iss
757 *entered first by mistake at foot of 30r, then erased; entered again at top of 31r with no comma*

751/752 The circled X shows where the revision on 32v was to go.
756 The addition and the cross are in pencil, in DW's hand.

33

Two losses had we to sustain
We lost both Waggoner and Wain. 196
Accept O Friend for praise or blame
The gift of this adventurous song
~~A Catastrophe as you~~
~~Adventure ... song~~
~~Be free to think ...~~
~~Have thought ... times and long~~
For ~~But what~~ I have and what I miss
I sing of these, it makes my bliss
Nor is it I who play the part
But a shy spirit in my heart
That comes and goes, will sometimes leap
From hiding-places ten years deep
Sometimes, as in the present case
Will shew a more familiar face
Returning like a Ghost unlaid
Until the debt I owe be paid 20
Forgive me then for I had been
On friendly terms with this Machine.
(+) ~~... the Wain ...~~
Anxious ... had we
We had a speaking Diary
Which in this uneventful Place
Gave to the days a mark & name
By which we knew them as they came

Sometimes, as in the present case
Will shew a more familiar face
Returning like a Ghost unlaid
Until the debt I owe be paid
Forgive me then for I had been
⊗*On friendly terms with this Machine.*
~~*In him a Chieftain of his race*~~
A living Almanack had we
We had a speaking Diary
Which in this uneventful Place
to the days
Gave ~~*every day*~~ ^ *a mark and name*
them as they
By which we knew ~~*it when it*~~ *came*

---

767 *no period*
had}
769 we } we
771 place
772 every *del in pencil to* to each

---

765 WW's line number, which here as elsewhere incorporates revisions (on 32ᵛ), reflects the separation in the fourth canto between the main text and the lines to Charles Lamb.

Yes I, and all about me here
Through all the changes of the year
Had seen him through the mountains go
In pomp of mist or pomp of snow
Majestically huge and slow
Or with a milder grace adorning
The Landscape of a summer's morning
When Grasmere smooth'd her liquid plain
The moving image to detain
And mighty Fairfield with a chime
Of echoes to its march kept time
When little other business stirr'd
And little other sound was heard
In that delicious hour of balm
Stillness, solitude and calm
While yet the Valley is array'd
On this side with a sober shade
On that, is prodigally bright
Crag, lawn and wood with rosy light
But most of all thou lordly Wain
I wish to have thee here again
When windows flap and chimney roars
And all is dismal out of doors
And sitting by my fire I see
Eight sorry Carts, no less a train!
Unworthy Successors of thee

[34[r]]

Yes I, and all about me here
Through all the changes of the year
Had seen him through the mountains go
In pomp of mist or pomp of snow
Majestically huge and slow
Or with a milder grace adorning
The Landscape of a summer's morning
When Grasmere smooth'd her liquid plain
The moving image to detain
And mighty Fairfield with a chime
Of echoes to its march kept time
When little other business stirr'd
And lit*tle other sound was heard*
In that delicious hour of balm
Stillness, solitude and calm
While yet the Valley is array'd
On this side with a sober shade
On that, is prodigally bright
Crag, lawn and wood with rosy light
But most of all thou lordly Wain
I wish to have thee here again
When windows flap and chimney roars
And all is dismal out of doors
And sitting by my fire I see
Eight sorry Carts, no less a train!
Unworthy Successors of thee

---

776 *torn margin; last letter missing*
786 And little
788 *no comma*
792 *no comma*
794 the {e

35

Come straggling through the wind and rain
And oft as they pass slowly on
Beneath my window one by one
See perch'd upon the naked height
The summit of a cumb'rous freight
A single Traveller and there
Another, then perhaps a pair
The lame the sickly and the old
Men, Women heartless with the cold
And Babes in wet and starveling plight
Which once be weather as it might
Had still a nest within a nest
Thy shelter and their Mother's breast
Then most of all, then far the most
Do I regret what we have lost
Am grieved for that unhappy sin
Which robbed us of good Benjamin
And of his stately Charge which none
Could keep alive when he was gone

[35r]

Come straggling through the wind and rain
And oft as they pass slowly on
Beneath my window one by one
See perch'd upon the naked height
The summit of a cumb'rous freight 60
A single Traveller and there
Another, then perhaps a pair
The lame the sickly and the old
Men, Women heartless with the cold
And Babes in wet and starvling plight
Which once be weather as it might
Had still a nest within a nest
Thy shelter and their Mother's breast
Then most of all, then far the most
Do I regret what we have lost
Am grieved for that unhappy sin
Which robbed us of good Benjamin
And of his stately Charge which none
Could keep alive when he was gone 74

---

800 *torn margin; last two letters missing*

804 fr{ei / ieght}

817 {C / c} harge

818 gone. *In the left margin WW has written* 68 *and directly below it* 388; *in this early line tally,* 388 *is WW's total for both sections of the "Third Part," the* 320 *lines of the main section and the* 68 (*miscounted for 67*) *lines of the Epilogue.*

On facing 32v WW has written in pencil

[?5]	438
305	305
75	5
	7 7
	818

According to WW's line count, there are 438 lines in the combined first and second parts (he continues MW's line numbers, which extend to line 378 of the "Second Part," to the close of that part); 305 *is probably WW's count of* 320 *at the end of that section of the "Third Part" preceding the Epilogue, with ll. 532–533, 580, and 606–607 subtracted. Finally,* 75 *seems to refer to the Epilogue after the ten lines to Lamb were added (WW's line counts are often inaccurate, and the number should probably be 77).*

The numbers to the left seem to be WW's working figures; those to the right his final figures.

Hoar with the frost-like dews of dawn
Across ~~this~~ yon meadowy bottom look
Where close fogs hide their parent brook
And see, beyond that Hamlet small,
The ruined Towers of Threlkeld hall
Lurking in a double shade
By trees and lingering twilight made.
There at Blencathara's rugged feet
Sir Lancelot gave a safe retreat
To noble Clifford: from annoy
Concealed the persecuted Boy
Well pleased in rustic garb to feed
His flock and pipe on shepherds reed
Among this multitude of hills
Crags woodlands, waterfalls, & rills
Which soon the morning shall enfold
From east to west in ample vest
Of massy gloom & radiance bold

The mists, that oer the streamlets bed
Hung low, begin to rise and spread.
Even while I speak, their skirts of grey
Are smitten with a silver ray
But what see you that glitters bright
Like a flood of rainbow light

[35v] [606–609]

Hoar with the frost-like dews of dawn
yon
Across ~~that~~ meadowy bottom look
Where close fogs hide their parent brook
And see, beyond that Hamlet small,
The ruined Towers of Threlkeld hall
Lurking in a double shade
By trees and lingering twilight made.
{e
There at Bl{ancathara's rugged feet
o}
Sir Lancel}t gave a safe retreat
To noble Clifford: from annoy
Concealed the persecuted Boy
Well pleased in rustic garb to feed
His flock and pipe on shepherds reed
Among this multitude of hills
Crags woodlands waterfalls & rills
Which soon the morning shall enfold
From east to west in ample vest
Of massy gloom & radiance bold

The mists, that oer the streamlet's bed
Hung low, begin to rise and spread.
Ev}
Th}en while I speak, their skirts of grey
Are smitten with a silver ray.
—But what is yon that glitters bright
Like a cloud of rainbow light

These lines, which run over onto 36r, are a development of drafts on 28v.

36

Like? — it is a purple cloud
Or a rainbow-coloured shroud
Such as doth round Angels blaze
Travelling along heavenly ways
Slowly, slowly up the steep
Of Castrigg doth the Vapour creep
Neither melting nor dissolving
Ever high and higher gliding
Glorious as at first it showed
Winding with the winding road
And with that bright empurpled steam
And partly hidden by the gleam
The ~~slow-paced~~ stately Waggon is ascending
With faithful Benjamin attending
Apparent now beside his team
Now lost amid the purple gleam
And with him goes his Sailor Friend
By this time near their journey's end
And after their high minded riot
Sickening into thoughtful quiet
As if the morning's pleasant hour
Had for their joys a killing power

They ~~are~~ drooping [illegible] 80 [illegible]

[36^r] [610–634]

Like?—it is a purple cloud
Or a rainbow-coloured shroud
Such as doth round Angels blaze
Travelling along heavenly ways
Slowly, slowly up the steep
Of Castrigg doth the Vapour creep
Neither melting nor dividing
Ever high and higher gliding
Glorious as at first it showed
Winding with the winding road
And with that bright enpurpled steam
And partly hidden by the gleam
stately W
The ~~slow paced~~ w aggon is ascending
With faithful Benjamin attending
Apparent now beside his team
Now lost amid the purple gleam
F
And with him goes his Sailor friend
By this time near their journey's end
And after their high minded riot
Sickening into thoughtful quiet
As if the mornings pleasant hour
Had for their joys a killing power

They are drooping &c
turn back

See note to 35^v. The instruction at the end directs the copyist to 28^r, l. 634.

[36v] [118–122]

Good proof of this the country gaind
One day when Ye were vexd and straind
~~Com~~ }
~~Un~~ }~~pelled unworthy stripes to bear~~
Entrusted then to other's care ~~unworthy~~
~~stripes~~
~~Unworthy st~~
And forced unworthy stripes to bear[?d]

~~As God would [?would] have on that day~~
~~I c~~
~~I chanced to pass~~

~~Angered ye~~
~~Ye [?plunged~~ was it]
~~I saw you~~ piteously abusd
Plunged in anger and confused
I [?spake] my voice was like a charm
Ye took your ranks ~~the waggon~~
and with one mind
Pulled [?steadily] and safe from harm
Your burthen followed close[?] behind
Moved [?~~like~~] like a Vessel by the wind.

The drafts, together with the drafts on the inside back cover, precede the drafts on 6v.

37

301
171
190
196
74

932

[Inside back cover] [118–122]

We climb contented with our lot
Yet here upon this very spot

Here was it on this
~~Twas here upon~~ this [?~~ver rug~~] rugged spot
Which [?now] contented with our lot
We [?climb] that piteously abusd
[?In] plunged in anger & confused
~~I chanced to~~ it [?happen]
As
[?] } chance would have ~~on that~~ day
jeopardy
I [?saw] you in your jeperdy

I
~~Ye~~ } ~~spaak~~
A
~~One~~ word from me was like a charm
Your ranks were taken with one mind
And the huge burthen
~~The burthen follow'd~~ safe from harm,
Moved like a Vessel by the wind.

301
171
190
196
74
932

Faintly visible penciled line numbers at the foot of the page are modern. Gordon Wordsworth, in his brief account of this manuscript printed by T. J. Wise in *Two Lake Poets* (London, 1927), p. 23, refers to pp. 54, 70, and 71, and four times mentions the date 1819. The line numbers in ink represent WW's line counts of Cantos 1, 2, and 3, Canto 4 without the Epilogue, and the Epilogue.

Benjamin the Waggoner MS. 3 (1812)

Transcriptions with Selected Photographic Reproductions

Benjamin the Waggoner MS. 3 (1812)

Benjamin the Waggoner MS. 3 is contained in DC MS. 72, where it is followed by *Peter Bell* MS. 6, *Artegal and Elidure*, and an early draft of the opening lines of the "Vernal Ode." The leaves, in gatherings of 12, measure 11.5 by 18.5 centimeters; the paper is wove and is watermarked "Holland & Co / 1808." The notebook contains 95 leaves (6^{r} through 34^{v} are devoted to MS. 3), of which the first two and final two are pasted-down endpapers. It is professionally bound in marbled paper boards, with gilt-tooled red calf backstrip and outer corners. On the front board, John Carter has written: "Waggoner, / & / Peter Bell."

The fair-copy transcription of MS. 3 is in the hand of Sara Hutchinson, but most corrections were made by Mary Wordsworth. Unless otherwise noted, all in-line revisions over erasures appear to have been entered first above the line by Mary Wordsworth in pencil; the word to be altered was then erased, along with the pencil, and the in-line correction made in ink. In most cases, traces of pencil remain visible. Visible letters in erased words that are otherwise conjectural, shown in the footnotes, are given in boldface type. Footnotes also identify a distinctive form of deletion, made as a series of regular, short, curved strokes; these "caterpillar" deletions overscore several passages here, as in other manuscripts, at early stages of neat, careful revision. An example may be seen in the photograph on p. 319.

MS. 3 diverges much further from MS. 1 than does MS. 2. Therefore, while the transcription that follows has been keyed to the MS. 1 reading text by bracketed numbers in the right margin, the text has also been given line numbers of its own in the left margin. Unlike MS. 2, most of MS. 3 has not been complicated with messy drafts, and a full set of photographs seems unnecessary. The opening page (leaf 7^{r}), following this headnote, is offered primarily for illustration; but photographs of eight difficult pages—leaves 22^{v}, 23^{r}, 23^{v}, 28^{r}, 28^{v}, 29^{r}, 29^{v}, and 30^{r}—are presented following the text.

Benjamin the Waggoner

'Tis spent — this burning day of June,
Soft darkness o'er its latest gleams are stealing
~~Its latest gleams are going out,~~
The Night-hawk is singing his frog-like tune
~~While restlessly he wheels about~~
On restless pinions wheeling
That solitary Bird
Is all that can be heard
In silence deeper far, than that of deepest noon.

Now that the Children are a-bed
The ~~little~~ tiny Glow-worms nothing dread,
Rich prize as their bright lamps would be,
Forth they peep in company

MS. 3,7r

[7^{r}]

Benjamin the Waggoner

~~*[?and his] Waggon*~~

'Tis spent—this burning day of June,
Soft darkness oer its latest gleams are stealing
~~*Its latest gleams are going out*~~,
The Night-hawk is singing his frog-like tune [3]
~~*on restless pinions wheeling*~~
~~*While restlessly he wheels about*~~
On restless pinions wheeling
That solitary Bird
Is all that can be heard
In silence deeper far, than that of deepest noon.

Now that the Children are a-bed [8]
tiny
The ~~*little*~~‸*Glow-worms nothing dread,*
Rich prize as their bright lamps would be,
Forth they peep in company

[7^{v}]

And shine in quietness secure
On the mossy bank by the cottage door
As safe as on the loneliest moor.
In the sky and on the hill [13]
Every thing is hush'd and still;
The clouds shew here and there a spot [15]
Of a star that twinkles not.
The air as in a Lion's den
{*Is* *c*}
{ *[?C*]} *lose and hot, and now and then*
Comes a tired and sultry breeze
With a haunting and a panting [20]
Like the stifling of disease.
The mountains seem of wondrous height
And in the heavens there is a weight—

A photograph of this page is provided following the headnote. On the preceding recto, 6^{r}, SH wrote, then erased:

[?'Tis Benjamin]
The Waggoner

title Deletion by erasure.
2 Revision written first in ink, then erased and rewritten.
3/4 Deletion by erasure.
11 Erased was probably the reading of MS. 2: "come."

But the dews allay the heat,
And the silence makes it sweet. [25]

Hush! there is some one on the stir!
—'Tis Benjamin the Waggoner

[8r]

Who long hath trod this toilsome way
Companion of the night or day.
That far-off tinkling's drowsy chear,
Mix'd with a faint yet grating sound,
In a moment lost and found,
The Wain announces, by whose side
Along the banks of Rydale Mere
He paces on, a trusty Guide;
Listen! you can hardly hear.
—Hither he his course is bending [29]
Now he leaves the lower ground,
And up the craggy hill ascending,
Many a stop and stay he makes,
Many a breathing fit he takes. [35]
Steep the way and wearisome,
Yet all the while his whip is dumb.

The Horses have work'd with right good-will
And now have gained *the top of the hill;*

[8v]

He was patient,} *they were strong*,} [40]
And now they smoothly glide along,}
Gathering breath, and pleased to win
The praises of good Benjamin.
Heaven shield him and from ill defend,
For he is their never-failing *Friend,* [45]
From all mishap and every snare!
But why so early with this prayer?—
Is it for threatenings in the sky,
Or for some other danger nigh?
No, none is near him yet, though he [50]
Be one of much infirmity.
For at the bottom of the Brow

---

47 Erased was probably the reading of MS. 2: "are up at."
53 Erased was probably the reading of MS. 2: "Father and th**eir**."

Where once the Dove and Olive-bough
Offered a greeting of good Ale
To all who entered Grasmere Vale [55]
And call'd on him who must depart
To leave it with a jovial heart—

[9r]

There, where the Dove and Olive-bough
Once hung, a Poet harbours now
A simple water-drinking Bard [60]
Why need our ~~Traveller~~ Hero then (though frail
His best resolves) be on his guard?—
He marches by secure and bold
Yet while he thinks on times of old
It seems that all looks wondrous cold.
He shrugs his shoulders, shakes his head, [65]
And for the honest Folk within
It is a doubt with Benjamin
Whether they be alive or dead.

No danger's here, no none at all
Beyond his wish is He secure— [70]
But pass a mile and then for trial
Then for the pride of self-denial
If he resist that tempting door

[9v]

Which with such friendly voice will call; [74]
If he resist those casement panes
And that bright gleam which thence ~~will~~ fall
Upon his Leaders' bells and manes
Inviting him with chearful lure—
For still, though all be dark elsewhere
Some shining notice will be there,
Of open house and ready fare.
The place to Benjamin full well [78]
Is known and for as strong a spell
As used to be that sign of love [80]
And hope the Olive-bough and Dove.
He knows it to his cost, good Man!
Who does not know the famous Swan?

---

72 Erased was probably the reading of MS. 2: "**Thi**n**k**i**ng** on the."
91 The correction is the copyist's.

Uncouth although the object be
An image of perplexity
Yet not the less it is our boast
For it was painted by the Host

[10r]

His own conceit the figure plann'd
'Twas colour'd all by his own hand
And Ben with self-dissatisfaction
Could tell long tales of it's attraction.

Well! that is past—and in despite
Of open door and shining light.
And now good Benjamin essays
The long ascent of Dunmail-raise
And with his Team is gentle here
As when he clomb from Rydale Mere.
His whip they do not dread: his voice
They only hear it to rejoice.
Their efforts and their time they measure
To stand or go is at their pleasure
He knows that each will do his best
And while they strain and while they rest
He thus pursues his thoughts at leisure

[10v]

Now am I fairly safe tonight
And never was my heart more light
I've been a sinner I avow
But better times are coming now.
A sinner lately worse than ever
But God will bless a good endeavour
And to my soul's delight I find
The evil One is cast behind.
Yes, let my Master fume and fret
H
I} ere am *I with my Horses yet.*
~~*When I was gone he felt his lack*~~
~~*And was right glad to have me back*~~.
My jolly Team he finds that ye
Will work for nobody but me.
Let Simon flog and Arthur curse
He knows they only make bad worse.
Good proof of this the Country gain'd
One day when ye were vex'd and strain'd

---

127 Erased was probably the revised reading of MS. 2: "**I**'m here and."
128–129 Deleted first in pencil, then in ink by "caterpillar" strokes.

[11^r]

Entrusted then to other's care
And forc'd unworthy stripes to bear.
Here was it, on this rugged spot
Which now contented with our lot
We climb, that piteously abused
e
Ye plunged in anger and confus's}d
As chance would have it, passing by
I saw you in your jeopardy;
A word from me was like a charm
The ranks were taken with one mind
B
And your huge b}urthen safe from harm
Mov'd like a vessel in the wind.
—Yes, without me up hills so high
'Tis vain to strive for mastery
~~*Let force and flattery both be tried*~~
y
~~*This Monster at our heels must lie*~~ [120]
~~*Midway upon the bleak Fell-side*~~
~~*As dead as Bowder Stone; to stir*~~

[11^v]

~~*No more till Ben be Waggoner.*~~
tough
Then grieve not jolly Team! though [125]
Our road be sometimes steep and rough
But take your time, no more I ask
I know you're equal to your task—
And for us all I'll sing the praise
Of Rydal heights *& Dunmail raise* [130]
t e
And of hi} ir fellow *Banks and Braes*
For though full oft they make you strain
And halt for breath, and halt again
Yet to their sturdiness 'tis owing
still
That side by side we ~~thus~~^are going.

While Benjamin in earnest mood [134]
His meditations thus pursued, [135]

150–154 Deleted first in pencil, then in ink by "caterpillar" strokes.
160–161 The revisions, probably over the readings of MS. 2—"our good friend here" and "his brother"—were first entered above the lines in pencil.
165 Deletion in pencil.

153 The Bowder Stone in Borrowdale is often described in guides to the Lake District as the largest stone in England.

A storm which had been smother'd long
Was growing inwardly more strong
And in it's struggles to get free

[12ʳ]

Was busily employ'd as he.
The thunder had begun to growl
He heard not too intent of soul.
The air was now without a breath
He mark'd not that 'twas still as death.
But now some drops upon his head
Fell with the weight of drops of lead
He starts, and at the admonition
Takes a survey of his condition.
The road is black before his eyes
Glimmering faintly where it lies
Black is the sky, and every hill
Up to the sky is blacker still—
A huge and melancholy room
ver
Hung round and o[?'er h]} hung with gloom
Save that above a single height
Is to be seen a lurid light
Above Helm-crag, a streak half dead

[12ᵛ]

A burning of portentous red
by is seen
And ~~near~~ that ~~lurid~~ light^ full well
sage
Th' Astrologer ~~dread~~ Sydrophel
Where at his desk and book he sits
curious
Puzzling on high his ~~wicked~~^wits
+*He whose domain is held in common*
antient
With no one but the ~~central~~ Woman
b
Cowring h} eside her rifted cell
~~With [? ? ? ?] W[?oman]~~
As if intent on magic spell

---

189 The revision, probably over the reading of MS. 2—"a sullen"—was first entered above the line in pencil.
194 The cross is in pencil. Erased was probably the reading of MS. 2: "from Quarter in the North." WW's lines at the foot of the page, meant for insertion here to replace ll. 194–197, are in pencil.
195 Erased was probably the reading of MS. 2: "For mischief **looks** or sends **it forth**."
196 The original line probably read, as in MS. 2: "Sharing his wild domain in common."
197 The original line probably read, as in MS. 2: "With southern Neighbor the old Woman." Above the line WW wrote in pencil, erased, a revised version of the original line.

Dread
A Pair that spite of wind and weather ,
Still sit upon Helm-crag together !

The Astrologer was not unseen
By solitary Benjamin;
But total darkness came anon [170]
And he and every thing was gone.
batter'd
The rain rush'd down the road was
+ *As with the weight of billows shatter'd*

He
Whose ~~wild~~ domain is held in common
With no one but the central Woman
Cowering beside her rifted cell
As if intent on magic spell

[13r]

The Horses are dismay'd nor know
Whether they should stand or go [175]
And Benjamin is groping near them
Sees nothing and can scarcely hear them
He is astounded, wonder not
With such a charge in such a spot
Astounded in the mountain gap [180]
By peals of thunder clap on clap!
With now and then a dismal flash
And somewhere as it seems a crash
Among the rocks; with weight of rain [184]
And rattling motions long and slow
That to a dreary distance go
'Till breaking in upon the dying strain
A rending o'er his head begins the fray again.

Meanwhile uncertain what to do [190]
And oftentimes compell'd to halt

[13v]

The Horses cautiously pursue
Their way without mishap or fault

217 Erased was probably the reading of MS. 2: "sullen."

And now have reach'd that pile of stones
Heap'd over brave King Dunmail's bones,
He who had once supreme command
Last King of rocky Cumberland,
His bones and those of all his Power
Slain here in a disastrous hour.

        ile
    Wh{en passing through this narrow *strait*
(Stony and dark & desol ate)   *gate*
Benjamin can faintly hear
A voice that comes from some one near,
A female voice a voice of fear.
                    V
"Stop" says the v{oice "whoe'er you be
Stop, stop, good Friend, and pity me"—
And less in pity than in wonder
Amid the darkness and the thunder

[14r]

Good Benjamin with prompt command
Summons his Horses to a stand.

                ys
    "Now tell," sa{id he, "in honest deed
Who you are and what you need."
Careless of this adjuration
The Voice to move commiseration
Still prolong'd it's supplication—
"This storm that beats so furiously
This dreadful Place! Oh! pity me!"

    While this was said, with sobs between
            tears
And many ~~sobs~~, by One unseen
F
There came a flash a startling glare
And all Seat-Sandal was laid bare
'Tis a not a time for nice suggestion
And Benjamin without further question
Taking her for some way-worn Rover
Said, "mount and get you under cover."

---

231 The first overwriting is in pencil; erased beneath the second was probably the reading of MS. 2: "stony."

232 The original line probably read, as in MS. 2: "('Tis little wider than a **gate**)." MW's "gate" toward the margin is in pencil.

[14v]

Another Voice, in tone *as hoarse*
As a swoln brook with rugged *course,*
th
Cried out "Good Bro[?]}er why so fast?
I've had a glimpse of you,} {avast!
Let go, or since you must be civil,
Take her at once for good and evil."

"It is my Husband" softly said
The Woman, as if half afraid.
By this time she was snug within
Through help of honest Benjamin
She and her Babe, for Babe she had
No wonder then her heart was glad.
near
And now the same strong voice more
Said cordially, "my Friend, what chear?
Rough doings these! as God's my judge
The sky owes somebody a grudge
We've had in half an hour, or less,

[15r]

A twelvemonth's terror and distress
But Kate give thanks for this, and ride
C[?on]t[?ented]—
Contended— *and be pacified.*

Then Benjamin entreats the Man
Would mount too quickly as he can.
The Sailor, Sailor now no more
But such he had been heretofore
To courteous Benjamin replied
"Go you your way and mind not me
For I must have, whate'er betide,
My Ass and fifty things beside
Go, and I'll follow speedily."

The Waggon moves and with it's load
Descends along the sloping road
And to a little Tent hard by
Turns the Sailor instantly

---

257 Erased was probably the reading of MS. 2: "that was."
258 Erased was possibly the reading of MS. 2: "stony."
276 The overwriting misspells the penciled revision, above the line; erased was probably the reading of MS. 2: "In quiet."

[15v]

For when at closing-in of day
The Family had come that way
Green pasture and the soft warm air
Had tempted them to settle there—
Green is the grass for Beast to graze
Around the stones of Dunmail-raise.

The Sailor gathers up his Bed
Takes down the Canvas overhead
And after farewell to the Place—
A parting word though not of grace—
Pursues, with Ass and all his store,
The way the Waggon went before.

[16r]

If Wytheburn's lowly House of Prayer,
{D
As lowly as the lowliest {*dwelling,*
{*ey's*
Had, with it's Belfr{*y's humble stock,*
A little Pair that hang in air,
Been Mistress also of a Clock
(And one too not in crazy plight)
telling
Twelve strokes that Clock would have been
Under the brow of old Helvellyn
It's bead-roll of midnight
Then when the Hero of my Tale
Was passing by, and down the vale
(The vale now silent hush'd I ween
As if a storm had never been)

[16v]

Proceeding with an easy mind
And little thought of Him behind
Who, having used his utmost haste
Gain'd ground upon the Waggon fast
And now is almost at it's heels
And gives another lusty cheer

---

303 Revision in pencil.
304 Comma deleted by erasure.
320 The line appears to have been omitted by mistake; WW supplied it in pencil, which was erased as the line was recopied in ink by SH.

For spite of rumbling of the wheels
A welcome greeting he can hear— [290]
It is a fiddle in it's glee
Dinning from the {*Cherry Tree*.

Thence the sound, the light is there
As Benjamin is now aware
Who neither saw nor heard—no more [295]
Than if he had been deaf and blind
Till startled *by the Sailor's roar—*
He hears the sound and sees the light
And in a moment calls to mind
That 'tis the Village {*Merry-night*. [300]

[17^r]

Although before in no dejection
He gladdens at the recollection [302]
His heart with sudden joy is filled
His ears are by the music thrilled
His eyes take pleasure in the road
Glitteing before him bright and broad
And Benjamin is wet and cold
And there are reasons manifold
yearning
That make~~s~~ the good tow'rds which he's [305]
e
Look fairly like an honest ~~y~~{*arning*.

Nor has thought time to come and go
To vibrate between yes and no.
For cries the Sailor "glorious chance [309]
That blew us hither—dance Boys, dance{,
Rare luck for us!—my honest Soul
I'll treat thee with a friendly Bowl."
He draws him to the door "come in

---

324 Underlined first in pencil, then in ink.
327 The curved line was intended to transpose "saw" and "heard."
329 Erased was probably the reading of MS. 2: "rouz'd **up**." The dash may have been meant for the line above.
332 Underlined first in pencil, then in ink.
338 Obviously "Glittering" was intended.
342 The correction is the copyist's; deletion by erasure.
346 Alteration in pencil.

[17v]

Come, come" cries he to Benjamin
And Benjamin—ah! woe is me!
Gave the word, the Horses heard
And halted though reluctantly.

we
Blithe Souls and lightsome Hearts have
Feasting at the {*Cherry Tree*

This was the outside proclamation
This was the inside salutation;
What bustling jostling high and low
A universal overflow
What tankards foaming from the tap
What store of cakes in every lap.
What thumping stumping overhead
The thunder had not been more busy
With such a stir you would have said
This little Place may well be dizzy
'Tis who can dance with greatest vigour

[18r]

'Tis what can be more prompt and eager—
As if it heard the fiddle's call
The pewter clatters on the wall
The very bacon shews it's feeling
Swinging from the smoky ceiling

A steaming Bowl, a blazing Fire
What greater good can heart desire:
'Twere worth a wise man's while to try
The utmost anger of the sky;
And in the fury of its blast
To seek for thoughts of painful cast
If such be the amends at last.
Now should you think I judge amiss
The Cherry Tree shews proof of this—
For soon of all the happy there
Our Travellers are the happiest pair

---

355 Underlined first in pencil, then in ink.
365 Erased was probably a copyist's mistake, repeating the conclusion of l. 363: "busy." The correction is probably the copyist's.
375/376 In pencil.
376 Erased was probably the reading of MS. 2: "even."

All care with Benjamin is gone
A Cæsar past the Rubicon

[18v]

He thinks not of his long long strife.{—
The Sailor, Man by nature gay
Hath no resolves to throw away
{th
And he ha{*s now forgot his Wife*
Hath quite forgotten her, or may be
{*laid*
Deems her happier ~~where~~ {*she ~~lies~~*
{, {,
~~Knows the very truth~~{*~~I wis~~*{
Within that warm & peaceful bed
~~That she is better where she is~~
Under cover
Terror over
Sleeping by her sleeping Baby.

With Bowl in hand
(It may not stand)
Gladdest of all the gladsome band
Amid their own delight and fun
They hear when every dance is done
They hear when every fit is o'er
The fiddle's squeak that call to bliss
Ever followed by a kiss

[19r]

They envy not the happy lot
But enjoy their own the more.

jocund Travellers
While thus the~~y sit and thus they~~ fare
Up springs the Sailor from his chair
Limps (for I might have told before
That he was lame) across the floor
Is gone—returns and with a prize
With what? A Ship of lusty size
A Vessel following at his heels
{ *b*
Upon a frame that goes {[?]*y wheels*

387 Overwriting in pencil.
389 Added punctuation in pencil.
399 The line appears to have been omitted by mistake, then written in.
411 The correction is the copyist's.

A gallant stately Man of War
Sliding on a sliding car.
Surprize to all but most surprize
To Benjamin who rubs his eyes
Not knowing that he had befriended [380]
A Man so gloriously attended.

[19v]

"This" cries the Sailor "a third rate is
Stand back and you shall see her gratis;
This was the Flag Ship at the Nile,
The Vanguard; you may smirk and smile, [385]
But, pretty Maid, if you look near
You'll find you've much in little here;
A nobler Ship did never swim
And you shall see her in full trim;
I'll set, my Friends, to do you honour [390]
Set every inch of sail upon her."
So said so done; and masts, sails, yards
He names them all and interlards
His speech with uncouth terms of art
p
Accomplished in the Showman's art [395]
And then as from a sudden check
Cries out "'tis there, the Quarter-deck
On which brave Admiral Nelson stood
A sight that would have rouzed your
blood

[20r]

One eye he had which bright as ten [400]
Burnt like a fire among his men.
{at
Let this be Land and th{is be Sea
Here lay the French and thus came we—"

Hush'd was by this the fiddle's sound
The Dancers all were gathered round
And such the stillness of the house [406]
You might have heard a nibbling mouse
While borrowing helps where'er he may
The Sailor through the story runs
Of ships to ships and guns to guns [410]
And does his utmost to display

---

431 Revised first in pencil by WW, then in ink by SH.

The dismal conflict and the might
And terror of that wondrous night.
"A Bowl, a Bowl of double measure"
Cries Benjamin "a draught of length
To Nelson, England's pride and treasure

[20v]

Her bulwark, and her tower of strength!"
When Benjamin had seized the bowl
The Mastiff from beneath the Waggon,
Where he lay watchful as a Dragon,
Rattled his chain 'twas all in vain
For Benjamin, triumphant Soul!
He heard the monitory growl
Heard, and in opposition quaff'd
A deep, determined, desperate draf{u / ght
Nor did the battered Tar forget
Or flinch from what he deem'd his debt
Then like a Hero crown'd with laurel
Back to her place the Ship he led
Wheel'd her back in full apparel
And so, Flag flying at mast head{,
Re-yoked her to the Ass —} anon—
Cries Benjamin we must be gone
Thus after two hours hearty stay
Again behold them on their way{! / .

[21r]

Right gladly had the Horses stirr'd
When they the smack of greeting heard—
whip's loud notice
The ~~smack of greeting~~ from the door
The sign that they might move once more:
You think these doings must have bred
In them disheart'ning doubts and dread
No, not a Horse of all the eight
Although it be a moonless night
Fears either for himself or freight.

---

461 The correction is the copyist's.
468 Addition in pencil, probably by WW.

For this they know and know full well,
And this it pleases me to tell
That Benjamin with half his brain {s}
Is worth the best with all their pain {s}
And if they had a prayer to make

[21ᵛ]

The prayer would be that ^ {t} {he {y} *might take*
With him whatever comes in *course*
The better fortune or the worse
them
That no one else may have business near
And drunk or sober he should steer them {—
{— *So forth in dauntless mood they fare*
And with them goes the guardian Pair.

Now Heroes for the true commotion
And triumph
The triumph *of your late devotion—*
Can aught on earth impede delight
Still mounting to a higher height
And higher still a greedy flight!
Can any low-born care pursue her?
Can any mortal clog come to her?
It can—if chance a strong desire,
out *Such as did soon lay hold of these,*
Should rise and set the throat on fire

[22ʳ]

And nothing by to give {us / ~~it~~} *ease.*
What wish you with that spacious Mere

---

482 The line appears to have been omitted by mistake, then entered in pencil and overwritten by SH in ink.
483–484 The added letters appear to be SH's.
486 Caret in pencil.
487 Erased was probably a copyist's mistake: "**of**."
494 The revision above the line is in pencil; erased was probably the reading of MS. 2: "blessing."
501 The "out" and the line in margin, which was drawn first in pencil then in ink, marked deletion of ll. 500–555 for the 1819 printing.
503 The "t" of the underwriting was erased, and the "i" incorporated in the "u" of the overwriting.

And all it's weight of water near?
But wise are they and self-denial
Prefer to such a dangerous trial!

But Benjamin in his vexation [474]
Possesses inward consolation [475]
He knows his ground and hopes to find
A Spot with all things to his mind
An upright monumental Stone
With purest water trickling down
~~*A spring that doth but faintly bleed*~~
~~*And yet sufficient for their need*~~
A slender Spring yet kind to Man
A cordial true Samaritan
Close to the Highway pouring out [480]
It's offering from a chink or spout

[22v]

Whence all, howe'er tired {and / or} drooping,
May drink at leisure without stooping.

Cries Benjamin "where is it, where?
Voice it hath none but must be near."
—A star declining to the west [486]
It's image faintly had impress'd
Upon the smooth and dewy block
The surface of the upright rock
And he espies it by this sign [490]
And both there take a draught divine
Could happier more convenient place
Be given in fortune's utmost grace
They have a comfort in their madness
And feel that this is sober gladness. [495]

Ah! dearest Spot! dear Rock of Names
From which the pair thus slaked their flames
Ah! deem not this light strain unjust
To thee and to thy precious trust
That file which gentle, brave, and good, [500]
The near in friendship and in blood,
The hands of those I love the best

514–515 Deleted first in pencil, then in ink by "caterpillar" strokes.

534–551 See photographs of 22v and 23r at the end of the text. This "Rock of Names" passage was entered in the bottom margins of 22v and 23r in accordance with WW's instructions to his copyist, entered on MS. 2, 23r: "Checks I think the interest and stops the progress therefore better out, do as you think best, Let the lines however be put in the Margin."

Committed to thy faithful breast.
Their hands and mine dear Rock! when we,

[23^r]

Have rested by the side of thee.
No, long as I've a genial feeling
Or one that stands in need of healing
Thy power shall last—oh! thought of pain
That would impair it or profane!
Take all in kindness then as said
With a fond heart though playful head
And thou thy record duly keep
Long after we are laid asleep.

[23^r]

As winds by pausing do grow stronger
How fierce when they can pause no longer!
So back again the tempest rush'd
That for a moment had been hush'd
No notions have they not a thought
That is from joyless regions brought.
And while they coast the silent Lake
Their inspiration I partake
Share their empyreal spirits—yea
enraptur d ,
With their ~~exalted~~ vision see
The pomp of radiant imagery
O, fancy, what a jubilee!
~~*shifting*~~ ~~*clad in*~~
~~*The moving pictures, and the gleams*~~
What shifting pictures clad in gleams
Of colour bright as feverish dreams
~~*Commingling as they come and go*~~
;
~~*With rocks, clouds, stars, majestic*~~ *show*
~~*Repeated in the flood below,*~~
Earth, spangled sky, and lake serene

557–558 Erased were probably the readings of MS. 2:

Not one that is not highly w
Beside the spring and

561 Erased was probably the reading of revised MS. 2: "Behold the."
565 Semicolon added in pencil.
566 Erased was probably the reading of revised MS. 2: "lake."

[23^{v}]

Involved and restless all—a scene
x
mutual e[?]} altation
Pregnant with ~~rare imagination~~
Rich change and multiplied creation!

out ~~*Brave world for Poet's eye to see*~~
~~*O Fancy, what a jubilee!*~~
This sight to me the Muse imparts [522]
And then what kindness in their hearts
What tears of rapture, what vow-making
Profound entreaties and hand-shaking [525]
What solemn vacant interlacing
As if they'd fall asleep embracing.
Then in the turbulence of glee
And in the excess of amity
Says Benjamin "that Ass of thine [530]
He spoils thy sport and hinders mine
If he were tether'd to the Waggon
He'd drag as well what he is dragging [535]
And we, as Brother should with Brother
Might trudge it along side each other." [537]

Forthwith obedient to command,
The horses make a quiet stand;
And to the Waggon's skirts was tied [538]

[24^{r}]

The Creature by the Mastiff's side
(The Mastiff not well pleased to be [540]
So very near such company)

This new arrangement made the {*w* / [*?th*]*ain*}
Through the still night proceeds again;
No moon hath ris'n her light to lend,
But indistinctly may be kenn'd,
The {*Vanguard following close behind* [546]
Sails spread as if to catch the wind.

567–568 The "out" and the line in margin, which was drawn first in pencil, then in ink, marked deletion of ll. 567–568 for the 1819 printing.

583 A photograph of 23^{v} is provided at the end of the text. Erased was possibly "to Benjamin's**s**."

584 Erased was probably "**p**atient."

585 Erased was probably "**h**e."

589–592 Erased were possibly the readings of MS. 2:

And staggering to the Rock once more
They drank as deeply as before
Their burning faces they bedew'd
And thus their journey all renew'd

589 The revision in the final word is the copyist's.

593 Underlined first in pencil, then in ink.

"Thy Wife and Child are snug and warm
Thy Ship will travel without harm
I like" said Benjamin "her make and stature [550]
And this of mine this bulky Creature
Of which I have the steering, this,
Seen fairly, is not much amiss
We want your streamers, Friend, you know
But all together as we go [555]

[24ᵛ]

We make a kind of handsome show [556]
Among the hills from first to last,
We've weather'd many a furious blast
Hard passage forcing on, with head
Against the storm and canvas spread;
I hate a Boaster—but to Thee
Will say't who knows't both land and sea
The unluckiest Hulk that sails the brine
Is hardly worse beset than mine
When cross winds on her quarter beat
And fairly lifted ^ [*from*] *my feet*
I stagger onward—Heaven knows [*how,*] [?~~*not*~~]
But not so pleasantly as now!
Poor Pilot I—by {[*snows*] ~~*storms*~~} *confounded*
And many a foundrous pit surrounded.
Yet here we are by night and day
Grinding through rough and smooth our [*way*]
Through foul and fair our task fulfilling [559]

[25ʳ]

And long shall be so yet {,} *God willing!"* [560]

"Plague on the whooping and the howl,"
Replies the Tar, "of yon Screech owl"
But instantly began a fray
That called their thoughts another way,
The Mastiff, ill-conditioned carl [565]
What must he do but growl and snarl
Still more and more dissatisfied

613–614 The corrections are the copyist's; the possible "not" is deleted by erasure.
616 Underwriting erased.
617 Erased was possibly "By."
621 The added comma is in pencil.

With the meek comrade at his side
Till, not incensed though put to proof
The Ass uplifting a fore hoof [570]
Salutes the Mastiff on the head
And so were better manners bred
And all was calmed and quieted.

"Yon Screech Owl," says the Sailor turning
Back to his former cause of mourning, [575]

[25^v]

"Yon Owl! pray God that all be well
'Tis worse than any funeral bell
As sure as I've the gift of sight
We shall be meeting Ghosts to-night"
—Said Benjamin "this Whip shall lay
A Thousand if they cross our *way.*
I know that Wanton's noisy station
I know him and his occupation [581]
The jolly Bird hath learnt his cheer
On the banks of Windermere
Where a tribe of them make merry
Mocking the Man~~t~~ that keeps the Ferry [585]
Ha‸[l] looing from an open throat
Like Traveller[s] shouting for a Boat
The tricks he learnt at Windermere
This vagrant Owl is playing here
That is the worst of his employment [590]
He's in the heigth of his enjoyment."

[26^r]

This explanation still'd the alarm
Cured the foreboder like a charm
This, and the manner and the voice
Summon'd the Sailor to rejoice [595]
His heart is up he fears no evil
From life or death from *man or devil,*

642 Erased was probably the reading of revised MS. 2: "come this"; the revision was first entered in the left margin in pencil.
648 Deletion by erasure, correcting false start.
649 The caret is in pencil.
650 The revision is in pencil.
651 An erased pencil draft, illegible, in the left margin may be related to this line.
654 SH's underlining evidently indicates that the letters should be reversed.
660 The correction is the copyist's; the erasure may have mended an error in transcription, although it appears that the same words lay underneath.

He wheel'd and making many stops
-tops
Brandish'd his crutch against the mountain
And while he talked of blows and scars
Benjaming among the Stars

{—
Beheld { a dancing—and a glancing
Such retreating and advancing
As, I ween, was never seen
In bloodiest battle since the days of Mars.

[26v]

Thus they with freaks of proud delight
Beguile the remnant of the night
And many a snatch of jovial song
Regales them as they wind along
While to the music, from on high,
The Echoes make a glad reply.—
But the sage Muse the revel *heeds*
No~~r~~ farther than her Story needs
Nor will she servilely attend
The loitering journey to it's end.
Blithe spirits of her own impel
The Muse, who scents the morning air,
{ansported
To take of this tr{ ~~iumphant~~ Pair

[27r]

A brief and unreproved farwell
To quit the slow-paced Waggon's side
And wander down yon hawthorn dell
With murmuring Greta for her Guide
—There doth she ken the awful form
Of Raven-Crag black as a storm
Glimmering through the twilight pale!
{B
And Gimmer Crag his tall twin {brother
{O
Each peering forth to greet the {other.
And rambling on through St. John's Vale,
Along the smooth unpathway'd plain

---

664 Deletion by erasure.
675 Erased was probably the reading of revised MS. 2: "**ir** **t**rium**ph**."
681 Deletion by erasure.
689–690 The added capitals seem to be SH's.

693 *By sheep-track or through cottage lane,*
694 *Where no disturbance comes to intrude*
695 *Upon the pensive solitude*{., ~~,~~}
696 *Her unsuspecting eye, perchance,*
697 *With the rude Shepherd's favour'd glance*
698 *Beholds the Faeries in array,*
699 *Whose party-coloured garments gay*

[27[v]]

And yonder [?where] the vapours creep
A{And / long and}

700 *The silent company betray,*
701 *Red, green, and blue; a moment's sight!*
702 *For Skiddaw-top with rosy light*
703 *Is touched and all the band take flight.*
704 *—Fly also Muse! and from the dell*
705 *Mount to the ridge of Nathdale Fell*
706 *Thence look thou forth o'er wood and lawn*
707 *Hoar with the frost-like dews of dawn*
708 *Across yon me*{*a* / ~~*d*~~}*dowy bottom look*
709 *Where close fogs hide their parent brook*
710 *And see beyond that Hamlet small,*
711 *The ruined towers of Threlkeld Hall*
712 *Lurking in a double shade*
713 *By trees and lingering twilight made.*
[?Where]
714 | *There at Blencathara's rugged feet*
715 in | *Sir Lancelot gave a safe retreat*
716 | *To noble Clifford: from annoy*
717 | *Concealed the persecuted Boy*

[28[r]]

And yonder amid vapour & steam
Half [?hidden along] Castriggs side

718 | *Well pleased in rustic garb to feed*
719 | *His flock, and pipe on Shepherd's reed*

---

695 Comma erased.
699/700 Draft in pencil. All drafts here and below through ll. 752/753 seem to relate to revision of ll. 718–747.
708 Mistake in transcription erased; corrected by copyist.
714 The alternate reading is in pencil, as is the "in" in margin.
715 The "in" and the line in margin, which was drawn first in pencil, mark WW's decision to include ll. 714–724 in the 1819 printing after considering their rejection.
717/718 Draft in pencil.
718 See photograph of 28[r] at the end of the text.

720 *Among this multitude of hills*
721 *Crags, woodlands, waterfalls and rills*
722 *Which soon the morning shall enfold*
723 *From east to west in ample vest*
724 *Of massy gloom and radiance bold.*

[?Now smooth the] vapours & [?]
Scatter[?ing oercast] [? ? ?]

725 *The mists that o'er the streamlet's bed*
726 *Hung low, begin to rise and spread—* ×
~~*In their detachments, multiplied*~~
727 ~~*Even while I speak, their skirts of gray*~~
And lo! where smoothly urged they sweep
728 ~~*Are smitten with a silver ray.*~~
Along, up Castrigg's naked steep
729 *—But what is yon that glitters bright* [608]
Half
730 *Like a cloud of rainbow light*
731 *Like?—it is a purple cloud*
732 *Or a rainbow-coloured shroud*
733 *Such as doth round Angels blaze*
734 *Travelling along heavenly ways*

[?Volums{e/s}], ~~and~~

[28^v]

×*Even while I speak their skirts of grey*
Are smitten by a silver ray
And lo! up Castrigg's naked steep,
~~*silently*~~
~~*Which suddenly the vapours sweep,*~~
~~*The stately*~~

735 ~~*Slowly, slowly up the steep*~~
(Where smoothly urged the vapours sweep
736 ~~*Of Castrigg doth the vapour creep*~~ [615]
Along—and scatter and divide
737 ~~*Neither melting nor dividing*~~
Like fleecy clouds self multipied)
738 ~~*Ever high and higher gliding*~~
The mists that oer the streamlet's bed
739 ~~*Glorious as at first it showed*~~
~~*Hung low begin to rise and spread*~~
740 ~~*Winding with the winding road*~~ [619]
~~*And look, while smoothly urged they sweep*~~
741 ~~*And with that bright empurpled steam*~~
~~*Along, up Castrigg's naked steep*~~
742 ~~*And partly hidden by the gleam*~~

726/727–730 Revision in the autograph of SH. Deletions by "caterpillar" strokes.
729–734 The vertical line is in pencil, as is the final half line of draft.
735 See photograph of 28^v at the end of the text. Underneath the revisions in top margin are three illegible lines in WW's pencil, beginning: "[?I]/ A/ A/."
735–742 Deleted by "caterpillar" strokes, as is "the" in l. 746, below.
741/742 Beneath the revision WW penciled a line now illegible beginning "And."

hoary
~~*Half hidden by the glittering steam.*~~
743 *The stately Waggon is ascending*
744 *With faithful Benjamin attending*
745 *Apparent now beside his team*
a glittering steam
746 *Now lost amid ~~the purple gleam~~*
~~*For while I speak the vapours grey*~~
~~*Are smitten by the solar rays*~~
747 *And with him goes his Sailor Friend* [628]
748 *By this time near their journey's end*
749 *And after their high-minded riot* [630]
750 *Sickening into thoughtful quiet*
751 *And if the morning's pleasant hour*
752 *Had for their joys a killing power.*

And lo half [?hid in] glittering steam
The stately waggon [?slowly the]

[29r]

[? ?]
(Where smoothly urged the vapours sweep
Along [?and scatter] & divide
Like fleecy [?clouds] self multiplied)
[?streaming]

753 *They are drooping weak and dull*
754 *But the Horses stretch and pull* [635]
755 *With encreasing vigour climb*
756 *Eager to repair lost time*
757 *Whether by their own desert*
758 *Knowing that there's cause for shame*
759 *They are labouring to avert* [640]
760 *At least a* portion *of the blame*
761 *Which full surely will alight*
762 *Upon his head whom in despite*
763 *Of all his faults they love the best*
764 *Whether for him they are distress'd* [645]
765 *Or by length of fasting rouze'd*
766 *Are impatient to be house'd.*
767 *Up against the hill they strain*
768 *Tugging at the iron chain*
769 *Tugging all with might and main* [650]
770 *Last and foremost every horse*

752/753 WW's draft is in pencil. The three partly legible lines of draft at the top of 29r overwrite three illegible lines.

760 See photograph of 29r at the end of the text. Erased was probably the reading of MS. 2: "li**ttl**e."

770 Underneath the revisions in the bottom margin WW drafted four lines in pencil, now illegible; in the top margin of 29v WW drafted three or four more lines in pencil, also illegible.

To the utmost of his force.
And the smoke and respiration
~~*Blends*~~ *Rising like an exhalation*
moving shroud
Blends with the mist a ~~*purple cloud*~~
iss} ~~*cloud*~~ *}*
To form, an undis }olving shroud} cloud

[29ᵛ]

~~*To form a rainbow coloured shroud*~~
~~*Such as doth round Angels blaze*~~
~~*Travelling*~~
~~*An un*~~

771 ~~*To the utmost of his force*~~
~~Th~~}
~~T}hence that purple clouds formation~~
772 ~~*And the smoke and respiration*~~
{~~*That*~~} *ranging round*
~~*T{hat } involves them as they go*~~
~~*Where the road winds to and fro*~~
{~~*ing*~~
773 ~~*Rise{s like an exhalation*~~
[?Seems] a
774 *Which with slant ray the merry Sun*
775 *Takes delight to play upon.*
[?Blends] with each floating exhalation
776 *Never surely old Apollo,*
777 *He or other God as old,*
778 *Of whom in Story we are told,*
779 *Who had a Favorite to follow*
780 *Through a battle or elsewhere*
781 *Round the object of his care*
782 *In a time of peril threw*
783 *Veil of such celestial hue*
784 *Interpos'd so bright a screen*
785 *Him and his enemies between*

786 *Alas! what boots it, who can hide*
787 *When the malicious Fates are bent*

[?Glorious as] at [?first it showed]
Winding with the winding road.

[30ʳ]

[?Here is] a radiant cloud formation
For that smoke & [?respiration]

771/772 See photograph of 29ᵛ at the end of the text. WW's line is in pencil.
775/776 WW's line is in pencil.
787 Below and to the left of the line a word, perhaps "**Whe**nce," was written, probably by MW, then erased. WW's lines in the bottom margin are in pencil.

Blends with each floating exhalation
That

On working out an ill intent
Can destiny be turn'd aside?
No—sad progress of my Story
Benjamin! this outward glory
Cannot shield thee from thy Master
Who from Keswick has prick'd forth
Sour and surly as the north
And, in fear of some disaster,
Comes to give what help he may
Or to hear what thou canst say
If as needs he must forebode
Thou hast loitered on the road
Peace to his spirit anxious wight
~~*He sees the Waggon welcome sight*~~
[*?For*] *what he seeks is now in sight*
~~*Of Castrigg, sees the vapour light*~~
~~*Glimmering through the vapour bright*~~
~~*Soon as he beheld he knew it*~~
~~*And the Waggon glimmering through it*~~
Yet, trust the Muse,
~~*Glad sight, and yet*~~ ^ *it rather hath*
Stirr'd him up to livelier wrath

For what he seeks is
now in sight

[30^v]

Which he stifles moody Man
With all the patience that he can
To the end that at your meeting
He may give thee decent greeting

There he is resolved to stop
Till the Waggon gains the top
But stop he cannot must advance
Him Benjamin by lucky chance
{*and instantly is ready*
Espies {~~*him*—~~}

788 See photograph of 30^r at the end of the text. WW's lines in the top margin are in pencil.
799/800 The line is in the autograph of SH.
800 The line may originally have read as MS. 2: "He is waiting on the height."
800/801 The conclusion of the erased line was "**sight**."
804 The correction may have been drafted in pencil by WW, below the line.
805 WW's draft in the bottom margin is in pencil.
813 The revision was first entered above the line in pencil; erased was probably the reading of MS. 2: "And."
814 Deletion of "him—" from the original short line was by erasure.

~~In a moment he is ready~~ [695]
Self-collected, poised, and steady
And to be the better seen
Issues from his radiant shroud
From his close-attending cloud
With careless air and open mien [700]
Erect his port and firm his going
So struts yon Cock that now is crowing

[31ʳ]

And the morning light in grace [703]
Strikes upon his lifted face
Hurrying the pallid hue away
That might his trespasses betray.
But what can all avail to clear him [707]
Or what need of explanation,
Parley or interrogation
For the Master sees alas! [710]
That unhappy Figure near him
Limping o'er the dewy grass—
Where the road it fringes sweet
Soft and cool to way-worn feet—
And O indignity! an Ass [715]
By his noble Mastiff's side
{ *Tethered to the Waggon's tail*
{ *~~And the Ship in all her pride~~*
And the Ship in all her pride
Following after in full sail;
Not to speak of Babe and Mother [720]

[31ᵛ]

Who, contented with each other
like leafy
And ~~as~~ snug as} Birds in ^ arbour
—}

Find,} within,} a blessed harbour.

With eager eyes the Master pries
through
Looks in and out and through and [725]
Says nothing till at last he spies

---

818 Erased was probably the reading of MS. 2: "**orth** from out his."
822 Erased was probably the reading of MS. 2: "As"; the correction was first entered above line in pencil, with a penciled caret.
837 SH skipped a line, then inserted it over erasure.
842 Revisions first entered in pencil, the second overwritten in ink. Deletion by "caterpillar" strokes.
843 The added commas are in pencil.

A wound upon the Mastiff's head
A wound where plainly might he read
What feats an Ass's paw can do.
But drop the rest and give the sense
The sum of all the consequence.
'Twas, briefly, that this aggravation
This complicated provocation
A hoard of grievances unseal'd
All past forgiveness it repeal'd.
blood
And thus, and through distemper'd
On both sides, Benjamin the good,

[32ʳ]

The patient, and the tender-hearted
Was from his Team and Waggon parted
When duty of that day was o'er
Laid down his Whip and serv'd no more.
Nor could the Waggon's self survive
The want of Benjamin to drive
Each steep unmanageable hill
Call'd for his patience or his skill—
Guide after Guide
It linger'd on ~~a month or so~~
Successively the service tried
~~What came of it I do not know~~
In vain is
But sure it is that through th~~at~~ night,
And what the morning brought to light,
Two losses had we to sustain
We lost both Waggoner and Wain.

Accept, O Friend! for praise or blame
The gift of this adventurous Song
A record which I dared to frame

[32ᵛ]

Though timid scruples check'd me long
They check'd me and I left the theme
{in spite of many}
Untouch'd, {~~untouch'd in spite~~} a gleam
Of fancy which thereon was shed
Like pleasant sunbeams shifting still

---

868 The revision of "that" may be the copyist's.
877 Mistake in transcription caught before completion of line and erased; correction by copyist.

Upon the side of a distant hill.
But Nature might not be gainsaid
For what I have and what I miss
I sing of these, it makes my bliss
Nor is it I who play the part
But a shy Spirit in my heart
That comes and goes, will sometimes leap
From hiding-places ten years deep.
Sometimes, as in the present case
Will shew a more familiar face
Returning like a Ghost unlaid
Until the debt I owe be paid.
Forgive me then for I had been

[33r]

On friendly terms with this Machine.
In him, while he was wont to trace
space
Our Roads, through many a long year's
A living Almanack had we
We had a speaking Diary
That in this uneventful Place
Gave to the days a mark and name
By which we knew them when they came.
Yes, I, and all about me here
Through all the changes of the year
Had seen him through the mountains go
In pomp of mist or pomp of snow
Majestically huge and slow—
Or with a milder grace adorning
The Landscape of a summer's morning
When Grasmere smooth'd her liquid plain
The moving image to detain
And mighty Fairfield with a chime

[33v]

Of echoes, to his march kept time
When little other business stirred
And little other sound was heard
In that delicious hour of balm
Stillness, solitude, and calm
While yet the Valley is array'd
On this side with a sober shade

---

898 The revision was first entered above the line in pencil; erased was probably the reading of MS. 2: "Which."

On that is prodigally bright
Crag, lawn, and wood, with rosy light.—
But most of all, thou lordly Wain!
I wish to have thee here again
When windows flap and chimney roars
And all is dismal out of doors
And sitting by my fire I see
Eight sorry Carts, no less a train!
Unworthy Successors of thee
rain
Come straggling through the wind and
And oft as they pass slowly on

[34r]

Beneath my window, one by one
See perch'd upon the naked height
The summit of a cumbrous freight
A single Traveller, and there
Another, then perhaps a pair
The lame, the sickly, and the old,
Men, Women heartless with the cold,
And Babes in wet and starv~~e~~ling plight
Whi
[?*Had*] } *ch once, be weather as it might,*
Had still a nest within a nest
Thy shelter and their Mother's breast—
Then most of all then *far the most*
Do I regret what we have lost
Am grieved for that unhappy sin
Which robb'd us of good Benjamin
And of his stately Charge which none
Could keep alive when he was gone.

---

945 In the upper left corner of leaf 34v WW has written in pencil

64
292
142
169
280
———
947

As is often the case, WW's apparently careless counting makes it difficult to determine at what stage of the text's development the line tally was made. Basically, 64 seems to refer to the Epilogue (although it is also included in the fourth-part count), 292 to the first part without the deleted lines, 142 to the third part without the deleted lines, 169 to the second part (perhaps without line 320), and 280 to the fourth part, including all or almost all of the deleted lines.

Whence all, howe'er tried and drooping,
May drink at leisure without stooping.

Cries Benjamin "where is it, where?
Voice it hath none but must be near."
— A star declining to the west
Its image faintly had impress'd
Upon the smooth and dewy block
The surface of the upright rock
And he espies it by this sign
And both there take a drought divine
Could happier more convenient place
Be given in fortune's utmost grace
They have a comfort in their madness
And feel that this is sober gladness.

Ah! dearest Spot! dear Rock of Names
From which the pair thus slaked their flames
Ah! deem not this light strain unjust
To thee and to thy precious trust
That file which gentle, brave, and good,
The near in friendship and in blood,
The hands of those I love the best
Committed to thy faithful breast.
Their hands and mine dear Rock! when we,

MS. 3, 22[v]

As winds by pausing do grow stronger
How fierce when they can pause no longer!
So back again the tempest rush'd
That for a moment had been hush'd
No notions have they not a thought
That is from joyless regions brought.
~~And~~ while they coast the silent Lake
Their inspiration I partake
Share their empyreal spirits—yea
With their ~~[illegible]~~ enraptured vision see,
~~The pomp of radiant imagery~~
O, Fancy what a jubilee!
~~to see & [illegible]~~ ~~clad in~~
~~The [illegible] pictures, and the gleams~~
What shifting pictures clad in gleams
Of colour bright as feverish dreams.
~~Commingling as they come and go~~
~~With rocks, clouds, stars, majestic show~~
~~Repeated in the [illegible]~~,
Earth, spangled sky, and lake serene

Have rested by the side of thee.
No, long as I've a genial feeling
Or one that stands in need of healing
Thy power shall last— oh! thought of pain
That would impair it or profane!
Take all in kindness, then as said
With a fond heart though playful head
And thou thy record duly keep
Long after we are laid asleep.

MS. 3, 23r

Involved and restless all — a scene
Pregnant with rare imagination mutual exaltation
Rich change and multiplied creation!
Brave world for Poets eye to see
out O Fancy, what a jubilee!

This sight to me the Muse imparts
And then what kindness in their hearts
What tears of rapture, what vow-making
Profound entreaties and hand-shaking
What solemn vacant interlacing
As if they'd fall asleep embracing
Then in the turbulence of glee
And in the excess of amity
Says Benjamin "that Ass of thine
He spoils thy sport and hinders mine
If he were tether'd to the Waggon
He'd drag as well what he is dragging
And we, as Brother should with Brother
Might trudge it along side each other."

Forthwith, obedient to command,
The horses make a quiet stand;
And to the Waggon's skirts was tied

MS. 3, 23^{v}

Well pleased in rustic garb to feed
His flock, and pipe on shepherd's reed
Among this multitude of hills
Crags, woodlands, waterfalls and rills
Which soon the morning shall enfold
From east to west in ample vest
Of massy gloom and radiance bold.

The mists that o'er the streamlets bed
Hung low, begin to rise and spread
And lo! where smoothly urged they sweep
Along up Dunmail's naked steep
But what is yon that glitters bright
Like a cloud of rainbow light
Like?—it is a purple cloud
Or a rainbow-coloured shroud
Such as doth round Angels blaze
Travelling along heavenly ways

MS. 3, 28r

\+ Even while I speak their skirts of grey
Are smitten by a silver ray
And lo! up Castrigg's naked steep,
the stately
Strains hardly up the steep
(Where smoothly urged the vapours sweep
Along and scatter and divide
Like fleecy clouds self multiplied)
The stately Waggon is ascending
With faithful Benjamin attending
Apparent now beside his team
Now lost amid the glittering steam
And with him goes his Sailor Friend
By this time near their journey's end
And after their high-minded riot
Sickening into thoughtful quiet
As if the morning's pleasant hour
Had for their joys a killing power.

MS. 3, 28v

They are drooping weak and dull
But the Horses stretch and pull
With encreasing vigour climb
Eager to repair lost time
Whether by their own desert
Knowing that there's cause for shame
They are labouring to avert
At least a portion of the blame
Which full surely will alight
Upon his head whom in despite
Of all his faults they love the best
Whether for him they are distress'd
Or by length of fasting rouz'd
Are impatient to be housed.
Up against the hill they strain
Tugging at the iron chain
Tugging all with might and main
Last and foremost every horse
To the utmost of his force
And the smoke and respiration
~~Blends~~ Rising like an exhalation
Blends with the mist a ~~[illegible] [illegible]~~ moving shroud
To form an undissolving ~~[illegible]~~ cloud

MS. 3, 29r

Scene
Which with slant ray the merry Sun
Takes delight to play upon.
Never surely old Apollo
He or other God as old,
Of whom in Story we are told,
Who had a Favorite to follow
Through a battle or elsewhere
Round the object of his care
In a time of peril threw
Veil of such celestial hue
Interpos'd so bright a screen
Him and his enemies between.

Alas! what boots it, who can hide
When the malicious Fates are bent

MS. 3, 29[v]

On working out an ill intent
Can destiny be turn'd aside?
No—sad progress of my Story
Benjamin! this outward glory
Cannot shield thee from thy Master
Who from Keswick has prick'd forth
Sour and surly as the north
And, in fear of some disaster
Comes to give what help he may
Or to hear what thou canst say
If as needs he must forebode
Thou hast loitered on the road
Peace to his spirit anxious wight
The [illegible] thing [illegible] seeks is now in sight
[illegible]
[illegible]
[illegible]
[illegible]
[illegible]
Yet trust the Muse,
[illegible] it rather hath
Stirr'd him up to livelier wrath

MS. 3, 30r

Manuscripts of 1836

Transcriptions

Never golden haired Apollo
Nor blue eyed Pallas nor the Idalian Queen
When each was Pleased a favorite chief to follow
Through accidents of peace or war
In a perilous moment threw
Around the object of their care
So veil by [illegible]
Interposed to baffle a screen
Him & his enemies between. —

After the line (page) —
Can any mortal clay come to her,
Stood the words in the MSS
[illegible] and then followed [illegible]
which the [illegible] which has been suppressed
Part of the suppressed verses shall here be given
[illegible] a gratification of private
feeling which the well-disposed reader will
find no difficulty in excusing

"It came —" [illegible]
But Benjamin in his vexation
Possesses inward consolation
He [illegible]
[illegible] to him [illegible]

[1r] [1819 ll. 683–692]

Never golden haired Apollo
Nor blue eyed Pallas nor the Idalian Queen
When each [?was] *Pleased a favorite chief to follow*
Through accidents of peace or war,
In a perilous moment threw
Ar
R }*ound the objects of* ~~[?their]~~ *care* (*celestial* above ~~[?their]~~; ~~s~~ of objects struck)
A
[?In]} *veil so* ~~bright~~ *to mortal view* (*rich* above ~~bright~~)
bri[?ght]
Interposed so ~~bright~~ *a screen—*
Him & his enemies between!—

["Rock of Names" Addition, ll. 19–29]

After the line (page) [?~~can~~]
Can any mortal clog come to her,
Stood the words
in the Mss
"It can— —and then followed an incident
h
Which ~~the a was~~ which {was been suppressed.
Part of the suppressed verses shall here be given
~~for a [?] by to~~ a gratification of private
feeling which the well-disposed reader will
find no difficulty in excusing
"It can— — " " "
But Benjamin in his vexation
Possesses inward consolation.
He knows his ground & hopes to find
A spot with all things to his mind

The upper passage is in pencil in the hand of Edward Quillinan, the lower in ink in WW's hand. The Idalian Queen was Aphrodite, the Roman Venus; the town of Idalium in Cyprus was sacred to her.

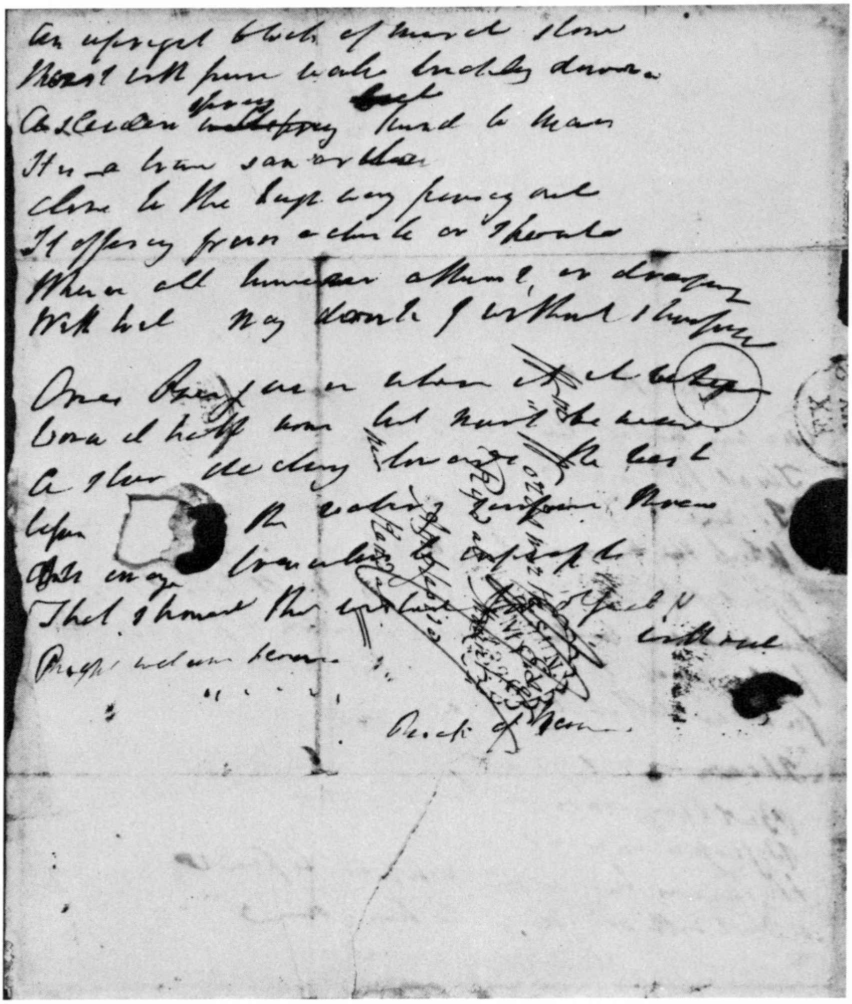

[1v] ["Rock of Names" Addition, ll. 30–44]

An upright block of mural stone
{Moist
{[?] with pure water trickling down—
spring but
A slender ~~wellspring~~ kind to Man
—}
It is {a true samaritan
Close to the highway pouring out
It offering from a chink or spout
Whence all howeer athirst, or drooping
With toil may drink & without stooping

Cries Benjamin where is it where
Voice it hath none but must be near.
A star declining towards the West
Upon the watery surface threw
{Its
{And image tremulously impresst
That showed the wished for object &
withdrew
Right welcome service
" " " "

Rock of Names

Wm Wordsworth, Esq
Rydal Mount,
Ambleside
near Kendal.

In ink, in the hand of WW.

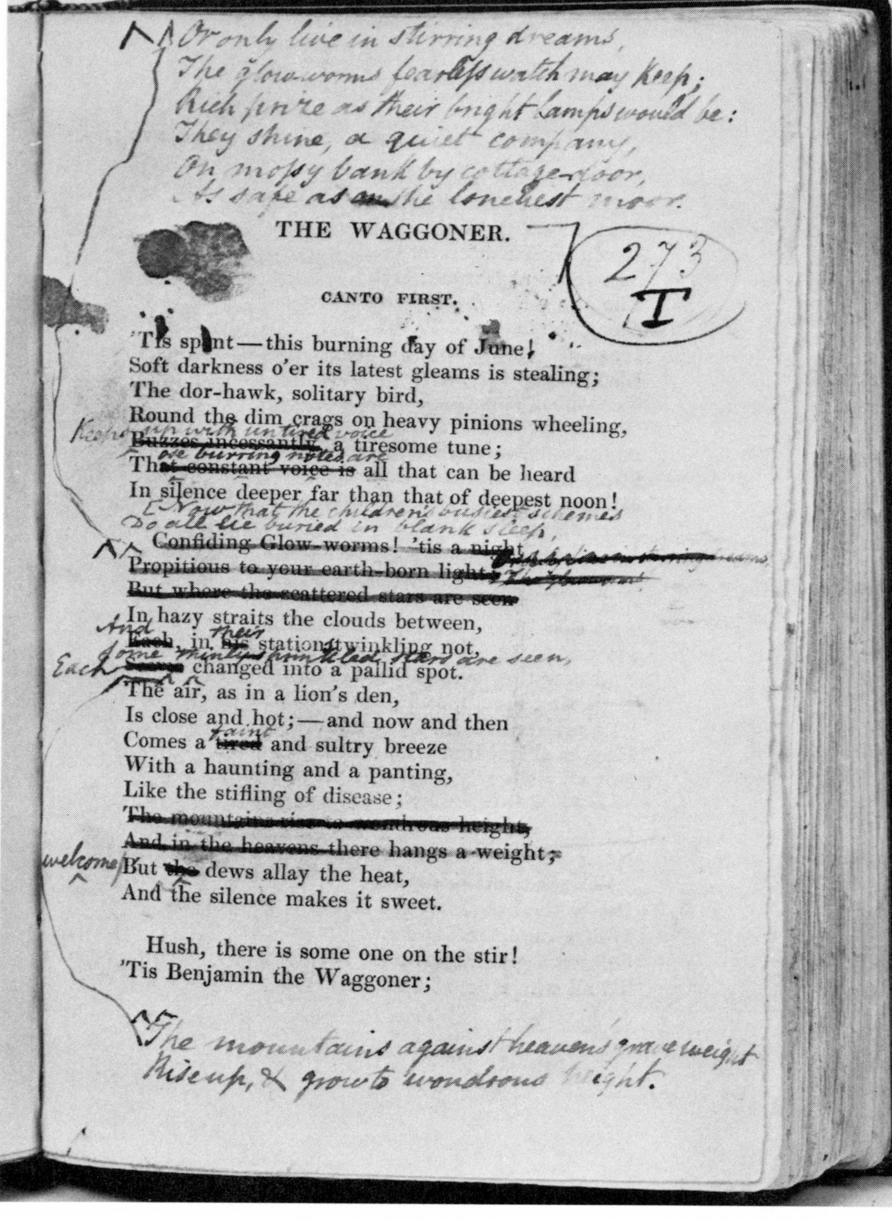

Or only live in stirring dreams,
The glow-worms fearless watch may keep;
Rich prize as their bright lamps would be:
They shine, a quiet company,
On mossy bank by cottage-door,
As safe as ~~on~~ the loneliest moor.

THE WAGGONER.

273
T

CANTO FIRST.

'Tis spent—this burning day of June!
Soft darkness o'er its latest gleams is stealing;
The dor-hawk, solitary bird,
Round the dim crags on heavy pinions wheeling,
Keeps up with untired voice
~~Buzzes incessantly,~~ a tiresome tune;
ose burring notes are
Th~~at constant voice is~~ all that can be heard
In silence deeper far than that of deepest noon!
Now that the children's busiest schemes
Do all lie buried in blank sleep,
~~Confiding Glow-worms! 'tis a night~~
~~Propitious to your earth-born light;~~
~~But where the scattered stars are seen~~
In hazy straits the clouds between,
And their
~~Each,~~ in ~~his~~ station twinkling not,
Each Some thinly-sprinkled stars are seen,
~~Seems~~ changed into a pallid spot.
The air, as in a lion's den,
Is close and hot;—and now and then
Comes a ~~tired~~ faint and sultry breeze
With a haunting and a panting,
Like the stifling of disease;
~~The mountains rise to wondrous height,~~
~~And in the heavens there hangs a weight;~~
But ~~the~~ welcome dews allay the heat,
And the silence makes it sweet.

Hush, there is some one on the stir!
'Tis Benjamin the Waggoner;

The mountains against heavens grave weight
Rise up, & grow to wondrous height.

[p. 191] [1819 ll. 1–23]

^^*Or only live in stirring dreams,*
The glow-worms fearless watch may keep;
Rich prize as their bright lamps would be:
They shine, a quiet company,
On mossy bank by cottage-door,
As safe as on the loneliest moor.

THE WAGGONER.

CANTO FIRST.

'Tis spent—this burning day of June!
Soft darkness o'er its latest gleams is stealing;
The dor-hawk, solitary bird,
Round the dim crags on heavy pinions wheeling,
Keeps up with untired voice
^**~~Buzzes incessantly,~~ a tiresome tune;**
ose burring notes are
Th~~at,~~^ ~~constant voice is~~ all that can be heard
In silence d^eeper^ far than that of deepest noon!
[Now that the children's busiest schemes
Do all lie buried in blank sleep,
^^**~~Confiding Glow-worms! 'tis a night~~**
or only live in stirring dreams,
~~Propitious to your earth-born light;~~ ~~*The glowworms*~~
~~But where the scattered stars are seen~~
In hazy straits the clouds between,
And *their*
~~Each,~~ in ~~his~~ station {*s* twinkling not,
Some thinly-sprinkled stars are seen,
Each **~~Seems,~~^changed into a pallid spot.**
Th^e air, as in a lion's den,
Is close and hot;—and now and then
faint
Comes a ~~tired~~ and sultry breeze
With a haunting and a panting,
Like the stifling of disease;
~~The mountains rise to wondrous height,~~
~~And in the heavens there hangs a weight;~~
welc^ome| **But^ ~~th^e~~ dews allay the heat,**
And the silence makes it sweet.
Hush, there is someone on the stir!
'Tis Benjamin the Waggoner;

^^*The mountains against heaven's grave weight*
Rise up, & grow to wondrous height.

The hand of the revisions is EQ's.

Cried out, "Good brother, why so fast?
I've had a glimpse of you — *avast!*
Or, since it suits you to be civil,
Take her at once — for good and evil!"

"It is my Husband," softly said
The Woman, as if half afraid:
By this time she was snug within,
Through help of honest Benjamin;
She and her Babe, which to her breast
With thankfulness the Mother pressed;
And now the same strong voice more near
Said cordially, "My Friend, what cheer?
Rough doings these! as God's my judge,
The sky owes somebody a grudge!
We've had in half an hour or less
A twelvemonth's terror and distress!"

Then Benjamin entreats the Man
Would mount, too, quickly as he can:
The Sailor, Sailor now no more,
But such he had been heretofore,
To courteous Benjamin replied,
"Go you your way, and mind not me;
For I must have, whate'er betide,
My Ass and fifty things beside, —
Go, and I'll follow speedily!"

The Waggon moves — and with its load
Descends along the sloping road;
And to ~~a little tent hard by~~ his rough nightly domicile,
Turned the Sailor instantly;
For when, ere closing-in of day,
The Family had come that way,
With caution placed and built with skill,
A little mockery of a tent,
Which in its sheltering nook hard by
Had weathered the fierce element—

[p. 199] [1819 ll. 260–265]

The Waggon moves—and with its load
Descends along the sloping road;
his
And to ~~a little tent hard by~~ *nightly domicile,*
ed *rough*
Turn s the Sailor instantly;
ere
For when, ~~at~~ closing-in of day,
The Family had come that way,
With caution placed, and built with skill,
A little mockery of a tent,
Which in its sheltering nook hard by
Had weathered the fierce element—

The hand of the revisions is EQ's. The printed "s" on "Turns" and the printed "at" were erased.

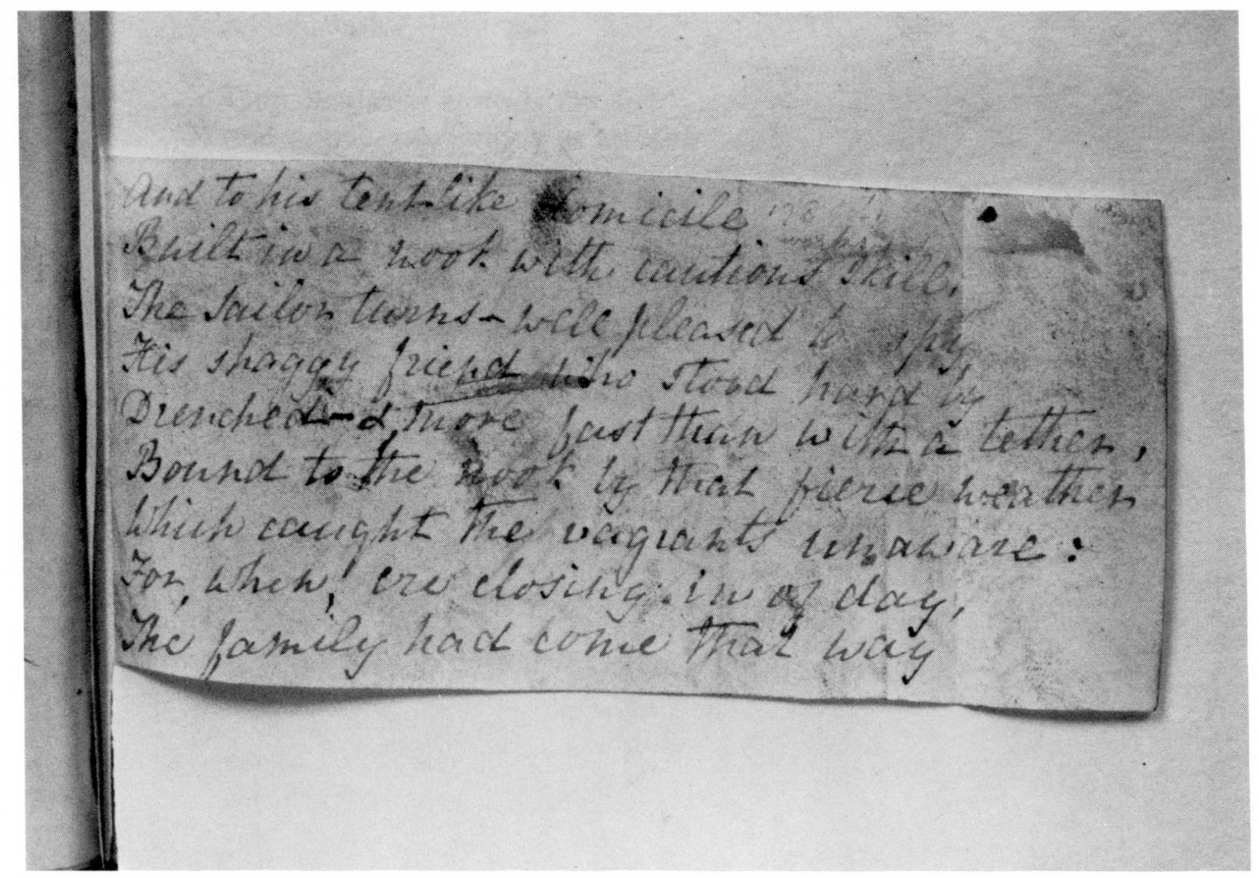

And to his tent-like domicile
Built in a nook with cautious skill,
The Sailor turns—well pleased to spy
His shaggy friend who stood hard by
Drenched—& more fast than with a tether,
Bound to the nook by that fierce weather
Which caught the vagrants unaware:
For, when, ere closing-in of day,
The family had come that way

[pp. 198/199 interleaf] [1819 ll. 262–265]

And to his tent-like domicile
Built in a nook with cautious skill,
The Sailor turns—well pleased to spy
His shaggy friend who stood hard by
Drenched—& more fast than with a tether,
Bound to the nook by that fierce weather
Which caught the vagrants unaware:
For, when, ere closing in of day,
The family had come that way

The hand is Dora's. At the end of the first line is a later penciled note, probably by the binder, locating the passage: "198 Vol. 1 / works."

Keyed to the text by EQ's "See alteration" and "ditto" in the right margin at p. 212, next to ll. 651–657.

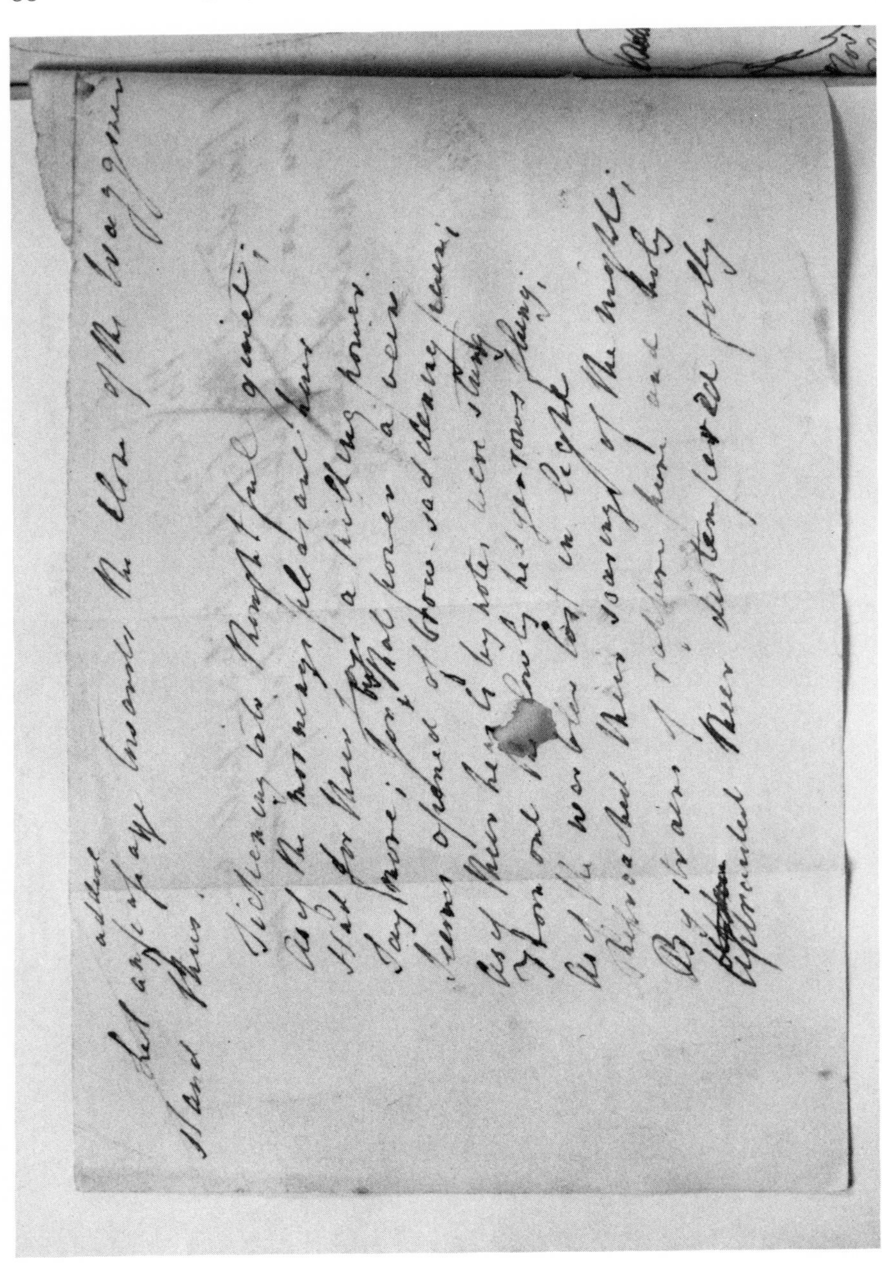

[pp. 212/213 interleaf] [1819 ll. 655–657]

added
n
Let a ^pa page towards the Close of the Waggoner
stand thus.

Sickening into thoughtful quiet;
As if the mornings pleasant hour
Had for their joys a killing power.
by
Say more; for ^ that power a vein
Seems opened of brow-saddening pain;
As if their hearts by notes were stung
From out the lowly hedge-rows flung;
As if the warbler lost in light
Reproached their soarings of the night;
By strains of rapture pure and holy
~~Up[?bra]~~
Upbraided their distempered folly.

On the reverse of the sheet is a deleted note in WW's hand:

Notice
At the close of the fifth Volume will be
given an alphabetical list of ~~the the~~
the Miscellaneous Poens.

Never golden-haired Apollo,
Nor winged Hermes, nor the Idalian Queen,
Pleased each some favourite Chief to follow
Through accidents of peace or war,
In a perilous moment threw
Round the object of that care &c

Whether, by their own desert,
Knowing there is cause for shame,
They are labouring to avert
At least a portion of the blame,
Which full surely will alight
Upon *his* head, whom, in despite
Of all his ~~faults~~ failings, they love ~~the~~ best;
Whether for him they are distrest;
Or, by length of fasting roused,
Are impatient to be housed;
Up against the hill they strain,
Tugging at the iron chain,
Tugging all with might and main,
Last and foremost, every horse
To the utmost of his force!
And the smoke and respiration,
Rising like an exhalation,
Blend with the mist, a moving shroud
To form, an undissolving cloud;
Which, with slant ray, the merry sun
Takes delight to play upon.
Never ~~Venus or Apollo,~~ golden-haired Apollo ~~golden-haired Apollo~~
~~Pleased a favourite chief to follow~~
Through accidents of peace or war,
In a ~~time of peril threw~~ perilous moment threw
~~Round the object of this care,~~ of that care
Veil of such celestial hue;
Interposed so bright a screen
Him and his enemies between!

Alas! what boots it? — who can hide,
When the malicious Fates are bent
On working out an ill intent?
Can destiny be turned aside?

Nor winged Hermes, nor the Idalian Queen
Pleased each some favourite Chief to follow

[p. 213] [1819 ll. 662–696]

Never golden-haired Apollo,
Nor winged Hermes, nor the 'Idalian Queen,
Pleased each some favourite Chief to follow
Through accidents of peace or war,
And in a perilous moment threw
Round the object of that care &cet

Whether, by their own desert,
Knowing there is cause for shame,
They are labouring to avert
At least a portion of the blame,
Which full surely will alight

Upon *his* head, whom, in despit *e* **~~e~~**
failings
Of all *his* ~~faults~~, they love ~~the~~ best;
Whether for him they are distrest;
Or, by length of fasting roused,
Are impatient to be housed;

Up against the hill they strain~~+~~ ,
Tugging at the iron chain~~+~~ ,
Tugging all with might and main~~+~~ ,
Last and foremost, every horse
To the utmost of his force!

And the smoke and respiration ,
Rising like an exhalation,

Blend~~s~~ with the mist~~+~~ , **a moving shroud,**

To form~~+~~ , **an undissolving cloud;**
Which, with slant ray, the merry sun
Takes delight to play upon.
golden-haired ~~Apollo~~
~~Never Venus or Apollo,~~ *~~golden haired~~*
some *~~Apollo~~*
~~Pleased a favourite chief to follow~~
Through accidents of peace or war,
In a ~~time of peril threw~~ *perilous moment threw*
t *~~at~~*
~~O'er~~ **~~Round the object of h~~ ~~is care~~,** *of that care*
Veil of such celestial hue;
Interposed so bright a screen
Him and his enemies between!

Alas! what boots it?—who can hide ,
When the malicious Fates are bent
On working out an ill intent?
Can destiny be turned aside?
Nor winged Hermes, nor the Idalian Queen,
each
Pleased ‸ some favourite Chief to follow

The hand of most revisions is EQ's. Single printed letters and marks of punctuation shown as deleted were erased.

Alterations & Additions to the Waggoner—Canto 4—

p. 212 (of 1832 Edition) Print according to the alterations underlined (which however are not to be in Italics.)

Apparent now beside his team-
Now hidden by the glittering steam

~~Drooping are they, and weak, and dull~~
Sickening into thoughtful quiet;
As if they by the notes were stung
From out the lowly hedge-rows flung;
As if the warbler lost in light
Reproached their soarings of the night,
Upbraided their distempered folly
By strains of rapture pure and holy;
As if the morning's pleasant hour &ce

---

p. 213

Whom in despite
Of all his failings they love best

Takes delight to play upon.
Never golden-haired Apollo,
Nor Blue-eyed Pallas, nor the Idalian Queen,
When each was pleased ~~a~~ ^some favourite c} C} hief to follow
Through accidents of peace or war,
In a perilous moment threw
Around the object of celestial care
A veil so rich to mortal view,
Interposed so bright a screen—
Him and his enemies between!

---

p. 214. ________________ *this outward glory*
Fails to shield thee from they Master,

Comes to give what help he may;
Perhaps to hear what thou canst say
If, as he cannot but forebode
Thou hast been loitering on the road!
His fears, his doubts may now take flight—

---

pp. 212–214 In these verse passages, EQ has underlined words and punctuation that differ from the text in the 1832 *PW*.

Appendixes

Appendix I

Coleridge and *Benjamin the Waggoner*: Transcriptions and Photographic Reproductions of Coleridge's Proposed Revisions to MS. 1

Shortly after Coleridge's return from Malta he read *Benjamin the Waggoner* for the first time, and at once proposed to Wordsworth some revisions to the poem. Coleridge's participation in the development of *Benjamin*, the evidence for which exists in the form of an unsigned note and two verse passages in his hand in MS. 1, remained long unrecognized. These suggested changes, and Wordsworth's drafts written in reaction to them, are of considerable interest and are too complex to be presented with clarity in the *apparatus criticus* of MS. 1 variant readings to MS. 2. Therefore, both transcriptions and facing photographs are presented below.

The passages that first troubled Coleridge appear on leaves 4^r and 6^r of *Benjamin the Waggoner* MS. 1 (DC MS. 56). (For a description of MS. 1, see the headnote to the MS. 2 transcription.) Coleridge responded on the facing versos, leaves 3^v and 5^v; most of Wordsworth's consequent drafts are on the same versos, but he also made a few revisions to the original fair copy. Coleridge's first perplexity concerned Wordsworth's somewhat uneasy shift from a third-person reference to "Ben" to a direct address of the Waggoner as "thou"; he was also uneasy about the figure of speech in which Wordsworth has a *door*, rather than windows, "Look at thee with so bright a lure." The objections seem well founded, especially in the second instance. The numerous drafts in which Wordsworth tried to come to terms with Coleridge's suggestions indicate that he took them very seriously. Notice, for example, Wordsworth's attempt, in his interlinear draft within the first Coleridge note, to deal with the light falling on the "old mossy High-way Wall"—"Brighten / That stands right [?surely] / This Highway"—before deciding to retain the "casement panes" but have their light fall instead upon the "Bells and Manes" of the two lead horses. Coleridge's push toward consistency was useful; and the increasing particularity of "sober Simon" and "sneaking Relph" is a valuable addition reflected in Wordsworth's subsequent "Let Simon flog and Arthur Curse," although "Relph" is rather obviously designed to rhyme with "itself."

In two respects, however, Coleridge's influence may have been unfortunate. First, although "Dead as a cheese upon a shelf" is precisely the kind of rustic Wordsworthian metaphor that Coleridge tended to dislike—and which has resulted in some ridicule, and from which Wordsworth himself was pulling back by 1806—it is vivid and appropriate in this context; one is sorry to see it lost. More important, by rectifying the inconsistency in the first passage in favor of third-person reference rather than direct address—"If he resist" rather than "If thou resist"—a valuable immediacy seems to be lost in the connection between the amused, sympathetic, but somewhat detached narrator and Benjamin.

In a personal and rather peripheral matter, Coleridge's familiarity with this poem may help to explain a rather enigmatic notebook entry that Kathleen Coburn dates "November–December 1806": "The Rock of Names—indignant answer to Australis" (*The Notebooks of Samuel Taylor Coleridge*, vol. 2 [1804–1808], Text [London, 1962], entry 2950). Australis was Southey; and there is some basis for speculating that Coleridge may have praised the "Rock of Names" passage in *Benjamin* to Southey, and that Southey may have responded by questioning the propriety of Coleridge's and Sara Hutchinson's having linked their names by carving them together on the rock. Southey's attitude toward Coleridge's relationship with Sara Hutchinson was no secret, and this would not have been the only occasion on which Coleridge became indignant about it.

A photograph, reduced in size, faces each page of the following transcription. Complete photographs of both rectos are presented, although only those fair-copy passages to which Coleridge responded have been transcribed.

+ From disuse of reading poetry, and thinking like a Poet, I am probably grown dull; but this × line I did not discover the meaning or construction, for some minutes of endeavor. Might I propose the addition of " will call,

[3v]

[?If] he resist those casement panes
bright
[?And] that ~~stray~~ gleam which there
will fall
Upon his Leaders Bells and Manes
Inviting him
~~[?Greeting] thee with a~~ chearful lure
F}
B} or sure though all be dark elsewhere

+ *From disuse of reading poetry, and thinking like a Poet, I am probably grown dull; but this X line I did not discover the meaning or construction, for some minutes of endeavor. Might I propose the addition of*
"will call,
If he resist those casement Panes
Which o'er his Leader's Bells & Manes
Bright[?ėn]
Will make th'old mossy High-way Wall
That stands right [?surely]
Look at him with so bright a Lure:—
This Highway
For surely if——

panes}
If he resist those casement [?that]}
strong
And that [?strong] gleam
That chearful light which there [?will]
fall
Upon [?his]
[?R]

All in pencil except "he" (l.1), the "Up" of "Upon" and "his Leaders" (l.3), and deletion lines in ll. 2 and 4.

It is a doubt with Benjamin
Whether they be alive or dead

No danger's here, no none at all
Beyond his wish is ~~he~~ secure
But pass a mile and then for trial
Then for the pride of self-denial
If ~~thou~~ he resist that tempting door
Which with such friendly voice will call
Look at ~~thee~~ him with so bright a lure
For surely if no other where
Candle or lamp is burning there

The place to Benjamin full well
Is known and for as strong a spell
As used to be that sign of love
And hope the Olive-bough and Dove
He knows it to his cost good Man!
Who does not know the famous Swan?
Uncouth although the object be
An image of perplexity
But what of that it is our boast
For it was painted by the Host
His own conceit the figure plann'd
'Twas coloured all by his own hand,

[4r]

No danger's here, no none at all
He
Beyond his wish is {He / *Ben secure*}
But pass a mile and then for trial
Then for the pride of self-denial
he
If ~~thou~~ resist that tempting door
Which with such friendly voice will call +
meet him
×*Look at ~~thee~~ with so bright a lure*
~~Will hail thee~~
~~For surely if no other where~~
For sure though all be dark elsewhere
Candle or lamp is burning there

All interlinear revisions are in pencil.

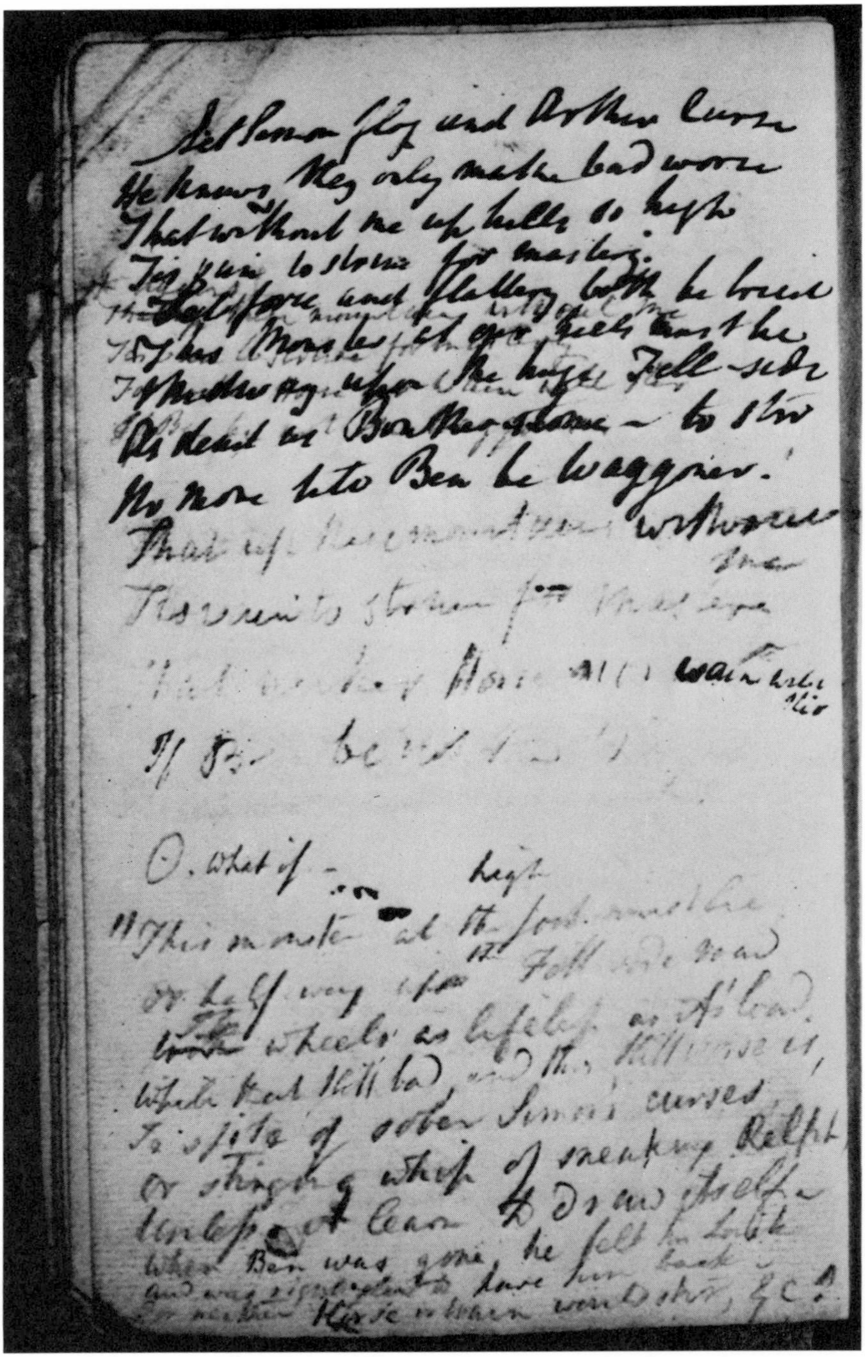

[5^{v}]

Let Simon flog and Arthur Curse
He knows they only make bad worse
That without me up hills so high
Tis vain to strive for mastery
Let force and flattery both be tried
This Monster at our heels must lie
Midway upon the huge Fell-side
As dead as Bowther-stone— to stir
No more till Ben be Waggoner.

*Against
~~That up~~ these mountains without me
Tis vain to strive for mastery
For neither Horse nor Wain will stir
If Ben be not the Waggoner.

That up these mountains without
me
Tis vain to strive for mastery
That neither Horse nor Wain will
stir
If Ben be not the Waggoner

Q. what if—
high
"*This monster at the foot must lie*
the
Or, half-way up~~on~~ Fell-side road
Its
~~With~~ wheels as lifeless as it's load
While that Hill bad, and this Hill worse is,
In spite of sober Simon's curses,
Or stinging whip of sneaking Relph,
Unless it learn to draw itself.—
When Ben was gone, he felt his Lack
And was right glad to have him back—
For neither Horse or Wain would stir, &c?

All in pencil except the 9-line draft beginning "Let Simon flog"; in the second occurrence of the words "Wain will stir / If Ben," faint pencil has been reinforced with ink.

I'm here and with my Horses yet!
~~When I was gone he felt his lack~~
~~And was right glad to have me back~~
My jolly Team he finds that ye
Will work for nobody but me
with hills so steep and high
This Monster at our heels must lie
~~When I was gone he felt his lack~~
~~And was right glad to have me back~~
Then grieve not jolly Team! though tough
Our road be sometimes steep and rough
But take your time no more I ask
I know you're equal to your task
And for us all I'll sing the praise
Of our good friend here Dunmal-raise
And of his brother Banks and Braes
For plain it is that they['ve] been the tether
By which we have been kept together

While Benjamin in earnest mood
His meditations thus pursued
A storm which had been smothered long
Was growing inwardly more strong
And in its struggles to get free

[6r]

114 *I'm here and with my Horses yet*
When I was gone he felt his lack
115 ~~*He makes a mighty noise about me*~~
And was right glad to have me back
116 ~~*And yet he cannot do without me*~~
117 *My jolly Team he finds that ye*
118 *Will work for nobody but me*
119 ~~*Finds that*~~ *with hills so steep and high*
120 *This Monster at our heels must lie*
As dead as Bowder-stone—to stir
121 ~~*Dead as a cheese upon*~~ *a shelf*
No more till Ben be Waggoner
~~*itself*~~ } ⊙
122 ⊗ ~~*Or fairly learn to draw* [?*a shelf*]~~ }
~~felt~~ }
123 ~~*When I was gone he* [?*knew*]~~ } ~~*his lack*~~
124 ~~*And was right glad to have me back*~~

120/121, 121/122, 122/123 In pencil.

Appendix II

T.J. Wise and *Benjamin the Waggoner* MS. 2

Most of Wordsworth's verse manuscripts and much of his and his family's correspondence, as well as much important Coleridge, De Quincey, and Lamb material, were still in the poet's possession at his death. These papers came at last into the hands of his grandson, Gordon Graham Wordsworth, who in the 1930s gave most of them to the Dove Cottage Wordsworth Library in Grasmere. T. J. Wise, whose forgeries of nineteenth-century pamphlets and thefts from the British Museum have since made him notorious, planned bibliographies of the works of both Wordsworth and Coleridge and also collected their works. It was probably inevitable that he would be drawn to Gordon Wordsworth.

After an extended epistolary courtship, which included the gift of copies of a number of his bibliographies, Wise wrote:

My dear Wordsworth,

I am delighted to know that you found something to interest you in Vol. V of the Catalogue. I am now hard at work on the Swinburne portion of Vol. VI. After Vol. V with its Shelleys, I look forward with greatest pleasure to Vol. VII with its Tennysons and its Wordsworths. With Tennyson I am satisfied; but I fear you will not think I have found sufficient success to be worthy of Wordsworth, for I have never been able to find a single Wordsworth manuscript. But at least the printed books are good!

Most Sincerely Yours
Thos. J. Wise[1]

Wise had been astute in calculating the generosity and naiveté of his friend; on Christmas Eve, 1924, Gordon Wordsworth sent what must have been the expected response:

My dear Wise,

It is altogether wrong that your wonderful library should contain none of Wordsworth's verse in manuscript. It is almost a reflection on the poet, and certainly a reproach to his grandson who is proud to call himself a friend of yours. I take it the ideal specimen would be a well-known poem, complete, signed, in good condition, and as well written as would be consistent with its being characteristic, but I have

[1] This letter is at the Wordsworth Library.

never seen any document of Wordsworth's that combined these qualities. You know what an untidy and reluctant writer he was, and how he always had willing scribes at hand. When he did write it was generally in a flimsy notebook, or on scraps of paper rescued from the waste paper basket, and with pencil or the worst of homemade pens.

It gives me great pleasure to be offering you two specimens, one from the drawing room, and one from the workshop; but please do not feel bound to accept both or either if you consider them to be out of place in your treasure-house. I know you like your Manuscripts to be spotless, and this "Waggoner" is sadly toil-stained.[2]

So this is how Wise came to own MS. 2 of *Benjamin the Waggoner* (now Ashley 4637), which after his death was to go with the bulk of the Ashley Library to the British Museum.

Wise's ownership of the manuscript might not seem at first to present a problem; despite his numerous fabrications of fraudulent first editions, he has not been accused of attempting to forge letters or manuscripts. There is a problem, however, in connection with William Wordsworth's note on leaf 1^{r}:

This Poem was at first ~~writ~~ thrown
under {of
off ~~from~~ a lively impulse {, feeling
during
~~in~~ the first fortnight of the month
6}
of Jan^{ry} 180 } and has since
at several times been carefully revised
retouched &
and with the Author's best efforts, inspirited
W Wordsworth

This note provides Wordsworth's most precise date for the poem's composition; and it assumes added importance because, beginning with the stereotyped edition of 1836, Wordsworth dated the poem "1805." Although the fair copy in MS. 2 was transcribed by March 29, 1806, this note was added much later, possibly in 1836. Wordsworth must not at first have recalled the year of composition, for in the note, which is in ink, he wrote only "180". The number "6" was then added in pencil. Although it is often very difficult to be certain about the handwriting of a single letter or number, the hand is not uncharacteristic of Wordsworth. Despite this evidence of his lapse of memory, had he added the number later it would still have possessed considerable authority.

The Dove Cottage archives, however, contain an uncatalogued memorandum, signed by Gordon Wordsworth, dealing with this manuscript of *Benjamin*. Gordon Wordsworth quotes the entire note, which he apparently copied shortly before giving the manuscript to Wise. The number "6" is

---

[2] Quoted in *Two Lake Poets* (1927), the catalogue of Wise's Wordsworth and Coleridge collection, p. 24; the original is BL Ashley A. 4637.

missing, and the omission is clearly intentional, as the figures "180" are followed by a space and "sic" in brackets. Gordon Wordsworth's copy of Knight's 1896 edition of the *Poetical Works*, now owned by Dr. G. R. Jackson of London, contains a second transcript of the note, from which the "6" is similarly absent. So the number was not added by Wordsworth or any other member of the circle, but was certainly added after Gordon Wordsworth made his two transcripts of the note.

Who, then, wrote in the number? Gordon Wordsworth himself, as guidance for his friend Wise before sending him the manuscript? Someone on the staff of the British Museum? The number lacks the quiver so characteristic of Gordon Wordsworth's hand; and there is a terminal date for the addition which rules out any tampering after Wise's death. In *Two Lake Poets*, Wise's catalogue of his Wordsworth and Coleridge collections, the note is printed for the first time, and the date is present in full: "1806."

While one cannot be certain, Wise's motives are easy enough to understand: he doubtless gave way to a kind of laziness—an unwillingness to explain a gap in the note as he printed it, which led him to entertain the possibility that there might be some uncertainty about the date—and to a latent contempt for other bibliographers who seemed to him less clever and less worthy of scholarly respect than he. He could scarcely have known that John Carter and Graham Pollard would soon be on his trail.